눈 내리는 여름날

시드니에서 이민자로 살며 한글과 영어로 엮은 수필

눈 내리는 여름날

초판 1쇄 인쇄 | 2025년 10월 23일
지은이 | 권영규
펴낸이 | 이재욱(필명:이승훈)
펴낸곳 | 해드림출판사
주 소 | 서울 영등포구 경인로82길 3-4(문래동1가 39)
　　　　센터플러스빌딩 1004호(07371)
전 화 | 02-2612-5552
팩 스 | 02-2688-5568
E-mail | jlee5059@hanmail.net

등록번호　제2013-000076
등록일자　2008년 9월 29일

ISBN　979-11-5634-657-9

눈 내리는 여름날

시드니에서 이민자로 살며 한글과 영어로 엮은 수필

권영규 지음 | 삽화 Kay Yasugi

Snow on a Summer's Day

A Migrant's Life in Sydney - Bilingual Essays in Korean and English

Written by **Young Kyu (Yong) Kwon**
Illustrated by **Kay Yasugi**

해드림출판사

프롤로그

    2006년, 시드니 교민신문에 문예창작교실을 연다는 광고가 나왔다. 그 기사는 그렇잖아도 오랜 세월 글쓰기라는 꿈을 가슴에 담고 살아온 내게 거센 꿈틀거림으로 다가왔다. 비록 늦깎이에 들어섰지만 '바로 지금이 가장 빠른 시기'라는 한 동기부여 문구가 망설여지는 나에게 용기를 주었다. 그때 원로 소설가 이효정 선생님을 강사로 만난 것은 크나큰 행운이었다.

    글쓰기를 시작하며 처음엔 자서전이나 회고록 같은 단순한 기록이 목적이었지만, 10주 동안 계속된 창작교실 제4기를 수료할 즈음에는 '수필문학'이라는 장르의 매력에 깊이 빠져 있었다. 그렇게 나는 지금껏 수필을 쓰며 살아왔고, 일상이 글이 되는 기쁨을 알아 가고 있다.

    모국을 떠난 지 어느덧 반세기가 되어간다. 1978년부터 10년 동안 도쿄에서 직장생활과 출산, 육아에 전념하며 치열한 시간을 보냈고, 서울올림픽이 열리던 해에 호주로 이주했다. 그렇게 이어진 이민자의 삶 속에서, 나는 다양한 변화와 도전을 겪으며 오늘에 이르렀다. 인생의 후반부를 조금은 시간의 여유를 누릴 수 있는 지금, 나의 첫 수필집의 작품을 한글과 영어 번역으로 함께 펴내게 되었다. 거기엔 아쉬움이 담긴 개인적인 사연이 있다. 나의 아들딸이 엄마가 쓰는 한국어 수필을 온전히 이해하지 못하기 때문이다. 세 살 때부터 호주에서 자란 딸은 한국어로 된 문장을 제대로 이해하는데 어려움이 있다. 엄마가 무슨 글을 쓰는지 늘 궁금해하던 딸에게, 이참에 본격적인 한국어 공부를 권하고도 싶다.

 영어 번역은 전문 번역가의 힘을 빌리자니 엄청 비용이 들 것을 지레 겁먹고 개인적으로 도움을 받았다. 부족한 나를 비롯하여 번역과 감수를 도와준 딸 Kay와 딸의 친구들: Nancy Lee, Sunny Lee, Sue Hendroff, Philippa Russell, Kate Harris and Sungsin Ro에게 깊은 감사의 말을 전한다. 최근엔 AI의 도움을 받기도 했다. 2년 전에 시도 했을 땐 '모녀'라는 단어 번역을 못하길래 길고 긴 번역의 초안을 내가 직접 시도하고 딸의 도움을 받기로 했었다. 그러나 진도가 생각보다 느려 다시 AI를 이용해 보니 이번엔 '모녀'를 제대로 번역하는게 아닌가! 그 빠른 발전 속도에 크게 놀라 초안 번역 작업이 빨라졌다. 그러나 작가의 의도와 맞는 번역이어야 하고 AI도 실수를 하기 때문에 결국 문장 하나하나 나의 확인 과정을 거치고 영어 달인들의 도움을 받았다.

이 수필집에 실린 작품들은 오랫동안 한호일보(2023년 폐간), 한국신문 등 교민언론에 실렸던 글 중에서 한글과 영어를 나란히 수록하기 위하여 30편만 추렸다. 이 책의 제목 〈눈 내리는 여름날〉은 책 속에 실린 한 편의 수필에서 따온 것이다. 모국과 계절이 반대인 시드니의 어느 무더운 여름날, 나는 스테이트극장에 공연을 보러 갔었다. 극의 절정에서 종이눈보라가 관객석 위로 펑펑 쏟아졌는데 그 환상적인 순간에 나는 12월이면 언제나 눈이 내리는 북반구에서 온 이민자로서 애틋한 그리움에 젖어 들고 말았다.

모국의 추억을 소중히 간직하면서도, 또한 호주가 나에게 안겨준 따스함과 빛, 그리고 수많은 기회에 깊이 감사한다. 이 책은 내 아이들을 위해 쓴 것이기도 하지만, 동시에 나 자신과, 이민자로 살아온 많은 이들을 위한 작은 흔적이기도 하다. 비록 미숙한 글일지라도, 그것들은 한 이민자로서의 내 생각과 여정을 담고 있다. 이 글들이 다른 이민자들에게도 공감을 불러일으키고, 그들 역시 자신의 이야기를 나누게 되면 좋겠다. 무엇보다도, 글이 영어권 독자들의 마음에도 가까이 다가가길 바란다.

이번 수필집의 말미에는 감히 나의 첫 단편소설도 한 편 게재한다. 수필과는 또 다른 제3자의 삶을 성찰하고자 시도해 보았다. 아직은 서툴지만, 새로운 문학적 표현의 가능성을 조심스레 열어보고 싶었다.

2025년 6월 시드니의 겨울에
권영규

목차

프롤로그   4
부록   378

1부

제2의 고향 호주에 살어리랏다	12
거리의 아침 식사	17
눈 내리는 여름날	22
손님 월터	26
셰릴의 환갑 파티	30
아름드리나무	34
단출하게 살아가기	39
인연의 끈	44

2부

인연의 도미노	52
신부(新婦)의 표정 변천기	55
산모와 미역국	59
사랑의 힘	64
마지막이 된 배웅	68
내 마음에 쌓인 저금	72
향기로운 우정	77
아, 버지니아!	82

3부

이 시대의 바벨탑	91
바야흐로 휴대폰 시대	95
문화의 힘	99
제주도 해녀를 만나다	103
문화유산 계승의 힘	108
떳떳할 수 없는 역사	112
천재(天災)와 인재(人災)	117
우리 아주 멀리서 왔어요	122

4부

장인정신	129
새해를 맞으며	133
이 또한 지나가리라	137
영혼의 흔적은 어디에	142
인생의 황금기에서	146
인생 소나타	149

단편소설

- 아버지의 봄   153

1부

제2의 고향 호주에 살어리랏다

그날은 너무 오랫동안 우기가 계속되어 물속에 잠겨버린 마음을 보상이라도 해 주는 듯 모처럼 맑고 청명한 날씨였다. 우리 모녀는 그 유혹에 끌리듯 외출하여 시드니박물관까지 다녀왔다. 호주에서 산지도 오래되었건만 아이들이 어렸을 때 호주박물관을 여러 번 가본 이후로 오페라하우스에서 멀지 않은 곳에 시드니박물관이 있다는 걸 알면서도 여태 찾지 못한 것에 부끄러움을 느꼈다. 박물관에서는 작년 11월부터 How to move a zoo라는 전시회가 열리고 있었는데 마침 우리가 간 날이 끝나기 전날 이어서 축구 골대에 아슬아슬하게 골인하듯 들어가 관람할 수가 있었다.

1884년부터 30여 년간 시드니 최초의 무어파크동물원이 있던 자리에 지금은 시드니보이즈하이스쿨과 시드니걸즈하이스쿨이 들어서 있다. 동물원 주인의 장소 이전 계획에 따라 지금의 타롱가동물원으로 옮기게 되었을 때는 아직 오페라하우스와 하버브

릿지가 생기기 전의 일이다. 그 당시 228마리의 포유류 동물과 552마리의 조류와 64마리의 파충류를 옮기는 데만도 6개월이 걸렸다고 한다. 대부분 새장이나 우리 안에 넣고 차량으로 화물훼리 타는 곳까지 가서 하버를 가로질러 이동했는데 체중이 4톤이나 되는 코끼리는 배를 타기 위해 무어파크에서 지금 오페라하우스가 있는 곳까지 걸어야 했다.

매우 흥미로운 전시회에 다녀온 이야기를 듣고 호주 지인이 "무어파크에 있던 모든 동물들이 떠나고 새로운 동물들이 들어왔다."고 했을 때 처음엔 무슨 말인지 몰라 어리둥절했으나 이 말을 한 사람의 익살스러운 표현에 웃지 않을 수 없었다. 자신이 시드니보이즈하이스쿨을 나왔기에 학생들을 새로운 동물이라고 농담을 했던 것이다.

전시회장에는 그 당시 특히 인기를 끌었던 체중 4천 킬로그램의 코끼리가 걸었던 길과 동물과 사람들과 나무들이며 그 거리에 있던 건물들을 미니어처로 재현한 방이 따로 있었다. 코끼리가 가까이 걸어오는 모습을 보고 깜짝 놀란 말이 몸을 위로 치켜세우는 바람에 마차에 실었던 우유가 도로에 쏟아져 있는 모습도 미니어처로 만들어져 있다.

1916년 9월 24일, 이른 아침 5시 30분. 제씨(Jessie)라고 불리우는 코끼리의 90분에 걸친 여정이 시작되었다. 사육사 세 명과 함께 좁은 길을 통과하고 경전차 트랙을 건너는 등 신경 쓰며 걷다 보니 제씨는 발이 아픈 기색이었다 한다. 맥콰리 스트리트를 지나 지금 오페라하우스가 있는 곳까지 와서는 대기하고 있던 배에 타자마자 제씨는 난간에 코를 말고 큰 바윗덩어리처럼 꿈쩍도 하지 않고 선 채로 시드니하버를 건넜다. 상상만 해도 내 가슴이 뭉클해진다. 코끼리는 지능이 높고 기억력이 좋아서 30년 전의 사육사를 알아보았다는 이야기도 있는데 제씨는 배 위에서 동남아시아 고향의 자연 속으로 가고 있다고 생각했을까. 무어파크 동물원으로 되돌아가고 싶다고 생각하고 있었을까. 8살 때 호주에 와서 그동안 많은 사람들의 사랑을 받으며 살아온 제씨의 이야기는 88 서울올림픽이 있던 해에 우리 네 식구가 호주로 이민 온 때를 생각나게 한다. 우리 아들도 8살 때였다.

 같은 나이에 호주에 왔다고 해서 코끼리의 삶과 아들의 삶을 비교하고자 하는 건 아니다. 다만 제씨가 자의에 의해서 호주까지 온 게 아닌 것처럼 어린 아들은 부모의 결정에 따라 온 것이지 자의에 의한 것이 아니라는 점은 같다. 코끼리는 EQ 지수도 높다는데 제씨가 인간의 손에 이끌려 무리에게서 떨어져 멀고 낯선 호주 땅에 와서 동물원에 갇혀 살게 되었을 때 제씨의 스트레스를 우리는 상상할 수 있을까 싶다. 그러나 사육사에게 잘 길들어 갔으리라. 타롱가 동물원에서 오래오래 수많은 사람들의 사랑을 받으며 살다가 64살에 코끼리 천수를 다했을 때 온 시드니가 슬퍼했다고 한다.

 우리 가족이 시드니에 도착하여 3주쯤 되었을 때 마침 방학이 끝나고 학기가 시작되어 아들은 초등학교 2학년으로 입학하게 되었는데 지금도 나는 그 첫날을 잊을 수가 없다. 내 손을 잡고 가다가 저만치에 학교가 보이자, 아들은 가던 발걸음을 멈추었다. "엄마, 내 가슴에 손 좀 대보세요." 심장이 쿵쾅쿵쾅 뛰고 있었다. 들어가기 싫다는 아이가 안쓰러워 괜히 이민을 왔나 후회가 될 정도였다. 입학 수속을 마치고 나는 운동장 한 켠에 있는 화장실 앞까지 아들을 데리고 가서 Boy라고 쓰여 있는 곳에 가라고 일러 주고 혹시 수업 시간에 화장실에 가고 싶게 되면 선생님에게 이렇게 이렇게 말하라고 가르쳐 주고 나왔다. 오후 하교 시간까지 종일 마음 졸이며 기다리다가 데리러 갔을 때 운동장에서 같은 반 아이들과 놀고 있는 모습을 보고는 안도의 숨을 쉬었다. 영어 한마디 못 하던 아들은 참 다행스럽게도 새로운 환경에 적응을 잘했다. 딸은 또 어떤가. 호주에 왔을 때 세 살이던 딸은 다음 해부터 프리스쿨에 다녔는데 6개월이 될 때까지 반에서 언제나 입을 꼭 다물고 있었다. 그 쉬운 헬로우, 굿모닝, 땡큐, 쏘리 한마디 하지 않아 나를 걱정시켰다. 선생님은 '이 아이가 말은 알아듣는데 자신이 없어서 그러는 것 같다. 어느 날 갑자기 입을 열 것이라 생각한다.'라고 했는데 그 말이 적중했다. 어느 날 봇물 터지듯 말을 쏟아내기 시작해서 선생님과 부모를 놀래켰으니.

코끼리 제씨가 동남아시아 어느 초지에 계속 살고 있었더라면 상아를 노리는 밀렵꾼에 의해 죽임을 당했을 수도 있을 텐데 오히려 시드니의 동물원에서 보호받으며 사람들의 사랑을 받다가 천수를 다할 수 있어서 다행이라고 생각하는 건 나의 이기적인 발상일까. 우리 가족이 호주로 이민 오지 않았더라면 우리는 지난 30여 년 어떠한 삶을 살아갔을까. 한 번밖에 살 수 없는 인생이고 돌이킬 수 없기에 우리 부부는 호주에 정착하게 된 것을 후

회하지 않는다. 오히려 다행으로 생각할 때가 많은 건 그만큼 제2의 고향 호주에서의 생활에 알 듯 모를 듯 스며들어 이제는 자연스러운 일상이 되어버린게 아닐까.

(2022)

거리의 아침식사

해마다 1월 26일 '호주의 날' 경축일이 오면 우리 동네 사람들은 11번지 집 앞에 모여 아침 식사를 같이한다. 이 거리의 아침 식사는 마흔여 채의 집이 들어서 있는 우리 동네에서 20년 가까이 계속되고 있다. 매년 9번지 집에서 도맡아 우편함에 넣어주는 안내쪽지에는 올해도 그 집의 세 아들과 막내딸로 귀염받는 개 죠디의 이름이 실려 있다. 싱그러운 한여름 아침, 먹을 것을 담은 바구니와 접이식 의자를 들고 11번지로 향하는 사람들의 즐거운 모습들과 만난다. 늘 조용하던 동네 길이 이날만은 활기에 찬다. 요즘 세상에 이처럼 이웃들이 모여 살아가는 정담을 나누는 우리 동네 풍습이 정겹고 감사한 마음이 든다.

길가에 준비된 바비큐에서 굽는 베이컨과 소시지의 군침 도는 냄새가 동네로 퍼져나갈 즈음엔 커피향도 은은히 코를 자극하고 있다. 아침 산책길에 가끔 마주치는 부부, 일 년 내내 한 번도 못 만나는 이웃도 있고 다른 곳으로 이사 갔지만 이날을 기억하고 찾아오는 이들도 있다. 이날엔 모두 모여 오랜만에 만난 친척들처럼 서로 안부를 물으며 이야기꽃을 피운다. 우리 가족이 이 동네로 이사 온 지 십오 년 가까이 되다 보니 집 앞에서 공놀이, 자전거 타기를 하던 꼬마가 어느새 늠름한 청년이 되어 이름표 담당 도우미 역할을 하고 있다. 모두들 스티커에 이름과 번지수를 적어 가슴에 붙여서 일일이 몇 번지에 사는 누구라고 소개하지 않아도 된다. 이사 온 지 얼마 되지 않은 한 중국인 가족은 같은 피부색인 우리 식구를 보고 무척 반가워하는 표정인데 그 집 부인은 영어가 미흡하다며 연신 큰 미소로 대화를 대신한다.

일 년에 한번 갖는 아침 식사 모임은 네트워킹의 장이기도 하다. 이 동네에 처음 이사 왔을 때 초등학생이던 딸이 대학에서 초등교육학을 전공하고 졸업을 앞둔 때에 마침 이웃의 초등학교 교장선생님과 대화를 나누며 조언을 들을 수 있었다. 인형극 전문가가 되기 위해 열정을 쏟고 있는 딸의 이야기를 귀담아듣는 어떤 부인은 며칠 후 우리 집 우편함에 인형극과 관련된 신문 기사를 넣어 주기도 했다. 또한 옆집 할머니와 9번지 집 부인, 그리고 나, 우리 셋의 공통분모를 알게 되었을 땐 괜히 동지애 같은 것을 느끼기도 했다. 같은 은행을 옆집 할머니는 세계 제2차 대전 직후, 나는 수년 전, 그리고 9번지 집 부인은 현재 재직 중이다. 그는 어쩌다 길에서 만나게 되면 다른 지점에서 근무하게 되었다던가, 이젠 파타임으로 바꿔야겠다던가 슬슬 그만두어야겠다던가 하는 화제를 꺼내곤 한다. 맞장구쳐주며 들어주는 이웃이 있어 좋은 표정이다.

아침 식사를 마치고 한창 분위기가 무르익을 무렵 교장선생님이 일어서서 인사말을 하고 특기할 만한 동네 뉴스, 카운슬(구청)의 동네 가로수를 바꾸는 계획 등을 전한 다음 경품권 추첨을 한다. 한 집에 한 장씩 받은 티켓 번호는 각 집의 번지수와 일치하는데 당첨되는 두 사람은 동네 사람이 기증한 와인을 한 병씩 받게 된다. 늘 와인을 기증해 온 와인 소사이어티(Wine Society) 멤버였던 한 부인이 두 해 전에 뜻하지 않은 사고로 세상을 떠난 이래 우리 옆집 할머니가 두 병씩 기증하고 있다. 와인을 포장지로 싸서 작은 호주 국기를 꽂아 놓았는데 한 어린이가 뽑아준 행운의 당첨 번호가 우리 집 번지수 40번이 아닌가! 동네 사람들의 축하 박수를 받으며 올해는 분명히 좋은 해가 될 것이라는 기분에 몹시 흥분되었다.

재작년에 한국을 방문했을 때 나는 꼭 한번 가 보려고 벼르던 서울의 옛 동네를 찾아갔다. 우리 오 남매 중 셋이 태어난 집, 우리 형제들의 어릴 적 고향이자 지금도 가끔 꿈에 보이는 그 추억의 한옥이 아직 그대로 있는지 궁금해서였다. 지금은 반백 년을 훌쩍 넘은 남동생이 코흘리개 시절 골목대장 노릇을 했던 동네. 어릴 적엔 무척 커 보였는데 이제 보니 작고 비좁은 동네에 지나지 않았다. 열너덧 채의 작은 한옥들이 좁은 골목에서 마주 보며 자리하고 있는데 요즘 흔한 아파트가 들어서지 않아 한편 다행으로 생각되었다. 그 동네 길은 수 많은 사연들을 그대로 간직하고 있는 듯 보였다. 아들을 얻기 위해 무당까지 불러 굿을 하던 담장 넘어 집은 주차장으로 변해 있었다. 우리가 살던 집은 그대로 있는데 굳게 잠긴 대문 안을 들여다볼 수 없어서 아쉽기만 했다. 우리 집은 돈암시장 바로 옆에 있었다. 장 보러 올 적마다 들려 문간방 툇마루에 걸터앉아 담소를 나누던 어머니의 친구분들, 가까이 사셨던 친척 아주머니, 그리고 여고 시절 시장에서 뜨끈한 순대를 사 들고 우리 집을 자주 찾았던 단짝 친구의 얼굴이 아련히 떠올랐다. 이른 아침이면 대문 밖을 깨끗이 쓸곤 하셨던 돌아가신 아버지의 그리운 모습도 눈에 아른거려 한참 동안 발길을 뗄 수 없었다.

예전, 그 동네 사람들은 훈훈한 정을 나누었다. 1960년대 전화가 없는 집이 많던 시절엔 전화가 있는 집에서 친절을 베풀어 주었고, TV가 있는 집에 모여서 함께 운동경기나 드라마를 보기도 했다. 무슨 때면 떡도 돌리고 잔치 음식도 돌리고 동네 어른이 돌아가시면 함께 슬픔의 눈물을 흘렸다. 동네 꼬마들은 집 앞에서 딱지치기, 구슬따기, 공기놀이 등을 하며 노느라 정신이 없었고 밥 먹을 때가 되어 집에서 부르는 소리가 나서야 장난을 멈추고 뛰어가곤 했다. 그 후 수십 년이 지났으니, 세상이 달라진 것은 당연한 일이건만 옛 모습만 그대로 남아 있어 보이는 그 동네를 뒤로하며 나는 쓸쓸한 미소를 지었다.

'호주의 날' 저녁 무렵 바구니를 들고 우리 집 앞을 지나는 옆집 할머니에게 어딜 가시냐고 물으니 몇 집 건너 사는 노부부가 저녁 식사에 초대했다고 한다. 혼자 사시는 할머니는 모처럼의 초대에 멋지게 치장하고 즐거운 모습이다. 아침에 만나 벌써 친해

져서 저녁 초대까지 받게 된 것은 거리의 아침 식사 덕분이 아닐까. 채널10 촬영팀이 취재해 간 후 뉴스 시간 화면에 살짝 비춰주기까지 했으니, 호주에서도 그리 흔치 않은 일인가 보다. 나이 들어가며 때로는 모국이 더욱 그리워지는 나에게 외국에서 소수민족 이민자로 살면서 외로움과 이질감을 어찌 견뎌낼 것인가 했던 걱정은 이럴 때 하나의 위로가 된다. 좋은 이웃 만나서 정을 붙이고 살고 있으니 옆집 할머니처럼 나도 이 동네를 떠나지 못할 것 같다.

오늘날처럼 이웃과의 단순한 연결조차 귀해진 세상에서, 푸른 하늘 아래 동네 거리에서 나눈 아침 식사는 공동체의 온기를 되살려주는 작은 기적이었다. 삶이란, 어쩌면 그렇게 우연히 마주한 자리에서도 새로이 피어나는 것인지도 모른다.

(2008)

이 글을 쓴 것은 17년 전이었다. 그때는 살아 있는 한 이 동네를 떠날 수 없을 거라 믿었다. 하지만 삶의 흐름은 우리를 이사하게 만들었고, 그 시절의 마음은 지금도 내 안에 좋은 추억으로 남아 있다.

눈 내리는 여름날

바깥 기온은 섭씨 30도를 웃도는 한여름인데 실내에선 눈이 내린다?

나는 지금 시드니 시내 State Theatre에 앉아서 수백 명의 관람객들과 쇼가 시작되길 기다리고 있다. 무더위에 이름만 들어도 시원한 Slava's Snow Show라는 공연 타이틀이 호기심과 기대감을 갖게 한다. 내 앞엔 엄마와 같이 온 남자아이가 앉아 있고 그 두 줄 앞에서는 내 딸이 러시아어를 하는 노부부와 어린 손자가 좌석 찾는 것을 도와주는 중이다. 주위를 둘러보니 다양한 연령대의 사람들이 보이는데 대부분 가족과 함께 이 쇼를 보러 온 듯했다. 얼마 후 안내 방송이 시작된다. 핸드폰을 끄고 사진과 비디오 촬영은 금지한다는 내용이다. 이제 쇼가 시작되나보다 했을 때 중국어 안내가 나오고 한국어로 안내를 하더니 러시아어로도 한다. 그제사 나는 이 쇼가 국제순회공연을 하고 있다는 것을 새삼 깨달았다.

　팬데믹 이후 이 세상이 지금 어디에 와 있는가를 생각하면 놀랍기만 하다. 일 년전만 해도 이 극장 문은 굳게 닫혀 있었고 모든 좌석은 텅 빈 상태였다. 지금 내가 좌석에서 내려다보는 무대의 첫 장면은 황무지처럼 세팅되어 있는데 마치 지난 3년 동안 팬데믹으로 정지되었던 공연 비즈니스를 대변해 주는 듯 보였다. 이 쇼는 '슬라바'라는 러시아 사람이 30년 전에 시작한 광대극으로서 세계적으로 인기를 끌어왔다는데 지금은 그의 아들이 대를 이어 광대 캐릭터를 연기하고 있다고 한다. 광대는 대화 없이 옷과 분장과 몸의 움직임만으로 관람객들을 웃게도 울게도 한다. 공연이 시작되자 캐릭터들이 황폐한 땅에서 서로 연결고리를 찾느라 왔다 갔다 한다. 그러던 중에 주연 광대가 목에 걸고 있는 긴 끈이 다른 캐릭터가 들고 있는 끈과 연결되어있는 것을 알게 된다. 그 모습은 마치 우리가 록다운으로 집콕하는 동안 사람들을 만나지 못하고 있다가 지금은 나와서 이런 공연을 보고 있다는 사실과 일맥상통한다는 생각이 들었다.

　중간 휴게시간이 시작되기 직전, 거대한 거미줄이 무대 아래 객석 전체를 덮치며 관객들에게 엉킨다. 나는 메자닌 층 좌석에 앉아 이 드라마틱한 광경을 내려다보며 바로 얼마 전까지만 해도 사람들이 저 거대한 록다운이란 거미줄 안에 갇혀 있었던 사실을 떠올렸다. 록다운이 한창일 때 이사까지 한 우리 가족도 거미줄에 붙잡힌 양 오도 가도 못하고 지냈다. 매일 식구 중 한 사람만 가까운 식품점이나 슈퍼마켓에 갈 수 있도록 외출이 허용되어 남편만 밖에 나갔다가 왔을 뿐 나와 딸은 바깥세상과 단절된 채 지내지 않았던가.

쇼는 엄청난 피날레를 장식함으로 절정을 이루었다. 갑자기 무대에서 소용돌이 같은 흰 연기를 뿜어대더니 수백만 개의 하얀 컨페티로 눈 폭풍을 일으켜 관객석을 덮치는데 내가 앉은 메자닌 층까지도 눈발이 날아들었다. 한여름에 폭설이라니. 이것을 생각해 낸 러시아인 슬라바의 아이디어에 감탄하지 않을 수 없었다. 1929년에 완공된 고풍스러운 극장 안을 종이조각 눈으로 쌓이게 하다니 어찌 이런 신바람나는 일이 있을 수 있단 말인가.

해외에 사는 어린 손주들과 함께하지 못한 아쉬움이 크다. 작년 12월 초에 다니러 와서 한 달 반 이상을 함께 지내고 열흘 전에 떠난 아이들이 그립다. 삼 년 전 팬데믹이 발생하기 바로 전에 왔다가 간 후 발이 묶였다가 이번에 재회의 기쁨을 만끽하며 우리들은 여기저기 어린이들을 위한 공연을 보러 가곤 했다. 손주들과 이 꿈 같은 매직쇼를 함께 봤다면 이처럼 즐거운 추억 하나를 더 만들었을 텐데, 하는 아쉬움이 관람 내내 들었다.

사실 나는 이 광대 공연 내용은 이해하지 못했다. 어쩌면 의도적으로 관객들에게 해석을 맡기는 게 아닐까 싶기도 하다. 다만 광대와 다른 캐릭터들의 표정과 몸짓과 행동이 아이들을 까르르 웃게 했고 어른들도 웃고 박수치게 했다. 그들이 러시아어 노래를 립싱크로 부를 때 두 줄 앞의 러시아인 노부부는 손을 흔들고 박수를 크게 치며 좋아하는데 나는 하얗게 칠한 그들의 동그란 입술의 코믹한 움직임을 보며 웃고 있었으니 어쩌겠는가.

올여름 날씨는 꽤 여름답다. 작년 이맘때 폭우와 홍수가 계속되는 바람에 잃어버린 여름을 보상이라도 하듯 올해는 섭씨 30도가 넘는 무더위가 반갑기까지 하다. 코비드는 여전히 우리들을 위협하고 있지만 이제는 마스크 착용조차 개인의 의사에 맡겨져 있다. 종심(從心)을 넘긴 내가 모처럼 동심으로 돌아가 광대 슬라바의 Snow Show를 즐긴 것은 행복이었다. 관람 내내 마음껏 웃어댔고 가슴이 철렁하도록 놀라기도 했으니 이 얼마 만에 맛본 즐거움인가. 마치 코비드로 움츠려 지냈던 가슴속의 응어리가 뻥 터져 나오듯 속이다 후련했으니.

"엄마 어땠어?" 극장을 나오며 딸이 내게 묻는다. "나를 잊고 완전히 어린 시절로 들어갔다가 다시 돌아온 기분이네. 하하하" 거리의 열기가 다시 피부를 감싸기 시작했지만 내 안엔 여전히 흩날리는 눈발이 남아 있었다. 그 눈발은 팬데믹과 일상의 무게 속에서 얼었던 내 마음 한구석을 살며시 녹여주었다. 이맘때 진짜 함박눈이 내리는 모국의 겨울을 떠올리며 또다시 어쩔 수 없는 그리움에 젖어 든다.

(2023)

손님 월터*

요즘 한국엔 우리말 잘하는 외국인들도 많고 외국인들이 출연하는 TV 드라마나 인기 프로그램도 꽤 있다. 한국을 좋아하고 한국음식과 문화를 좋아하는 외국인을 만나면 그 사람에게 호감을 갖게 된다. 더욱이 호주에 살면서 이곳 호주인이 한국에 대한 조예가 깊거나 관심이 많은 것을 보게 되면 호감도는 더 높아진다. 그리고 상대적으로 호주에 살고 있는 우리들은 얼마만큼 호주를 알고 있으며 좋아하고 있는가를 생각해 보게 된다.

올해는 부활절 휴일과 다른 공휴일이 겹쳐서 휴일이 5일간 연속이었다. 시드니를 벗어나 어딜 가려 해도 휴가 떠나는 차량이 많은 시기를 피하는 우리 가족에겐 집에서 편히 뒹굴며 쉴 수 있

---

* 월터는 프라이버시를 위해 사용한 가명입니다

는 황금의 기회가 온 것이다. 이번에도 온갖 식재료를 냉장고에 꽉 채우고 집에서 휴가 보낼 준비를 했는데 뜻하지 않은 손님이 3일이나 우리 집에서 머물게 되었다. 쉰이 넘어 보이는 월터라는 초면의 호주 남자였다.

월터는 파트너와 함께 멜버른에서 활약하고 있는 인형극의 대가이다. 그곳에서 1,600Km나 떨어져 있는 브리즈번까지 인형극 공연에 필요한 것들을 작은 밴에 가득 싣고 혼자 운전하며 다녀오는 길이었다. 시드니에서 머물 예정이었던 인형극 동료 집에 부득이한 일이 생겨 갑자기 우리 딸에게 연락이 온 것이다. 초등학교 선생으로서 인형극을 교육에 활용하는 딸도 장차 호주에서 인형극의 대가가 되리라 기대하고 있는 우리 부부는 이 손님을 흔쾌히 받아들였다. 더욱이 딸이 멜버른에 갔을 때 받았던 이분들의 호의에 보답할 기회이기도 해서였다.

첫인상이 미국 배우 로빈 윌리암즈와 많이 비슷해서 혹시 친척 아니냐고 물었더니 간혹 같은 질문을 받는다며 웃음으로 대답한다. 비교적 작은 체구에 길지 않은 희끗한 머리를 뒤로 묶은 이 사람은 온화한 인상이다. 4월의 흐리고 으스스한 날씨 탓에 추워하는 이 손님에게 남편의 스웨터를 입히고 히터를 켜고 오붓하게 둘러앉아 한식으로 저녁 식사를 했다. 전기 철판에 먼저 등심구이로 시작해서 불고기와 LA갈비를 구워 상추에 싸서 먹고 마지막엔 철판에다 김치볶음밥을 만들어 밥공기에 내놓으니 이 손님의 표정이 참 행복해 보인다. 앞에 놓인 김치도 한 그릇 혼자 다 비운 월터는 김치볶음밥이 마음을 푸근하게 해 주는 음식이라고 좋아한다. 이제까지 한국 음식을 좋아하는 호주인들을 많이 보아 왔지만 김치볶음밥을 먹으며 행복해하는 오십 대의 호주 남자는 의외였다. 한국을 방문한 적이 있고 한국음식이 처음이 아니란 말을 듣기는 했어도 신기하긴 마찬가지였다. 딸이 멜버른을 방문했을 때 초대받아 갔더니 월터는 한국 식품점에서 구입한 요리책을 보고 직접 콩나물밥을 해 주었다고 한다. 그의 집에서 요리는 남편 전담이고 설거지는 파트너의 몫이라고 한다. 이 또한 놀라운 사실이지만 호주 남자가 콩나물밥을 다 만들다니!

월터의 파트너는 오페라 가수가 되고자 훈련을 쌓았던 사람이라고 한다. iPod에 담아온 그녀의 노래를 들으며 또한 감격하지 않을 수 없었다. 오페라 한 토막을 우리말로 번역해서 부르고 있다. 한국을 방문했을 때 시간이 모자라 발음을 제대로 익히지 못하고 부른 노래여서 비록 확실하게 알아들을 수 있는 말들은 '나는' 이라든지 '오페라 가수' 등 몇 개 안 되었지만 무척 감동적이고 멋진 노래였다. 여러 번 들으면 좀 더 이해할 수 있었겠지만, 월터가 멜버른으로 떠나기 직전에 들려 주어 아쉬움으로 남는다. 한글로 번역해서 노래 부르고자 했던 그 분의 마음에 감동 받은 나는 다음 기회에 두 분이 시드니에 오면 발음을 봐 주겠노라고 자청했다.

건축가의 길을 가다가 인형극의 매력에 빠져 파트너와 함께 올

인하고 있는 월터의 작품에는 건축가의 면모가 다분히 엿보인다. 그는 떠나면서 우리로 하여금 또 하나의 생각을 하게 만들었다. 바닥에서 천장까지 공연에 필요한 캐릭터들과 소품들로 빼곡히 쌓여 있는 그의 밴을 보며 힘드시겠다고 했더니 돌아온 말은 "힘들기 때문에 좋아하는 일입니다."

월터 커플 같은 손님이라면 우리 집 대문을 언제나 열어 놓아도 좋다는 생각이 든다. 나부터 호주와 호주적인 것에 좀 더 관심을 두다 보면 호주인들이 마음 문을 활짝 열게 되겠고 서로의 것들을 주고받을 수 있을 때 더욱 풍요로운 이민의 삶이 되지 않을까.

(2011)

셰릴*의 환갑 파티

친구 생일 파티에 다녀오며 나는 새삼스럽게 이런 생각이 들었다. 나이테가 늘어 가도 마음은 청춘이라고 자신 있게 말할 수 있어야 하겠다. 얼굴에 주름살이 늘어가도 마음만은 봄에 새롭게 피어나는 아잘리아의 연분홍빛을 닮으리라고. 그러나 아잘리아가 이른 봄에 그처럼 화사한 몸으로 살아나는 것은 거름을 주고 가지치기를 하며 손질을 해야 많은 꽃을 피우게 하는 진리를 배운다. 나도 내 마음에 거름 주는 일에 게으름을 피워서는 아니 되겠지.

나하고 비슷한 연배인 줄 알았던 셰릴이 나보다 사 년이나 아래라는 것을 안 것은 그녀의 60세 생일에 초대를 받고서였다. 그

---

* 셰릴은 가명입니다.

녀는 내가 십 년째 성경공부를 함께 하고 있는 열 명 그룹 '십자매'의 리더이다. 우리의 주소록에는 태어난 달과 날짜만 기록되어 있을 뿐 어느 해에 태어났는지는 적혀 있지 않다. 서양 여성들에게 나이를 묻는 것은 실례인 줄 알고 있는 터라 그녀가 내 또래로 짐작했을 뿐이다.

우리와 문화가 다르다고 그들을 우리식대로 대할 수는 없지 않은가. 우리나라 사람들은 조금 알게 되면 나이부터 묻는다. 상대방이 먼저 자기는 몇 살이라고 말하기도 한다. 의학의 발달로 수명이 길어졌고 70이 되어야 60 같이 보인다는 이유로 얼마 전부터 내 주변의 한국 사람들은 환갑을 그냥 넘기며 칠순에나 잔치하자는 게 상례가 되었다. 반면에 호주 사람들은 서른 살부터 숫자 뒤에 0이 붙는 나이가 되면 특별한 생일 파티를 연다. 내 딸의 여고 동창은 필리핀에 호주 외교관으로 가 있으면서도 자신의 서른 살 생일 파티를 위하여 휴가를 받고 호주에 다니러 올 정도로 자신의 생일을 챙겼다. 예순 살 생일은 더욱 뜻깊게 보낼 수 있도록 가족들이 많은 신경을 쓰기도 한다. 이처럼 호주 사람들은 생일을 중요하게 챙기는데 비해 나는 환갑을 슬그머니 지나쳐 버려 친구들과 즐거운 시간을 보낼 수 있는 특별한 기회를 놓친 것이 아쉽다.

셰릴의 생일 파티는 그녀의 집에서 오후에 티파티로 열렸다. 식탁 중앙을 아름다운 꽃들로 장식하고 오븐에서 구워 낸 음식들이며, 샌드위치, 작은 케이크들과 과일 등이 푸짐하게 놓인 것을 보며 공들여 준비한 것을 알 수 있었다. 아니나 다를까. 결혼해서 두 살 된 아들이 있는 데다 공부까지 계속하느라 늘 바쁘게 지내는 셰릴의 딸이 엄마의 특별한 날을 위해 혼자서 모든 음식을 준비했다며 인사말을 했다. 엄마 친구들에게 많이들 잡수시고 즐거운 시간을 보내시라고 덧붙였다. 얼마나 멋진 선물인가? 엄마의 친구들에게 직접 초대장을 보내고 정성껏 준비를 하며 엄마에 대한 사랑을 보여준 효녀. 쉽지 않은 일을 자신의 능력껏 최선을 다해 준 효심 덕분에 우리들은 샴페인 잔을 높이 들며 친구의 환갑을 축하해 주었다. 아늑한 분위기의 리빙룸에 둘러앉아 담소하는 부인들 중에는 유치원 때부터의 친구도 있고 여고 친구며 결혼식 때 들러리를 섰다는 친구도 있다. 자리를 바꿔가며 서로 다른 사람들과 이야기를 나누는 동안 특히 키 크고 마른 체구에 얼굴엔 주름이 가득한 마리아에게 마음이 끌렸다. 마리아는 전에 셰릴과 같은 교회에 다녔는데 은퇴한지 꽤 오래된 지금도 계속 무언가를 열심히 배우러 다니고 있는 그녀의 열정에 탄복했다.

리빙룸의 한쪽 벽엔 셰릴이 태어나서부터 지금까지 60년 동안의 삶이 사진으로 볼 수 있도록 붙여져 있었다. 사진 앞에 서니 어느새 그녀의 노모가 내 옆에 와서 설명해 주기 시작했다. 딸이 몇 살 때쯤 어디서 찍은 것이고 옆에 있는 사람들은 누구라고 일일이 짚어가는데 참 흥미로운 사실을 알게 되었다. 이 친구는 지금 한인타운이 되어가고 있는 리드콤(Lidcombe)에서 초등학교를 다녔고 이미 한인타운으로 알려져 있는 스트라스필드(Strathfield)에서 중고등학교에 다녔단다. 그녀는 자신이 어린 시절과 청소년기를 보냈던 동네가 한국 및 다른 소수민족들에 의해서 크게 달라지고 있다는 사실을 어떻게 받아들이고 있을까 궁금하기도 했지만, 어짜피 그네들도 영국에서 건너온 이민자들이 아니던가. 나는 이 친절한 노모가 불편해할 지도 모르는 사실을 구태여 그 자리에서 화제에 올릴 필요가 없다고 생각하며 다음 사진으로 시선을 옮겼다. 구순이 가까운 나이에 딸의 친구들과 어울리며 오래된 사진들을 또렷하게 열정적으로 설명하는 노모의 건강한 모습은 보는 이로 하여금 부러움을 사게 했다.

독일계 미국 시인 사무엘 울만이 78세 때 쓴 시구절을 떠올린다.

'청춘이란 인생의 어떤 시기가 아니라 마음가짐이다.
 …강인한 의지, 풍부한 상상력, 불타오르는 열정을 말한다…
나이를 먹는다고 우리가 늙는 것은 아니다. 이상을 잃어버릴 때 비로소 늙는 것이다… 머리를 높이 쳐들고 희망의 물결을 잡는 한 여든 살이라도 인간은 청춘으로 남는다.'

나도 몇 년 후 고희를 맞게 되면 친구들을 집에 불러 셰릴처럼 추억에 남을 멋진 파티를 하고 싶다. 그날에 나는 어떤 모습을 보여주게 될까….

(2014)

아름드리나무

요즘 나에게 이상한 버릇이 생겼다. 그것은 나무가 우거진 동네에 줄지어 서 있는 나무 중에서도 특히나 몸통의 한쪽이 잘려 나갔으나 우람하게 잘생긴 나무에게 눈길이 꽂힌다. 그 같은 나무를 발견하게 될 때면 예외 없이 발길을 멈추거나 차를 세우기도 한다. 그리곤 감탄 어린 시선으로 그 나무를 관찰하고 나서 나름대로 점수를 매기기도 한다.

집 앞에서 무심코 올려다본 유칼립투스 나무가 한쪽 팔을 잃은 모습으로 서 있다. 이층 베란다에선 저 멀리 양팔을 벌린 모양의 나무가 보이는데 마치 성자가 양팔을 올리고 있는 모습이어서 나는 수년 동안 그쪽을 바라보며 기도하는 마음을 가졌다. 한 가운데가 푹 꺼진 채 아문 상처를 안고 있으리라는 생각은 전혀 들지 않았다. 왠지 마음이 끌려 내 두 팔도 같은 모양으로 올리곤 복 받은 기분이 되곤 했다. 이제 와서 눈여겨보니 이곳저곳에서 우리들에게 싱그러움을 선사해 주는 나무들이 한글의 'ㄴ'자 모양으로 되어 있기도 하고 한쪽으로 기울어져 팔을 쭉 뻗은 것도 있다.

이런 나무들은 전깃줄이 지나가는 자리에서 볼 수 있다. 전선에 걸림돌이 되어 사람 손에 의해 잘려 나가고 말았으니, 나무의 입장으로는 불구의 몸이 된 셈이다. 그러나 그 나무는 굵은 가지가 잘려 나가 기형으로 보여도 아랑곳없이 푸른 잎을 무성하게 늘어뜨리고 있다. 땅속 깊이 뿌리를 내리고 있기 때문일 것이다. 이렇듯 꿋꿋하게 살아가는 나무를 보면서 나도 그 같이 대견한 삶을 살고 싶은 소망을 가져보곤 한다.

70년대 어느 봄날. 나를 데리러 온 신랑을 따라서 나는 일본행 비행기에 몸을 실었다. 김포공항에서 부모님과 동생 넷, 죽마고우들과 한바탕 눈물 바람을 치른 뒤 굵은 나무의 가지를 치듯 내 마음의 가지를 쳐서 가족에게 남기고 떠났다. 신혼의 단꿈이라던가 앞으로의 계획 따위에 부풀어 있기는커녕 내 마음은 베인 상처로 아파하면서 두 시간 남짓 하네다 공항을 향해 가는 내내 눈에선 우물을 판 듯 눈물이 멈추질 않았다. 색시 옆에서 신랑은 안절부절 어찌할 바를 몰라 했다.

내가 초등학생이었던 1950년대 후반엔 학교에서 반일 교육을 했다. 단체 관람했던 영화 '유관순'을 어린 학생들이 엉엉 울며 일본 놈들 나쁜 놈들이라고 주먹을 쥐었던 기억이 반세기가 훨씬 지난 지금도 머리 한구석에 남아 있다. 유관순의 모교가 나의 모교가 되었을 때는 내가 참 자랑스럽기도 했다.

우리는 '세계 평화와 정의와 화해를 위한 국제 청소년 회의'에서 처음 만났다. 그 후 누구 못지않게 민족적 자긍심이 강했던 내가 오 년 동안 끊임없이 날아드는 그의 편지 공세에 흔들리지 않으려고 애를 썼다. 괴로운 나머지 편지를 그만하라고 냉정한 마음을 보내기도 해 봤다. 처음엔 영어로 쓰던 편지가 차츰 한글로만 채워져 갔다. '나는 일본에서 태어났기 때문에 일본인일 뿐입니다.' 이런 말에선 특히 마음이 더욱 아팠고 편지마다 그의 정성과 애절함에 나의 마음이 서서히 기울고 있는 자신을 의식하곤 걱정이 밀려왔다.

도대체 어떤 사람이길래 오 년씩이나 내 딸에게 편지를 보내오는가 한번 만나고 싶다고 어머니가 말했을 때 내심 놀라웠다. 일제 강점기에 여고 시절을 보낸 어머니와 같은 반 친구들이 학생들을 따뜻하게 잘 대해 주었던 일본인 스승과 연락을 취하고 있던 터였기에 관심을 갖게 되었는지도 모른다.

그가 처음으로 우리 집에 인사를 온 날 우리말로 열심히 의사 표현하는 모습은 참 진실해 보였다. 만나기 전에는 일본 사람과의 결혼은 절대로 안 된다던 동생들과 걱정스러워했던 부모님으로부터 어렵게 허락이 떨어졌다. 한 달 후 그는 자기 부모를 모시고 다시 서울에 와서 결혼식을 올렸다. 가족의 허락부터 결혼식 날까지 한달 동안 나는 친지들의 질책을 감수해야 했다. 조상에게 면목이 없다고 큰아버지께선 결혼식에 참석지 않으셨다. 특히 내 아버지의 상심은 누구보다 컸었는데 큰아버지 역시 마음이 편치 않았던 것 같다. 비자 수속 문제로 나는 함께 떠나지 못하고 먼저 떠나는 그를 큰댁에서 공항 가는 길에 들르라는 연락이 왔다. 그때 기뻐하시던 아버지를 생각하면 가슴이 아려온다. 딸 때문에 마음 고생을 하셨으니…

 큰 키에 풍채 좋고 늘 근엄한 인상을 주시는 우리 집안의 어르신, 큰아버지는 안방에서 뒷짐을 지고 서 계셨다. 일어가 유창하신 큰아버지는 우리 둘이 올리는 큰 절을 선 채로 받으시곤 그에게 영어로 간단한 질문을 몇 가지 했는데 그는 우리말로 대답했다. '음… 너는 내가 생각한 왜놈이 아니구나.' 술상이 벌어지고 심지어 출국을 다음 날로 연기하라고 하셨다. 이것으로 어려운 고비 하나가 허물어져 갔다. 몇 달 후 내가 출국할 때 김포공항 출국심사대 직원도 대놓고 나에게 한마디 했다. 아깝다고… 우리나라의 70년대는 더욱 그런 시대였다.

 그 당시 일본 인구 일억이천만 명 중 신랑 하나만 보고 따라나섰던 나는 어디서 그런 용기가 났었는지 지금 생각해도 잘 모르겠다. 어떤 큰 힘이 내 인생의 행로를 이끌어 주고 있었다고 믿고 싶다. 강산이 한번 변한 세월을 동경에서 직장, 출산, 육아로 보내는 동안 진실한 친구가 있었음에도 불구하고 나는 정신적으로 온전히 자유롭지 못했다. 지금도 그렇지만 그 시절에도 일본의 정치가나 관료들의 망언에 분노하고 가슴에 생채기가 나기도 했다. 서울 88 올림픽이 개최되기 전이니까 모국의 위상이 날개를 달기 전의 일이다. 어느 날 나는 중요한 결정을 내리게 되었다. 두 아이를 위해서 인생의 나무를 옮겨심기로 했다.

 호주에서 뿌리를 내리기 시작한 지 26년. 처음엔 새로운 언어와 환경 속에서 아이들이 우여곡절을 겪기도 했지만 당당하게 한·일·호주의 세 문화를 받아들이며 이 땅에 깊이 뿌리 내리고 있다. 바야흐로 내 가족은 무성한 잎을 달고 아름드리나무로 자리를 지키게 되었으니 돌이켜 보면 모두가 감사할 따름이다.

(2014)

단출하게 살아가기

집을 줄여 이사를 앞두고 있다. 살아생전 마지막 집이 되기를 바라며 관리가 수월하고 역까지 걸어갈 수 있는 위치의 단층집이라는 두 가지 조건을 만족시키는 집을 찾은 것이다. 결코 쉽지 않은 일이었기에 대어를 낚은 기분이 이런 것일까 생각이 들기도 했다. 그러나 지금은 산더미처럼 쌓인 묵은 짐들을 버리고 또 버려야 하는 갈등을 겪고 있다.

인구조사 자료에 의하면 호주 사람들은 일생 동안 평균 일곱 번 집을 옮긴다고 한다. 꼽아보니 부모와 사는 동안 두어 번, 성인이 되어 독립을 한 경우도 있겠고, 결혼으로 작게 시작한 보금자리, 자녀 숫자가 늘어남에 따라 업사이징, 빈 둥지가 되면 다운사이징, 요양원 혹은 요즘 듣게 되는 어시스트 리빙(assisted living) 등 얼추 계산이 된다. 이렇게 집을 옮길 때마다 가구며 장식품, 옷과 책, 부엌살림 등이 풍선처럼 늘어났다 줄어들었다 했을 터인데 사람들은 어떻게 용단을 내리고 살림살이를 처분했을까. 다운사이징 단계에 와있는 내가 풀어야 하는 수수께끼다. 적십자사나 구세군 기부처에 보낼 박스와 버리는 물건 박스에 넣었다가 다시 슬쩍 꺼내어 이삿짐 쪽으로 옮기며 나 자신 한심한 생각이 들 때가 한두 번이 아니다. 우리 부부가 일하며 번 돈으로 하나하나 장만한 살림살이가 아닌가. 하지만 내려놓기가 이렇게 힘들어서야 이 세상을 떠나는 날 홀가분하게 자유로워질 수가 있기는 할까.

집 매매를 담당했던 부동산 에이전트 소개로 집 정리를 직업으로 하는 소위 정리 전문가 린이라는 여성이 우리 집엘 왔다. TV나 잡지에서만 어쩌다가 본 적이 있는데 정리는 물론 이삿짐을 싸고 새 집에서 정돈까지 맡아 해준다는 말에 귀가 번쩍 뜨였다. 나는 최근에 갑자기 높아진 혈압 때문에 힘든 일 하다가 병원 신세라도 지게 될까 봐 그녀에게 맡기기로 했다. 이 집에서 26년 사는 동안 사들인 부엌 용품 중에 곽에서 채 꺼내지도 않은 아이디어 제품이 나오거나 찾다가 없어서 사용하지 못하던 물건도 나왔다. 이제껏 남에게 공개한 적이 없던 살림살이를 온통 드러내 보여야 하니 부끄러운 마음이 들었지만, 나는 그녀를 향하여 오히려 나 자신을 책망했다. 하지만 그녀는 과연 경험 많은 프로답게 나의 기분을 적당히 살펴줄 줄도 알았다. 감자 깎기가 서랍에서 다섯 개가 나와 내가 난색을 보이자 자기도 어머니와 함께 살며 각자 선호하는 감자 깎기가 달라서 두 개를 갖고 있다면서 우리는 딸도 함께 사니까 세 개는 두라고 했다. 채칼도 여럿이고 칼은 또 왜 그렇게 많은지… 이제는 결혼해서 아이를 넷이나 낳고 사는 아들이 아기 때 사용하던 멜라민 밥그릇과 칸이 나누어진 접시도 어느 구석에서 나왔다. 이렇게 오래된 플라스틱 그릇은 기부 박스에 선뜻 넣지 못하고 주저하는 나를 지켜보던 딸이 '이제는 놓아주라'는 말대로 버릴 박스에 들어갈 위기에 처했을 때 린은 내 편을 들어 주었다. 그런 의미가 있는 물건은 가지고 있어도 된다고. 덕분에 나는 보이지 않는 탯줄이 아들과 아직 연결된 듯 묘한 기분이 들었다. 남들이 보면 오래된 소꿉장난 같은 공기와 접시지만 나에겐 거기에 밥을 담아 먹이던 첫아들의 귀여운 모습과 몇 해 후 태어나 그릇을 물려받게 된 어린 딸의 밥 먹는 모습도 필름처럼 눈에 어른거리니 쉽게 버릴 그릇이 아닌 것이다. 아아, 이렇게 끌어안고만 있다가 어찌할 것인가.

사반세기 이상 살며 정든 집을 떠날 때가 되었다는 생각이 서서히 들기 시작한 것은 우리 부부에게 겁이 덜컥 나는 사건이 있고부터였다. 앞뜰에선 남편이 사다리에서 톱질하다가 떨어지는 사고를 겪었고 뒤뜰에선 내가 나무 가지치기를 하다가 갑자기 뒤로 넘어져 벽돌 바닥에 머리를 부딪치는 일이 있었다. '탁!' 소리와 함께 머리를 부딪치는 순간 나는 단말마의 경험을 하기도 했다. 이뿐이랴. 일일이 나열하자면 머리가 아프다. 그렇다고 은퇴한 마당에 돈을 들여 사람을 부른다는 것은 남편에겐 언감생심이고 나 역시도 원하지 않는다. 그러나 예전처럼 힘을 못 쓰고 운동 삼아 천천히 할 수 있는 일도 제한되어 있지 않은가. 더 늦기 전에 결단을 해야만 했다. 살림살이도 단출하게 줄이고 집도 손이 거의 안 가는 아담한 단층집으로 옮기기로 했다. 그런데 막상 옮기자니 문제는 현재 가지고 있는 물건들을 대폭 줄인다는게 보통일이 아니다. 피아노를 비롯하여 자리를 차지하는 가구와 잡동사니들을 처분해야 하는 딜레마에 빠져있다. 책부터 처분한다는 사람들도 많지만 나는 친정아버지 책장에 있던 오십여 년 된 세계문학전집을 호주까지 가지고 와서 이젠 버리라는 동생들의 말에 아랑곳하지 않은 채 간직하고 있다. 살아 계셨으면 올해 99세가 되었을 아버지를 생각하면 아직도 그리움으로 가슴이 미어지는데 내 어찌 재활용 통에 던져버릴 수 있단 말인가.

나는 오래 살 것만 같다는 생각에 환갑도 칠순에도 잔치를 벌이지 않고 조용히 넘겼다. 어쩌면 나이 듦을 광고하는 것 같아 부끄러움을 피했다고나 할까. 옛적에 사람이 70년을 살기는 드물다고 희수(稀壽)라 했다지만 21세기 지금은 백세시대가 아닌가. 그런 내가 지금은 생각이 바뀌었다. 인간이 마지막 숨을 거두는 순간은 결코 나이대로 찾아오지 않음을 최근에도 경험하고 나니 그 마지막이 언제 나에게 닥쳐올지 모르지만, 이번에 이사를 가면 아끼던 그릇들을 아낌없이 사용하리라. 그릇장에 모셔만 두었다가 결국 처분해야 하는 상황이 온다면 억울하지 않겠는가. 일년에 한번 설날에만 빛을 보는 그릇들은 행여 깨질세라 갓난아기 다루듯 꼭 내가 설거지를 해왔다. 언젠가 딸에게 시집갈 때 가져가라고 했더니 자기가 좋아하는 것만 갖겠단다. 오십 대 중년여성인 린에게 나는 젊었을 때 왜 이런 그릇들을 사 모으는데 돈을 썼을까 반성한다고 했더니 그녀는 또 내 마음을 이해하듯 한마디

해준다. "괜찮아요. 그럴 때 행복했잖아요. 그러면 된 거예요."

　세상에서 거처를 옮기는데도 이렇듯 어렵고 진이 빠지는데 돌아올 수 없는 길을 갈 때는 그 마무리에 얼마나 할 일이 많을까. 아들네는 해외에 사니까 그렇다 치고 딸에게 너무 많은 짐이 되지 않도록 그때그때 정리하면서 살아가는 연습을 해야겠다고 다짐해 보는 것이다.

　(2021)

인연의 끈

코로나로 봉쇄가 한창일 때 이사를 하게 되었다. 벌써 2년 반 전의 일이다. 이사를 하던 그날은 하늘이 심술부리듯 비가 쏟아지다 말다를 반복했다. 이사 간 집 앞 담장에 덩치가 큰 야생 코카투(황관앵무새)가 꿈쩍도 하지 않고 앉아서 짐 나르는 사람들을 감시하듯 보고 있었다. 지능이 높다는 코카투는 나중에는 몇 마리가 떼를 지어 현관 앞 지붕과 시멘트 바닥에서 서성거렸다. 새로 이사 오는 사람들이 친절하게 자기네 무리에게 먹이라도 주지 않을까 싶었나 보다. 떼로 몰려오기라도 할까 봐 꾹 참고 먹을 것을 주지 않으니 똑똑한 이 녀석들은 두 번 다시 현관 주위에서 얼쩡거리지 않고 옆집의 키가 큰 나무 위에 모여 살고 있다. 태양광 솔라 패널이 설치된 옆집의 지붕 위는 코카투 배설물로 가려지기 일쑤다. 록다운 중이니 동네에 인적은 없고 새들에게 먼저 눈으로 인사를 한 셈이다.

이곳 사람들은 이사를 하면 대개 직접 구운 과자나 케이크 등을 들고 이웃집 문을 마치 신고식 하듯 두드린다. 그러나 봉쇄령으로 외출이 엄격히 제한된 때가 아닌가. 마스크를 쓰고 사회적 거리 두기를 한다 해도 남의 집 초인종을 누르거나 문을 두드린다는 것은 엄두도 못 낼 때였다. 그 대신 우리는 식구를 소개하는 글을 써서 초콜릿과 함께 예쁘게 포장하여 몇 집의 우편함에 넣었다. 다음날, 비가 쏟아지는데 현관문 두드리는 소리가 났다. 마스크를 쓴 부인이 앞집에 산다며 웰컴이라고 적은 카드와 오븐에서 막 구워낸 바나나 케이크를 들고 왔다. 카드에는 온 식구 이름과 네 자녀의 학년, 강아지 이름, 남편과 자신의 직업까지 적혀있다. 그녀는 록다운이 해제되면 만나자며 황급히 빗속으로 사라졌다. 우리 우편함에 카드를 넣고 간 이웃도 있었다.

호주에서 산 지 36년 만에 처음으로 울타리를 사이에 두고 한국 가족이 살고 있다. 지금은 가끔 안부를 묻고 지내는 정도지만 뒤뜰에 있던 나의 남편을 불러 상추 모종을 나눠주기도 한 친절한 분들이다. 간혹 마당에서 성년의 그 집 딸이 엄마- 하는 소리가 들려오면 비슷한 목소리의 내 딸이 나를 부르는 것으로 착각할 때도 있다. 바비큐를 하는지 갈비 굽는 냄새나 된장찌개 냄새라도 간혹 바람에 실려 우리 집 쪽으로 풍겨 오면 나는 괜히 기분이 좋다. 한국인이 한국적인 것에 자석처럼 마음이 끌리는 것은 당연하지 않은가.

26년 동안 살며 정들었던 동네를 떠나오니 그리운 마음에 가끔 그곳으로 드라이브를 간다. 사십여 채가 들어선 그 동네는 해마다 호주의 날(Australia Day)이 오면 동네 사람들이 거리에 모여 아침 식사를 같이하는 전통이 있다. 그동안 주민들의 연령이 높아지며 이 세상을 떠난 이웃도 여럿 있고 실버타운이나 요양병원 같은 곳으로 거처를 옮기기도 하니 지금은 동네 풍경이 달라진 듯하다. 동네 길에서 걷기운동을 하거나 개를 데리고 산책하는 동양인이 부쩍 눈에 띈다. 우리가 살던 집을 구입한 사람은 중국계였다. 새 주인은 아직은 멀쩡한 집을 부수고 새로 짓고 있다. 땅을 완전히 갈아엎는 바람에 색색의 철쭉이며 꽤 많던 꽃나무들이 뿌리째 뽑히고 흔적도 없이 사라져 버렸다. 특별한 이유가 아니면 법적으로 자를 수 없는, 하늘을 찌를 듯이 키가 큰 유칼립투스 몇 그루만이 제자리를 지키고 있다. 이제 그 집은 완전히 추억 속의 집, 사진으로만 볼 수 있게 된 것이다. 우리가 살던 집도 사라졌으니 나는 그 집 앞을 드라이브하며 지날 때면 유칼립투스 나무만 올려다보고 '안녕!' 인사한다.

새로 이사 온 지금 이 집에서 2년 이상을 살다 보니 정이 들었다. 집안에서는 동선이 짧아서 편리하고 전철역까지 평평한 도로를 따라 걸어갈 수 있는 거리에 있어서 더 나이들기 전에 잘 옮겼다고 식구들과 두고두고 이야기한다. 처음에는 봉쇄령으로 한 가구에서 한 사람만 하루에 한 번 슈퍼마켓이나 식품점에 갈 수 있도록 외출이 제한되던 때였다. 밖에 나가는 건 남편 몫이었다. 집 안에 묶여 있는 것이 갑갑하고 바깥세상이 궁금한 남편은 반경 5킬로미터 내로 허용된 한국 식품점에 들락거렸다. 나와 딸은 시쳇말로 '집콕'을 하며 이삿짐을 정리했다. 집을 줄여 이사를 하는 바람에 살림을 반 이상 줄여야 했는데 적십자사나 구세군을 비롯해서 모든 기부처가 문을 닫았고, 크고 작은 쓰레기를 처분하는 곳이 철문을 굳게 닫았었다. 지역 카운슬(구청)에서조차 픽업 서비스를 중단하는 바람에 결국 버릴 물건까지 끌고 이사를 오게 되어 이삿짐 트럭을 몇 대나 더 불러야만 했다. 집 안팎에서 눈꼴 사나운 모습으로 둘러싸여 있던 그 짐짝들을 처분하는 데는 상당한 시간이 걸렸다. 우리 집은 길 뒤쪽에 있어서 길에서 보이지 않기에 다행이었지만.

이 집에서 살게 된 것이 필연적이었다고 생각되는 재미있는 사실이 있다. 우리 집 개 이름이 루이(Louie)인데 하필이면 앞집 부인 이름이 루이즈(Louise), 그 옆집 고양이 이름이 루이스(Louis)다. 우리는 루이를 애칭으로 '루'라고 부르는데 앞집 부인의 애칭도 '루'라는 걸 알고는 기겁을 했다. 더 이상 밖에서는 크게 '루'라고 부르지 않는다. 게다가 옆집 한국인 가정에서 키우는 개 이름이 '리오(Leo)'인데 그 집 식구들은 강아지 때부터 키우는 그 개를 아기 부르듯이 리오, 리오 한다. 작년에 태어난 내 조카의 아들도 같은 이름이다. 아기가 우리 집에 올 때마다 우리들은 그 사랑스러운 아기를 리오, 리오…… 하고 불러댄다. 이사 온 후 새로 정한 동네 홈닥터의 이름도 닥터 리오! 우연의 일치라고 웃어넘기기보다는 이쯤 되면 예사롭지 않은 인연의 끈이 우리를 이곳으로 끌어당긴 것이지 싶다. 더 나아가서 우리가 고국을 떠나 하필 호주 시드니로 이주해 와 오랜 세월을 살게 된 일이며, 어쩌면 이 세상에서 마지막이 될 수도 있는 이 집에 둥지를 틀게 된 것 역시도 예삿일이 아니라는 생각이 든다. 우리가 모르는 절대의 섭리로 받아들일 수밖에 없지 않을까.

봉쇄령은 벌써 폐지되었고 아직 코로나로부터 자유로울 수는 없어도 사람들은 일상을 예전처럼 자유롭게 살고 있다. 우리가 이사 온 이 집에서 52년을 살았다는 노부부는 그 긴 세월 동안 동네에서 많은 변화를 겪었으리라. 영국계 백인인 그들이 반세기 전 이곳에 둥지를 틀었을 때만 해도 호주가 백호주의 깃발을 펄럭이던 때가 아니던가. 지금은 집 양쪽에 한국인과 중국인이 이웃하고 있으니 많은 변화를 경험했을 터이다. 이분들은 'Garden File(가든 파일)'이라고 적힌 폴더를 우리에게 남겼다. 나무를 살 때마다 묘목에 딸려 있던 품목표에 구입한 해를 적어서 보관해 왔을뿐더러 어디에 심었다는 것까지 분류해 놓았다. 관리법을 손수 자세히 적어 두기도 했다. 뒤뜰에 아가판서스(agapanthus)가 무리 지어 있던 자리를 지금은 깻잎과 상추가 차지하고 있는 것을 보면 어떻게 생각할까.

내일 지구가 멸망하더라도 오늘 사과나무를 심겠다고 한 스피노자의 명언을 따르고자 한 것은 아니나, 나는 사과나무를 심었다. 로열갈라와 핑크레이디 두 품종을 현관 앞에 나란히 심어 놓고 쌀뜨물을 부어가며 정성을 들인다. 사과가 주렁주렁 열리게 되면 이사 오던 날 현관 앞을 맴돌던 코카투 녀석들을 의식해서 그물을 씌워야 할 수도 있겠지만 사람만 먹겠다고 욕심을 부릴 수도 없지 않은가. 유년 시절 동네 집에서 떡을 하면 이웃들과 나누워 먹었던 훈훈함이 그립다. 이심전심 마음으로 통하며 편안하게 다가와 주는 한국인만이 갖고 있는 정이 그리울 때가 많다.

　우리 이웃들과 사과를 나누게 될 날을 상상하며 나는 저녁쌀 씻은 쌀뜨물을 들고 현관문을 나선다.

　(2023)

2부

인연의 도미노

얼마 전 딸아이가 나에게 선물한 DVD 가운데 '나비의 날갯짓'이라는 프랑스 영화(Le Battement d'Ailes du Papillon)가 있다. 대서양에서 나비가 날갯짓을 한 것이 태평양에 태풍을 불러일으킬 수 있다는 꽤나 미학적인 뜻을 담은 영화로 보통 사람들의 얽히고설킨 이야기들이 도미노처럼 연쇄 반응을 일으키며 운명처럼 전개되는 과정을 보여주고 있다.

… 할머니가 손자에게 과자를 주며 엄마한테 말하지 말라 했으나 아이는 엄마에게 말하고 엄마는 과자 통을 빼앗아 한 개를 꺼내 입에 넣자마자 맛없다고 차창 밖으로 던져 버린다. 길바닥에 떨어진 과자 조각을 비둘기가 먹고 날아가더니 사진 현상소 앞 지붕에 앉는다. 마침 사진을 찾아 가지고 나온 러시아 관광객이 문 앞에서 사진을 들여다보는데 비둘기 똥이 사진 위로 떨어진

다. 관광객은 다시 사진 가게로 들어가서 여자 종업원에게 좀 닦아 달라고 하는데 비둘기 똥을 닦던 여자는 사진 속에서 10년 전에 오해로 헤어진 남자 친구를 발견하고 놀란다.

영화니까 현실과는 거리가 먼 우연의 연속들이라고 생각한 스토리가 마치 필연 같은 결과를 가져오는 것을 보며 문득 떠오르는 친구가 있다. 70년대 초 국제 청소년 회의에 참석했던 나는 그 당시 한창 유행하던 '사랑해'라는 노래를 한 일본 여대생에게 기타를 치며 가르쳐준 적이 있다. 그녀는 대학 졸업 후 항공사에 취직을 했는데 회사의 크리스마스 파티에서 우연히 한 남자를 만나게 되었다. 워낙 큰 회사라 직원들끼리도 서로 모르는 사람이 많았다고 한다. 파티가 무르익을 무렵 한 남자 직원이 앞에 나와 노래를 부르기 시작하는데 수년 전 나에게 배웠던 바로 그 노래가 아닌가. 그녀는 반사적으로 일어나서 앞으로 나가 처음 보는 그 남자 직원과 함께 '사랑해'를 노래했는데 그는 서울지사에 근무하는 동안 배웠다고 한다. 두 사람이 결혼으로 골인하며 내 덕분이라고 감사 편지를 보내왔을 때 그들의 결혼에 내가 관여 되었다는 사실은 놀라운 기쁨이었다.

내 인연의 도미노도 운명처럼 찾아 왔었다. 여고 시절 일 년을 교환학생으로 외국에서 보냈고 대학생 때 회의 참석 명목으로 동경에 간 적이 있다. 귀국하여 얼마 되지 않았을 때 두툼한 우편 뭉치를 받았는데 회의 기간 사진을 담당했던 일본 측 대표 남자 대학생 H가 망원렌즈로 잡은 내 사진과 함께 편지를 보내왔다. 그의 한국에 대한 관심은 70년대 초에 시작되었다. 그가 나에게 5년 동안 보내온 편지는 처음엔 영어로 썼으나 조금씩 한글이 들어 가더니 나중엔 전체가 한글로 되어 있었다. 당시 유행하던 한국 대중가요를 즐겨 부르고 한국 관련 책들도 공부하듯 많이 읽는 등, 그의 관심은 진심이었다는 걸 나는 결혼 후에야 알게 되었다. 그는 수십 권의 공책을 작은 글씨로 빼곡히 채워가며 한국어를 거의 독학했다고 한다. 내가 그 고등학교에 다녔기에 교환학생 기회를 얻었고, 그것이 결국 H를 만나고 호주로 이민까지 오게 된 시작이 아니었을까. 묘하게도 그는 나의 친정아버지가 한때 다녔던 대학의 동문이기도 했다. 거의 40년 전 우리의 만남이 운명처럼 이어진 인연이었다는 생각을 간혹 하게 되는 이유이기도 하다.

프랑스 영화 속의 주인공은 아침 출근길 전철에서 좌석 맞은편에 앉아 있던 남자 승객을 같은 날 밤 뜻밖의 장소인 병원 밖 벤치에서 우연히 만나게 된다. 하루 동안 꼬리를 물고 이어진 일상의 해프닝 끝에 두 사람이 필연적으로 만나야 했던 사람들인 양 암시를 주며 영화는 막을 내린다.

그리고 보면 우리의 일상사는 한순간 한순간이 나도 모르는 사이에 어떤 도미노 대열에 붙어서 흘러가는 건 아닐까? 인연이라는 게 참 묘하기만 하다.

(2011)

신부(新婦)의 표정 변천기

코로나바이러스로 인하여 많은 시간을 집에서 보내며 산더미처럼 쌓인 사진과 비디오를 정리하던 중에 조카의 결혼식 비디오를 다시 보게 되었다. 우아하고 세련된 흰 웨딩드레스의 신부는 입장하며 연신 미소를 머금고 여유 있게 하객들과 눈인사까지 한다. 퇴장할 때는 환하게 웃으며 답례를 하고 있다. 때마침 그림에서 본 꽃가마 타고 시집가는 조선시대 혼례 행렬과 새색시의 무뚝뚝하고 굳은 표정, 그리고 70년대 나 자신의 결혼식 모습을 돌이키면 격세지감을 아니 느낄 수가 없다.

1920년부터 20년간 조선을 방문하며 판화와 수채화를 그린 파란 눈의 미혼여성이 있다. 영국의 화가이자 작가이기도 한 그녀 이름은 엘리자베스 키스(Keith). 그녀의 책 〈코리아-1920-1940〉를 번역함으로써 우리들에게 알려지지 않던 작품들이 책을 번역한 재미교포에 의해서 2006년이 되어서야 빛을 보게 되었다고 한다. 그림들은 그 당시 조선의 풍습이며 경관을 보여준다. 영국과 조선의 문화적 차이가 하늘과 땅같이 다를 진대 그 푸른 눈에 비친 조선이 얼마나 신기하고 흥미로웠을까.

엘리자베스는 '이 가난한 나라에' 깊은 애정을 가지고 사진 찍듯이 그림을 그렸다. 혼례 행렬, 서당에서 공부하는 아이들, 주막 등 자신의 나라와는 전혀 다른 풍습을 캔버스에 담았다. 그 당시 고요한 아침의 나라로 알려진 조그만 동방의 나라에 와서 그녀가 느꼈을 신비함. 그녀는 나라 잃은 조선인들을 연민의 눈으로만 보았을 뿐 아니라 이화학당의 아펜젤러 교장과 함께 3·1운동 때 감옥에 갇힌 여학생을 면회 갔던 일도 전한다.

또한 어느 초라한 주막을 묘사하며 그 집 문 위에 '달을 쳐다보는데 최고로 좋은 집'이라 쓰여 있었다고 전한 그녀 덕분에 비록 가난해도 이런 운치 있는 말로 객을 끌어들이고자 한 주인장의 유머에 정감을 느낀다. 막걸리 한잔 들이켜고 안주 삼아 달을 쳐다보던 가난한 나그네에게 주인은 부침개 한 점 얹어 주었을지도 모른다.

특히 원삼에 족두리 쓰고 앉아 있는 '한국의 신부'라는 그림과 설명이 내 마음을 움직였다. 연지 곤지 찍고 고개를 약간 수그린 채 눈을 감고 다소곳이 앉아 있는 새색시의 표정이 굳어 있다. 지쳐 보이는 얼굴이다. 그림에 대한 화가의 설명은 이러하다. '한국에서 제일 비극적인 존재! 한국의 신부는 결혼식 날 종일 앉아서 먹지도 눈을 뜨지도 못한다. 예전에는 눈에 한지를 붙이기도 했

다고 한다. 신랑은 온종일 친구들과 즐겁게 먹고 마시며 논다.'
남존여비 사상이 뼛속 깊이 녹아 있던 시대의 풍습에 따라 신부
는 그러려니 하고 석고처럼 굳은 얼굴로 앉아 있었겠지만 새색시
의 신세가 오죽 불쌍해 보였으면 가장 행복해야 할 결혼식 날의
신부를 제일 비극적인 존재라고 빗대어 표현했을까. 영국에선 상
상도 못 할 일이었을 터이니.

 돌이켜보건대 나의 결혼식은 엄숙한 분위기에 주눅이 들어 미
소도 짓지 못했고 그렇다고 얼굴이 굳지도 않은 중간 지점이었
다고나 할까. 흰 실크를 끊어다가 양장점에서 맞춘 웨딩드레스는
그 당시 나의 기호대로 지극히 단순한 디자인이었다. 원피스의 길
이를 길게 했을 뿐 목선은 전혀 파지지 않은 매우 수수한 드레스
였다. 새마을 운동이 한창일 때라 결혼식장에서 예물 교환이 금지
되었고 하객들에게 답례품이 허락되지 않았다. 영국 화가의 '시골
결혼 잔치'라는 그림엔 잔치 준비로 꽤 많은 여인들이 부산하게
일하는 그림이 있는데 나의 결혼 때는 잔치마저 생략되었다.

 철통같이 이어온 유교문화의 단단한 벽이 부숴져서 오늘날에
이른다. 경제성장과 더불어 결혼식 풍경이 완전히 달라진 지 이
미 오래다. 웨딩플래너라는 결혼 관련된 모든 일을 대행하는 컨
설팅업체까지 생긴 데다 여행이 자유화되었으니 신혼여행은 보
통 해외로 떠난다. 지금은 코로나바이러스로 하늘 길이 닫혀 있
지만 시드니에서도 한국에서 온 커플룩의 신혼여행객들이 자주
눈에 띄었다. 지금의 여성들은 많이 편해졌고 자유를 만끽하게
되었다. 가정에서도 남편이 도와주고 육아는 의례 같이 한다. 여

권 신장은 쌍수를 들어 환영하지만 지금은 자유가 위험할 정도로 풀어져서 오히려 절제가 있어야 하지 않나 싶을 정도이다.

여자의 일생에서 중대사인 결혼식 날 신부들의 얼굴 표정이 지난 한 세기 동안 참 많이도 변했다. 당면한 시대적 요소들이 그 표정에 한몫했다. 나는 조선 시대에 태어나지 않은 것이 다행이라는 생각이 들며 그렇다고 커플룩으로 신랑과 다닌다는 것도 내게는 얼굴 붉어지는 일일게다. 갑자기 앞으로 내 후손들은 또 어떤 모습으로 변화가 될지 그것이 자못 궁금해지는 것이다.

(2020)

산모와 미역국

 며느리의 출산일이 다가오자 이번엔 이미 세 번이나 딸의 산관한 사부인 대신 내 손으로 산관을 하리라 마음을 먹고 여장을 꾸려 아들네가 살고 있는 미국으로 떠났다. 여행을 할 때마다 좁은 기내에서 장시간 버텨내는 건 여전히 내게는 고역이다. 통로 석을 요청하여 자리를 잡고 자주 일어나 맨 뒤로 가서 스트레치를 하거나 걷기도 하며 산관하는데 체력이 달리지 않도록 신경을 썼다. 오 년 전 꼼짝하지 않고 앉아만 갔다가 건강을 해쳐 고생한 적이 있어서 이번 장거리 비행에 염려가 은근히 밀려들었기 때문이었다. 기내에서 저녁 메뉴로 한식을 선택했더니 더운물만 부으면 되는 인스턴트 미역국이 나왔다. 미역국이라는 흉내만 낸 국을 먹으며 며느리에게 국을 끓여주러 가는 시어미로서 비행기 안의 미역국이 예사롭지 않게 다가왔다. 분만과 미역국에 얽힌 나의 사연이 생각나기도 했고, 친정엄마가 불현듯 떠오르기도 했다.

결혼을 하고 나는 도쿄에서 살았는데, 1980년에 적십자 병원에서 한밤중에 첫 아이를 낳았다. 이튿날 아침 커튼을 친 옆 침대에서 구수한 미역국 냄새가 내 쪽으로 솔솔 스며들어와 나의 침샘과 눈물샘을 자극해 오는 게 아닌가. 옆 사람들이 조총련계인 것을 알고는 말도 섞지 못하고 말았지만, 나는 병원에서 나온 밍밍한 아침밥을 눈물과 함께 삼켜야 했다. 내가 초등학교 때 엄마는 여동생과 막내 남동생을 출산하고, 커다란 국그릇을 가득 채운 미역국을 특별한 음식이라도 하사받은 듯 맛있게 다 비우셨다. 당시 어린 생각에도 나는 이담에 시집가서 아기를 낳으면 엄마처럼 큰 사발에 미역국을 먹어야겠다는 야무진 생각을 했었다. 외할머니가 딸을 위해 끓여내 오신 그 구수하고 고소한 참기름 냄새가 온 방을 풍기던 그 미역국이 이국땅 낯선 침대에서 낯선 음식을 떠먹으며 그날따라 어찌나 그리웠는지 모른다.

장녀인 내가 두 아이를 낳을 때마다 아버지의 병환이 위중해서 엄마는 내게 올 수가 없었다. 엄마는 얼마나 이 딸이 안쓰러웠을까. 엄마는 얼마나 딸이 낳은 첫 손주를 보려고 한달음에 달려오고 싶었을까 하는 생각이 지금 내 마음을 파고든다. 당신 대신 여고를 갓 졸업한 동생에게 미역국 만드는 법을 가르쳐서 비행기에 태워 나에게 보내고, 속으로 많이 울었을 것이다. 동생은 내가 해산한 지 이틀 만에 부랴부랴 미역국을 들고 와서는 '언니' 하며 민망스러운 얼굴로 내 앞에 내밀었다. 형부가 사다 준 쇠고기로 국물을 내서 끓였는데 너무 짜서 다시 만들었더니 미역만 둥둥 떠있는 멀떡국이 되었단다. 그 당시의 미역은 지금 같지 않았다.

엄마가 미역을 일곱 번 박박 씻으라 했건만 두 번 씻고 깨끗해서 그냥 끓였더니 짜서 버리기를 여러 번 했다고. 어찌할 것인가. 그래도 나는 동생이 갸륵하기만 했다. 나는 지금도 동생이 당황해하며 만들었을 그 맹탕이 된 국에 동기간의 정이 담겨 있었기에 맛있게 먹었던 기억을 되살리며 미소 짓는다.

아들은 출근을 하고 배가 남산만 한 며느리가 6살 미만의 올망졸망한 세 아이를 데리고 공항에 나와 나를 반겼다. 아들네 집에 들어서면서 나는 팔을 걷어붙이고 부엌일부터 맡았다. 내가 도착하고 며칠 안 되어 예정일보다 빠르게 진통이 와서 병원으로 간 며느리가 단 90분 만에 순산을 하고 다음 날 퇴원하여 집으로 왔다. 점점 고령화 시대가 되어가는 판에 아이를 하나만 낳거나 아예 낳지 않겠다는 젊은 부부가 늘어나고 있는데 반해 우리 며느리는 넷이나 낳았으니 참 대견하고 존경스러운 생각이 들었다. 제 형제들을 쏙 빼닮은 모습으로 태어난 신비로움에 감탄하며 아기를 내 품에 안으니 너무나 좋아서 마음이 붕 뜨는 것 같았다. 나도 어쩔 수 없는 할머니인 것을 숨길 수가 없었다. 아들네 여섯 식구를 위하여 내 일손이 더 바빠졌지만, 마음은 마냥 행복했다.

그 옛날 외할머니가 내 어머니에게 끓여주었던 그런 미역국을 나는 며느리에게는 해줄 수가 없는 게 안타까웠다. 며느리는 임신 초기 갑상선에 문제가 생겨 요오드 성분이 많은 미역국을 먹을 수가 없었기 때문이다. 나는 고기로 진하게 국물을 내어 배추된장국을 푹 끓여 큰 사발에 담아 미역국을 대신했다. 며느리는 고마워하며 맛있게 잘 먹어 주었다. 멸칫국물에 뭇국, 시금칫국 콩나물국도 끓여댔다. 나는 자신 없는 음식은 요즘 식대로 인터넷에서 찾아가며 만들었다. 내가 해 주는 음식을 식구들이 모두 맛 있게 잘 먹으니, 아무래도 내 음식 만드는 솜씨는 엄마를 닮은 것 같다.

엄마는 60년대 초 요리 연구가인 왕준연 요리학원을 다녔다. 요즘처럼 프린터가 없던 시절이어서 손수 음식 만드는 법을 적은, 간장과 기름으로 얼룩진 공책을 지금도 나는 소중하게 간직하고 있다. 지금 살아 있다면 카톡으로 음식에 관한 정보도 배우고, 친구처럼 이런저런 얘기도 나누련만… 뇌졸중으로 쓰러져 말도 못하고 누워계시다가 세상을 떠나 못내 아쉽고 한이 된다. 엄마는 첫 손주인 내 아들의 돌상을 한국에서 차려주었다. 그 첫 손주가 이제 믿음직한 어른이 되었고, 좋은 아내를 맞아 아들, 딸 낳고 행복하게 사는 모습을 봤더라면, 대견스러워하는 모습이 눈앞에 어른댄다.

내 동생들은 내 입에서 나오는 말씨며, 일하는 모습이, 엄마를 닮았다며 신기해한다. 나 자신도 일상에서 문득 내 안에 엄마를 발견할 때가 있어 놀라곤 한다. 엄마가 지금 내 곁에 와 있는 건 아닐까. 미국에 오기 전 한국에 들러 가족묘에 있는 엄마에게 며느리 산관 잘하고 오겠다고 인사를 했는데 아닌 게 아니라 엄마의 영혼도 나를 따라 이곳에 같이 있는 것 같은 느낌이 들었다.

시드니 집으로 돌아온 후 산모용 미역을 사다가 엄마의 미역국을 끓이며 문득 언제부터 우리나라에서 산모가 미역국을 먹게 되었나 궁금해졌다. 인터넷 검색을 해 보니 고려 시대에 고래가 새

끼를 낳은 후 미역을 뜯어 먹고 상처를 낫게 하는 것을 본 사람들이 산모에게 미역을 먹인 것으로 전해진다. 이어서 조선 시대에도 흰쌀밥과 미역국을 먼저 삼신에게 바치고 나서 산모가 먹었다는 기록이 있다. 근자에 한국에서 유행하고 있는 산후조리원의 식단을 보니 하루 세 끼 일주일 내내 미역국이 나온다. 그러나 의학정보에 의하면 모든 산모에게 다 좋지는 않다는데… 하루가 다르게 급변하는 요즘 세태에 우리의 산모와 미역국의 풍습이 과연 얼마나 먼 후손들에게까지 이어지게 될까. 그들은 먼 조상인 우리들의 이야기를 산모 곁에서 전설처럼 들려줄지도 모른다.

(2018)

1980년 도쿄에서 첫아들을 출산하고

2017년 아들과 갓 태어난 아들의 넷째 아기.

사랑의 힘

　전철 안은 한산했다. 내 옆자리에는 금발의 귀여운 여자아이가 앉아서 앞에 서 있는 엄마에게 조잘대고 있다. 아이는 서너 살쯤 되어 보인다. 이 젊은 엄마 옆엔 유모차 손잡이를 잡은 젊은 아빠가 있다. 딸 옆에 빈자리가 있지만 그녀는 서서 가며 유모차 안의 아기를 연신 들여다보고 있다. 유모차 커버는 손잡이에서 앞쪽으로 반 이상 가려져 있어 나에겐 안이 보이지 않지만, 아기가 잠들어 있는 듯 조용했다. 5개월된 큰손자를 유모차에 싣고 다니던 즈음에 호주를 떠난 아들네를 생각하며 무심코 앞을 바라보다가 갑자기 이 젊은 아빠가 보인 행동에 나는 깜짝 놀라 그에게 말을 걸고 싶어졌다. 유모차 커버 위에 가로세로 한 뼘가량의 부분을 들 출 수 있게 되어 바로 밑의 투명비닐 막을 통하여 그가 아기를 들여다 보고 있는 듯했다. 얼마나 기발한 아이디어인가. 그것을 보는 순간 1·4후퇴 때 나의 부모를 생각했다. 엄마가 아기인 나를 포대기로 업고 윗부분을 담요로 덮어씌워 살을 에는 듯한 추위 속에서 피난민 대열에 끼어 남으로, 남으로 가면서 아버지는 내가 숨을 쉬고 있는지 수시로 담요를 들춰 보았다는 이야기가 생각났다.

당신 지금 저 부분 들춰서 아기 체크하는 거였어요?
네.
와~ 정말 좋은 아이디어네요. 난 이런 거 처음 봐요. 점점 더 편리한 세상이 되어가네요.

나는 어느새 수다스러운 아줌마 티를 내며 한국동란 1·4 후퇴 때 20대 젊은 부부였던 내 부모 이야기를 했다. '이렇게 살아 계셔서 기쁩니다.'라고 젊은이가 웃으며 말했을 때 열차는 목적지 역에 다다랐고 나는 고맙다고 인사하며 서둘러 내렸다. 개찰구를 나와 걸으면서도 내 머리 속에선 그 젊은 아빠가 손바닥만 한 커버를 들추고 아기를 들여다보던 아름다운 장면이 마치 유튜브 쇼츠처럼 반복해서 재현되었다. 문득, 이 젊은이도 내가 그랬던 것처럼 아이의 마음을 읽을 수 있으리라는 엉뚱한 생각이 들었다. 나는 아들이 어렸을 때 아이의 마음을 곧잘 읽을 수 있었다. 아니, 읽었다고 생각할 때가 많았다. 어린아이들은 단순하기 때문에 그럴 수도 있겠지만 합창하듯 동시에 내 입에서 아들과 똑같은 말이 나올 때마다 은근히 그런 생각이 들었다. 어린아이들을 키우는 여느 부모들은 다 마찬가지겠지만…
아들은 중학교 때 NSW주 지방의 야외학교에서 6개월을 보낸

적이 있다. 당시 학교가 학생들에게 가족들과 정기적으로 손편지를 하게한 덕분에 우리 식구들은 손편지로 소통하며 서로의 마음을 전했다. 기숙사 생활, 학업, 친구, 주위의 자연환경, 애완용이 된 캥거루에 대해서도 내 눈에 보이듯 자세히 적혀있었다. 그러던 어느 날, 그곳에서 6개월을 마치고 집에 가면 꼭 교회에 나가고 싶다고 교회에 데려가 달라고 써왔을 때 나는 아들의 마음에 큰 변화가 생긴 것을 감지했다. 사춘기를 겪으며 갑자기 어른스러워진 듯한 아이의 마음속을 내가 어찌 다 헤아릴 수 있으랴. 아주 오래전 친정어머니가 당신의 자녀를 두고 '그 아이 마음속에 한번 들어갔다 나오고 싶다'고 하신 말이 어렴풋이 생각난다. 어느덧 세월이 흘러 이제 아들은 불혹의 나이에 장로가 되어있다. 멀리 살고 있다고 내가 너무 그들의 삶을 미화하는 건 아닐지 모르나 늘 대화를 하며 이심전심하고 사는 듯한 아들 며느리가 내 아들 며느리여서 좋다. 그들은 서로가 열길 물속 한길 마음속 운운할 필요가 없는 삶을 살고 있는 듯이 보인다. 나는 어떤가. 가까운 사람들의 마음을 이해하지 못할 때가 얼마나 많았던가. 내가 사람들의 마음을 섭섭하게 하거나 상처를 주지는 않았는지…

  최근에 뜻하지 않은 일로 당분간 지팡이를 사용하게 되어 하나는 집안용, 다른 하나는 외출용으로 준비를 했다. 집안에서 사용하는 지팡이는 여러 곳에 체인점이 있는 D 점포 에서 저렴하게 구입했는데 세워 놓을 때마다 넘어지는 것을 방지하기 위한 부품도 겸해 구입했다. 지팡이에 부착하여 테이블이나 책상 같은 곳에 기억자 모양으로 걸쳐지니 깔끔하게 정리까지 된다. 외출용은

약국에서 꽃무늬에 반해 D 점포보다 몇 배 비쌌지만, 손잡이가 크고 대가 굵어 힘을 주었을 때 흔들리지 않아 안정감이 있다. 그러나 문제는 세워둘 때마다 옆으로 넘어지지 않도록 신경을 써야 하니 여간 불편한 게 아니다. 식당 같은 데서 딱 소리를 내며 옆으로 쓰러질까 여간 마음이 쓰이는게 아니다.

  무릎을 다쳤던 순간을 생각하면 마음에 찬바람이 스친다. 조심할걸… 그러나 이미 엎질러진 물이 아닌가. 지금 나는 며칠째 심한 감기몸살로 누워있으며 내 마음에도 지팡이가 필요했다. 어떤 상황에서도 넘어지지 않을 마음의 지팡이는 과연 무엇일까. 온갖 상념에 빠져들고 있을 때 아들에게서 전화 메시지가 들어왔다. 여기는 밤인데 그쪽은 새 아침이 밝아오는 시간이었다.

'오늘은 더 좋아지셨어요? 저희 식구들 모두 기도하고 있습니다.'

  나는 5살에서 12살까지 네 명의 손주들이 끼니때마다 서로 식기도를 하겠다고 나서는 것을 본 적이 있다. 그래서 나를 위해 기도한다는 아들 말에 마음이 환해져 옴을 느꼈다. 기도는 가족 간 사랑의 힘일 것이다. 그렇다. 나를 지탱해 줄 마음의 지팡이는 바로 사랑인 것을. 하늘의 크신 사랑, 가족들의 극진한 사랑, 그리고 지인들의 따뜻한 손길이며 위로 등이 나를 감동케 하며 힘이 되어주고 있다. 이웃을 네 몸 같이 사랑하라는 계명을 인간으로서 어찌 실행할 수 있을까. 다만 이웃을 미워하지 않는 것만이라도 실행하게 되기를 바랄 뿐이다.

  (2023)

마지막이 된 배웅

모든 이별은 마음에 치유되기 어려운 상처나 흔적을 남긴다. 그 이별 중에서도 혈육을 나눈 가족이나 마음을 나누고 지내온 친구와의 이별은 더 깊은 상처를 남긴다. 내가 겪은 마지막이 된 배웅은 오랫동안 나에게 텅 빈 세상, 허무한 나락을 경험하게 했다.

70년대 말. 갑자기 찾아온 병마로 아버지는 오른쪽 반신불수에다 언어장애까지 와서 온 가족을 충격과 절망에 빠뜨렸다. 뇌졸중이란 단어조차 주위에서 들은 적이 없었던 그 당시 아버지는 57세 젊은 나이였다. 장녀인 나는 결혼해서 동경으로 간 지 일 년이 되었고 나머지 동생 넷 중에 셋이 학생이었다. 그 후 나는 시드니로 삶의 터전을 옮겼고, 어머니는 시집간 딸네 집에 가보고 싶은 마음을 가슴에 누르며 13년을 단 하루도 빠짐없이 아버지 곁을 지켰다.

중환자실을 거쳐 처음 몇 년 동안은 위독하다는 연락이 오면 나는 비행기를 탔고 내 눈앞에서 아버지가 경련을 일으키며 온몸이 멍든 것처럼 보라색으로 변하는 것을 보게 된 적도 있었다. 아버지는 이 세상을 떠나려고 식음을 전폐하기도 했으나 어머니는 어떻게 해서든 회복시키려고 혼신을 다했다. 수소문하여 한의와 양의를 병행해서 치료에 임했는데 서울 토박이 어머니는 친척이나 지인 한 명 없는 지방 어디 어디에 침을 잘 놓는 한의사가 있다는 얘기를 듣기가 무섭게 싫다는 아버지를 무시한 채 어떻게 해서든지 모시고 갔다. 그 지성이 하늘에 닿았던가. 언젠가부터 경련이 멈추고 다리의 마비가 조금씩 풀리기 시작했다. 왼손으로라도 글을 써서 가족과 소통을 하면 좋으련만 의사표시는 왼손의 제스처로 했고, 어머니가 유일한 통역사가 되었다. 가족들에게 자신의 마음을 내보이기 싫어서였을까. 말하기 좋아하던 사람의 입에서 소리가 나질 않으니 아버지는 그렇게 냉가슴을 앓았다. 식사조차도 아내가 곁에서 떠먹여 드렸으니 미안한 마음이 컸으리라. 어머니와 자식들은 아버지가 그런 상태라도 살아 계시기만을 간절히 원했다.

아버지는 6남매 중 아들로는 막내였다. 막내가 갑자기 쓰러지니 위로 두 형님이며 누님들이 애절해 하셨다. 연로하신 큰고모님은 아버지의 병세를 아시면서도 나를 보실 때마다 눈시울을 붉히시며 '아빠 어떠시냐'고 물었다. 내 입에서 한가닥이라도 희망적인 말이 나오길 기대하시던 그 애절한 눈빛이 지금도 눈에 선하다. 그렇게도 막냇동생 걱정을 하시던 큰아버지, 둘째아버지 두 분이 70의 벽을 간신히 넘기고 먼저 별세하셔서 아버지가 칠순이 되던 그해에 나는 혼자서 속으로 긴장했다. 다행히 아버지는 병세가 많이 호전되어 비록 말을 못 하고 오른손 사용을 할 수는 없지만 혼자서 아파트 단지 내에 있는 이발소도 다녀오실 정도가 되었다. 어머니 덕분이었다. 좋아하는 맥주도 한잔하게 되었다. 안 된다고 하면 화를 내는 바람에 좋아지던 병세가 도루묵이 될까 봐, 드리게 되었다. 식구들은 그런대로 이런 생활에 익숙해져 집안에서 웃음소리가 들리게 되었을 때 나는 용기를 내어 아버지와 어머니를 호주에 모시고 오고자 했다.

아버지는 손사래를 치시며 '나는 아니고 엄마만 모시고 가라'고 왼손으로 말씀하셨다. 동생들도 모두 어머니가 호주에 다녀오시길 원했다. 아버지는 이제 많이 회복하신 데다 자기들이 잘 보살펴 드릴 테니 엄마는 아무 걱정하지 말고 호주에 잘 다녀오시라고 했다. 아아, 얼마나 애타게 기다리던 기회인가. 그러나 어머니 입장에선 병중에 있는 아버지 곁을 자식들보다 자신이 지키기를 고집하셨다. 결혼한 딸네 집에 왔다 갔다 하며 지내는 친구들이 늘 부러웠다는 어머니는 결국 처음으로 딸네 집엘 다니러 가기로 했다. 호주로 떠나는 날. 온 가족이 김포공항에 모였다. 아버지가 엄마를 배웅하러 공항에 나오셨다는 건 우리 가족 친지에겐 뉴스거리가 되었다. 60일만 헤어져 있다가 다시 반갑게 만날 터이니 서양 사람들 같으면 서로 끌어안고 인사를 하건만 우린 그냥 몸을 숙여 절을 하고 손을 흔들며 헤어졌다.

시드니 집에 와서 어머니와 나는 그동안 쌓였던 이야기를 끊임없이 나누었다. 어머니는 오페라 하우스 앞에서 햇빛에 반사되어 반짝이는 시드니 하버의 푸른 물결을 하염없이 쳐다보며 '속이 후련하구나' 하셨다. 그러나 운명은 딸과 잠시 행복한 시간을 보내고 있던 어머니를 그냥 두지 않았다. 호주에 온 지 오십일. 이제 열흘만 있으면 한국으로 돌아갈 텐데 한밤중에 남동생의 전화를 받았다. 아버지가 돌아가셨다는 마른하늘에 날벼락 같은 소식이었다. 쌍초상이 날까 두려워 협심증이 있는 어머니에겐 사실을 숨기고 아버지가 병원에 가셨다고만 했다. '내가 13년을 하루같이 돌봐드렸는데 내가 없을 때 무슨 일이 나면 절대로 안된다.'고 완강한 어머니의 믿음과 고집. 급히 한국에 도착해서 집으로 가는 도중에 내가 아버지 죽음의 진실을 말씀드려야 했을 때의 그 상황을 어찌 말이나 글로 표현할 수 있으랴.

어머니는 이미 돌아가신 아버지를 몸부림치며 배웅했다. 50일 전 김포공항에서 아버지의 입장에서도 자신의 죽음을 예견했다면 가장 힘들었던 배웅이 아니었을까.

나는 아버지와의 돌이킬 수 없는 사별을, 먼 길을 떠나시는 아버지를 배웅해 드렸다고 표현하고 싶다. 언젠가는 다시 만날 수 있다는 믿음으로.

(2023)

내 마음에 쌓인 저금

나는 여행 중 낯선 곳에서 길을 잃거나 복잡한 전철역에서 어느 쪽으로 가야 할지 모를 때 사람들에게 곧 잘 묻게 된다. 안내책자와 지도를 들고도 어리둥절하여 반대 길로 계속 가다가 목적지에서 더 멀어졌을 땐 난감하다. 이번 여행 중에도 이런 경우가 종종 있었다. 처음 간 프랑스와 스위스에서는 물론이고 모국에서도 예외는 아니었다. 나를 도와준 사람들이 없었다면 여행하기 어려웠을 텐데 여러 사람들의 도움을 받았다. 그들의 얼굴은 기억하지 못하지만 그들이 베풀어준 친절은 잊고 싶지 않아 마음속 깊은 곳에 귀중품 다루듯 간직해 두었다.

인천에서 파리행 비행기를 탔을 때 이야기를 나누게 된 옆자리의 승객은 내 딸 또래로 남태평양의 프랑스령 섬에서 농업 관련 일을 하는 엔지니어라고 했다. 공항에 마중 나온 그녀의 아버지가 친절하게도 나를 숙소까지 데려다주었으니 이렇게 고마울 데가 있을까 싶었다. 택시를 타고 시내로 가려 했는데 러시아워에 뒷길을 이용해서 편하게 데려다주었으니 누가 파리지앵을 콧대가 높다고 했던가.

파리에 도착한 둘째 날이었다. 노트르담 가까이에서 유람선을 타고 센강을 한 바퀴 돌며 개선문과 에펠탑 등 명소들을 처음 본 감격에 젖어서 숙소로 가는 도중에 그만 길을 잃었다. 지도를 손에 들고도 완전히 거꾸로 한참을 간 것이었다. 얼마를 걸었던지 올 들어 겪었던 족저근막염이 도져 발바닥에선 불이 나고 다리가 아파 길바닥에 주저앉고 싶은 것을 간신히 참으며 무겁게 발을 옮겼다.

횡단보도에서 신호등이 바뀌기를 기다리고 있는 젊은이에게 물으니 친절하게 내 눈에 익숙한 장소가 보일 때까지 데려다주었다. 여기서부터는 찾아갈 수 있다고 자신 있게 말했는데도 마치 엄마가 길 잃고 헤메던 아이를 보듯이 이 동양 아줌마를 걱정스러운 눈으로 보더니 공손히 인사까지 하고 되돌아갔다. 이 청년의 뒷모습을 보며 사십여 년 전 일본에서도 동경의 어느 큰 역에서 친절한 청년의 도움을 받은 것이 생각났다. 당시엔 언어가 전혀 통하지 않을 때인지라 청년은 아예 자기 돈으로 표까지 끊어서 나를 개찰구까지 데려다 주었다.

처음 방문한 프랑스에 대한 인상은 어제에 이어 좋은 느낌을 받았다. 프랑스 사람들은 특히 여성들에게 친절한 것일까 생각했지만 여성들에게도 도움을 받고 보니 꼭 그렇지만은 않은 것 같왔다. 프로방스로 가는 기차를 타고 여행 가방 두는 곳에 가방을 올리려 했을 때 맞은편에 자리를 잡고 있던 젊은 여성이 벌떡 일어나 무거운 나의 짐을 거뜬하게 올려 주기도 했다. 프랑스 사람들은 다 이렇게 친절한가 아니면 내가 운이 좋았던 것일까.

리옹의 거리에서도 도움을 받았다. 리옹을 떠올리면 군침부터 돈다. 명실공히 식도락의 도시로 유명한 프랑스 제2의 도시에서 일주일을 보내며 점심과 저녁 식사를 3코스로 즐겼다. 하루는 친구들과 프랑스 3대 셰프인 폴 보퀴즈의 이름을 딴 식재료 시장 '레알 드 리옹-폴 보퀴즈'에 갔다. 처음 보는 다양한 식재료들이 고급스럽게 진열되어 있는데 절로 탄성이 나올 정도였다. 친구들과 헤어질 때 길치인 나를 걱정하여 한 친구가 지나가는 사람에게 말을 걸었다. 말끔한 정장 차림의 이 젊은 남자는 마침 내가 가야 할 방향으로 걷는 중이었다. 짧은 불어 실력으로 나는 프랑스에 처음 왔으며 프로방스에서 여름학교에 다녀오는 길인데 산속에 있는 그 학교는 오래된 수도원을 개조한 참 아름다운 곳이라는 둥 떠듬떠듬 말하며 걸었다. 이 젊은이가 반대편에서 오고 있던 지인들을 만나게 되었는데 그들은 내가 일행인 줄 알고 손을 내미는 바람에 얼떨결에 악수까지 했다. 금세 헤어지지 않고 계속 이야기를 하기에 나는 슬그머니 일행에서 뒤처져 혼자 걷고 있는데 한참 있으니 그가 나에게 뛰어와서 미안하다고 했다. 전혀 모르는 사람에게 선의로 길 안내를 하면서도 최선을 다하는 태도가 놀라웠다. 조금 더 걷다가 자기는 건너편 건물로 가야 한다며 나더러 곧장 더 가서 왼쪽으로 돌면 된다고 가르쳐 주곤 좋은 여행되시라고 한마디 하는 예의까지 차리는 게 아닌가. 어쩌면 그리도 친절하고 신사적인지⋯ 프랑스 국민이라는 자부심에서 이렇듯 좋은 매너가 자연스럽게 나오는 것일까, 아니면 그들의 교육에서였을까.

귀국길에 한국엘 들렸다. 오 년 만이었다. 강남역에서 무인운전 시스템으로 운행되는 신분당선을 탔다. 정자역에서 내려 분당선으로 환승하기 위해 표시판을 따라가긴 했으나 전혀 방향감각이 없어서 한 학생에게 물었더니 그 옆의 중년 여성이 반대 방향에서 타야 한다고 친절하게 거들었다. 그녀는 내게 곧장 가서 엘리베이터를 타고 다음엔 계단을 올라가서 왼편으로 돌아 다시 계단을 내려가서 타면 된다고 했다.

나는 분명히 가르쳐 주는 대로 했는데 제자리걸음을 하고 말았다. "아니, 왜 이걸 타셨어요?" 깜짝 놀란 듯한 예의 그녀의 목소리에 나는 화들짝 놀라서 방금 급히 올라탄 전철의 문이 닫히기 직전에 얼른 뛰어내렸다. 이 촌극에 혼자 웃고 앉았을 부인을 생각하면 부끄러웠지만 그분이 아니었다면 마냥 반대 방향으로 가다가 결국 약속 시간에 늦었을 텐데. 지금 생각해도 신기하기만 하다. 조금 전 친절하게 가르쳐준 그 중년여성이 전철에 앉아 있다가 제자리걸음을 한 나를 보았으니 놀랄 수밖에⋯ 자초지종을 들은 여고 친구들은 나의 호주 촌뜨기 됨에 배를 쥐고 웃어댔다.

남이 나에게 순수하고 인간적인 친절을 베풀 때 진실로 감사함을 느낀다. 친절을 베푼 사람은 그의 선행을 곧 잊을지라도 베품을 받은 사람의 마음속엔 깊이 새겨져서 오랜 시간이 지난 후에도 기억 속에서 끄집어낼 수 있는가 보다. 99세에 시집을 낸 일본 할머니의 시 '저금'이 떠올라 그 시를 소개하고 싶다.

난 말이지 사람들이 친절을 베풀면 / 마음에 저금을 해둬
쓸쓸할 때면 그걸 꺼내 / 기운을 차리지
너도 지금부터 모아두렴 / 연금보다 좋단다. - 시바타 도요

(2016)

향기로운 우정

'사무치게 그리운 이가 있는 사람이 부럽다.' 어느 모임의 대화에서 이런 말을 한 그녀의 얼굴에선 쓸쓸한 느낌이 들어, 내 눈엔 마치 마른 꽃처럼 보였다. 나이 때문으로 미루기엔 아직 이른 그가 왜 이처럼 보였을까. 그 말을 들으면서 나는 자신을 돌아보게 되었다. 사실 우리 내외는 어린 남매를 데리고 호주로 이민 와서 아이들이 성인이 될 때까지 참으로 부지런하게 살아왔다. 그동안 내게 생존 외의 어떤 그리움에 젖어 본다는 건 호사였을 지도 모른다. 젊음이 다 지나가 버리고 이제 삶의 여유가 찾아왔다 싶은 이 기회를 놓칠세라 나를 위한 시간으로 채워 가려 마음을 다졌다. 인생에는 나이에 따라 그에 맞는 새로운 라이프스타일이 열려 있다는 말도 있지 않은가.

돌이켜 보면, 나에게 잊을 수 없는 따뜻한 친구가 있었다. 그녀는 우리 가족이 동경에서 살고 있을 때 천사처럼 내게 다가선 바다 건너 서양인이었다. 건축 분야에서 일하는 공무원인 그녀는 건축학을 공부하던 대학생 시절 방학 때마다 꽃꽂이를 배우기 위해 일본을 찾아온 열정이 넘치는 여성이었다. 지인의 부탁으로 그녀가 일본 체류 기간 동안 우리 집에서 함께 기거하곤 했는데 직장에 다니느라 바빴던 나를 많이 도와 주기도 했던 고마운 친구다.

2년 전 더위가 기승을 부리던 한 여름에 나는 딸과 함께 이 친구를 만나기 위해 파리에서 열차를 갈아타고 프랑스 남동부의 한적한 시골 역에 도착했다. 역사를 벗어나자 후끈 달아오른 아스팔트 열기가 얼굴에 훅 끼쳐왔다. 시골 마을답게 거리는 마치 무인도처럼 고즈넉하니 땡볕만 가득했다. 두리번거리는 내 시야에 한 여인이 부리나케 나를 향해 달려오고 있었다. 아리안느였다. 나도 그녀를 향해 마주 달려갔다. 우린 서로 얼싸안았다. 연신 내 볼에 뜨거운 입맞춤을 하는 그녀의 모습은 머리에 새치가 생겼을 뿐, 20대 젊었을 때 그 모습 그대로였다. 그녀 역시 내가 하나도 변하지 않았다며, 연신 나를 관찰하듯 내려보며 눈을 크게 뜨고 놀라워했다. 실로 삼십 년만의 해후였지만, 변함없는 마음으로 서로를 봐서인지 얼굴의 주름 따위는 눈에 들어오지 않은 듯싶었다. 그녀가 강력히 권하는 바람에 우리는 열흘간 그녀의 집에 머물면서 그동안의 회포를 끊임없이 풀어댔다.

아리안느의 집은 구석구석 그녀다운 따뜻한 마음으로 잘 꾸며져 있었다. 그녀는 네팔에서 두 남매를 입양해 키우고 있었는데 아기 때부터 입양한 아들은 이제 15살, 딸은 10살로 아이들은 네팔식 이름을 갖고 있다. 집안 여기저기에서 네팔의 문화를 엿볼 수 있는 휘장이며 그림과 장식들이 눈에 뜨였다. 그녀는 남편과 함께 네팔 아이들을 키우며 그들이 태어난 나라를 가까이 생각할 수 있도록 많은 배려를 하고 있는 것이 퍽 감동적이었다. 삼십년 전 내가 딸을 출산했을 때에도 이 친구는 보드랍고 포근한 실로 아기 포대기와 앙증맞은 모자까지 손수 떠서 보내주었다. 나는 그것을 아직까지 잘 보관하고 있다. 딸이 결혼하게 되면 손녀에게 대물림하리란 생각에서이다. 그뿐만 아니라 우리 아들이 세 살 때 자신이 직접 찍은 사진을 그림처럼 크게 프린트해서 골판지에 1984년도 달력을 만들어 보내 주기도 했다. 우리 부부는 연도와 상관없이 그 달력을 마치 명화라도 되는 양 감상하며 오래도록 벽에 걸어두었었다. 아리안느는 어른이든 아이든 그 마음을 헤아릴 줄 아는 따뜻한 친구여서 참으로 귀하게 여겨진다.

지금도 가끔 느닷없이 이 친구가 문득 떠오를 때가 있다. 열흘 동안 체류했던 그녀와 그 집의 향내에 취하게 되고, 아리안느와 그녀가 살고 있는 스위스가 그립다. 거실에서 아득히 보이던 그 유명한 알프스의 최고봉 몽블랑이며, 그녀와 기차를 타고 체르마트라는 산악마을까지 가서 다시 산악열차로 마테호른산이 코 앞에서 바라다보이는 곳까지 갔던 일. 그 거대한 산을 바라보며 샌드위치를 꿀맛처럼 먹었던 일들을 생각하면 지금도 그 산에서 뿜어내는 정기가 나를 둘러싸고 있는 듯한 착각이 들곤 한다.

좋은 친구를 가진다는 것은 또 하나의 인생을 갖는 것이라고 한다. 나는 결코 마른 꽃이 되지 않으리라. 내가 비록 풍란(風蘭)의 향기를 맡아본 적은 없어도 이름만으로도 마음이 끌리는 그

꽃처럼 서로에게 은은한 향기를 남기는 친구를 만나며 여생을 보내리란 꿈을 꾸어 본다.

(2017)

1983년 도쿄에서 아들 신지와 아리안느와 함께

2015년 스위스에서 아리안느와 딸 케이와 함께

Ariane과 작별하기 전날 딸이 그린 감사카드. 함께한 시간들을 그림으로 남겼다.

아, 버지니아!

국내선으로 갈아타고 목적지인 버지니아주의 한 지방 공항에 도착할 때까지 세 시간 남짓 걸렸다. 스무 명쯤 태운 경비행기가 기류에 흔들리며 하늘을 가로지르는 동안 나는 줄곧 좌석 양쪽 팔걸이를 꽉 붙들고 무사히 착륙하길 기도하고 있었다. '아! 버지니아!' 내 마음의 고향 버지니아에 37년 만에 다시 찾아가는 길이었다.

짐을 찾고 통하는 문을 나오는데 한산해 보이는 시골 공항에 누군가를 마중 나온 사람들이 서너 명 정도 눈에 띄었다. 양팔을 벌려 큰 종이를 펼쳐서 들고 있는 사람도 보였다. 관광객을 맞는 여행사 직원으로 생각하며 내 눈길이 그녀가 들고 있는 종이에서 얼굴로 옮겨지는 순간 그녀는 종이를 떨어뜨렸고, 나 역시 여행가방을 놓아버리고 "아~!" 하고 외치며 서로에게 달려갔다. 우리는 단숨에 껴안았고 그 간의 오랜 세월은 순식간에 사라졌다. 멀어진 시간이 다시 눈앞의 '지금'이 되었다. 나를 마중 나와 준 옛 친구 캐롤 이었다. 기쁨의 눈물과 웃음으로 범벅이 된 얼굴을 보고 또 보고 다시 얼싸안는 장면을 옆에서 누군가가 비디오를 찍고 있다는 걸 알아차린 것은 잠시 후였다. 그녀의 남편 레이몬드였다. 그 당시엔 대학생이었는데 이젠 백발에 그나마 머리숱이 거의 없어서 딴사람 같았다. 이제부터 열흘간 이 부부가 나를 타임머신에 태우고 1968년에서 1969년으로 돌아갔다가 다시 2006년으로 데려다 주게 된다. 우리들은 함께 추억의 길을 찾아 나선 것이다.

세계 제2차 대전 후 미국과 독일 간에 악화된 외교관계를 민간차원에서 개선 하고자 시작되었다는 국제 기독 교환학생 프로그램으로 당시 기독교 계통 여고에 다니던 나에게 일 년 동안 버지니아에 갈 기회가 주어졌다. 그때는 미국 비자는 물론 우리나라 외무부로부터 여권 받는 일조차 쉬운 일이 아니었던 걸로 기억된다. 어머니는 우리나라 문화를 소개하기 위하여 가야금과 고전무용을 속성으로 익히게 하시고 시집가는 딸에게 해 주시는 것처럼 한복도 여러 벌 마련해 주셨다. 요즘같이 비디오나 DVD가 있었다면 우리 문화를 쉽게 소개할 수 있었겠지만, 수박 겉핥기식으로 배운 실력, 춤추다가 틀려도 시치미 떼고 넘어갔던 일은 지금 생각하면 아찔하다.

나를 1년 동안 친딸처럼 돌봐 주신 미국 부모님은 아들 다섯에 딸 둘을 둔, 자식 많은 가정의 어른이었다. 일찍 결혼한 두 아들과 집을 떠나 대학에 다니는 큰딸을 제외하고도 여전히 대가족이었는데, 교회를 통해 처음으로 외국 교환학생인 나를 맡아 주시며 셋째딸처럼 여겨 주셨다. 일 년 동안 한 방을 함께 썼던 둘째딸 캐롤과 공항에서 다시 만났을 때의 감회는 정말 특별했다. "오! 영규, 이제야 왔구나!" 집에서 나를 기다리고 계시던, 이제는 많이 연로하신 미국 부모님은 기쁨의 눈물로 나를 맞아 주셨다. 거실의 커다란 벽 한 면을 빼곡히 채운 가족사진 속에는 이 행복한 가정의 이야기가 고스란히 담겨 있었다. 그중에는 나의 미국 고3 졸업 앨범 사진도 포함되어 있어 가슴이 뭉클했다. 주말에는 나를 위한 환영 파티가 열렸다. 일곱 남매와 그들의 가족, 부모님의 형제자매, 사촌들, 그리고 고등학교 동창들까지 70여 명이 모인 자리였다. 미국 아버지는 흥분된 목소리로 "주님, 감사합니다. 영규가 왔습니다!" 하고 감사의 기도를 올리셨다. 두 분은 늘 봉사 정신을 실천하며 사셨다. 나를 맡아 주신 일 역시 그 정신에서 비롯된 것이 아니었을까 싶다. 대가족을 돌보시던 그 시절에도 미국 어머니는 정기적으로 병원 봉사활동을 하셨고, 나는 가끔 봉사에 따라갔다. 병실에서 외롭게 누워 있는 노인 환자들에게 다정한 말을 건네고 정성껏 돌보시던 모습은 내게 큰 감동이었다. 그분들은 최근까지도 아프리카에 가서 학교를 짓고, 태풍 피해를 입은 뉴올리언스로 가서 목공일을 돕고 식사를 준비하시는 등 봉사의 손길을 멈추지 않으셨다. 어려움에 처한 이웃들을 향한 이분들의 지치지 않는 열정은 지금의 나를 되돌아보게 만든다.

내가 만 일 년 동안 고3으로 다녔던 학교에 찾아갔다. 밖에서는 하나도 변한게 없어 보이는데 알고 보니 학교 건물로 들어가는 모든 문들은 한군데를 제외하곤 다 잠겨져 있다. 1999년 세상을 충격 속으로 몰아넣었던 콜롬바인고교 총기 난사 사건 이후부터 그렇다는데 참으로 서글픈 현실이 아닐 수 없다. 우리 일행 셋 다 이 학교 졸업생들인데도 사무실로 가서 사인하고 선생님 한 분이 안내를 해 주셔서 학교 안을 둘러볼 수 있었다. 약간 달라진 곳도 있지만 체육관과 학교 식당은 예전 모습 그대로여서 감회가 깊었다. 당시 내가 미국에 도착한 다음 날부터 신학기가 시작되었는데 하루는 신문기자가 찾아와서 인터뷰를 하고 이런 기사를 실었다. '저 멀리 코리아에서 온 이 여학생은 사진을 찍을 때 잠시 기다려 달라고 한 후 안경을 벗고 콘택트렌즈를 끼고 나왔다. 십 대 소녀들의 예쁘게 보이려는 마음은 동양이나 서양이나 다 똑같다는 것을 증명했다.' 그때 나는 학교에서 유일한 동양인이었을 뿐 아니라 유일한 외국 학생이기도 했다. 역사 선생님은 출석 부르실 때마다 생소한 내 이름을 발음하기가 힘들어서 아예 "한국서 온 여학생(The girl from Korea)" 하고 부르셨다. 십 년이면 변한다는 강산이 거의 네 번이나 변하는 동안 교실에 늘어난 동양 학생들이 지금은 어떻게 호명되고 있을까 궁금하다.

열흘 내내 미국 부모님 댁에 머물면서 우리들은 쉴 새 없이 옛이야기와 그동안 살아온 이야기로 꽃을 피웠다. 내가 마치 어제 나갔던 딸이 오늘 돌아온 것처럼 자연스럽게 어울리고 있는 것을 매우 기뻐하셨다. 예전에 살았던 집을 지금 주인의 친절로 자세히 둘러볼 수 있었는데 영화 '바람과 함께 사라지다'에 나오는 그런 집이다. 1800년대 초에 지은 집으로 현재의 주인 부부가 직접 옛날의 모습대로 고쳐가는 중이었는데 거의 40년 전에 내가 지냈던 2층의 방이 옛모습 그대로 있어 놀라웠다. 쉐난도 밸리(Shenandoah Valley)에 위치한 이 집의 바로 옆에는 쉐난도 강이 냇물처럼 얕게 흐르고 있는데 당시 나는 중2의 쌍둥이 남동생과 강가에서 낚시를 하곤 했었다. 그때의 쌍둥이 중 식사 시간에 기도를 도맡아 하던 아이는 어느새 나이 오십의 목사님이 되어 있었다.

어느새 찾아온 작별의 시간에 우리 모두 손에 손을 잡고 함께 보낸 시간을 감사하며 무사히 잘 돌아가게 해 주시고 다시 만날 때까지 건강 지켜 주실 것을 미국 아버지께서 간절히 기도해 주셨다. 지나간 긴 세월 나의 친부모 형제들과 멀리 떨어져 해외에서 시작한 결혼생활, 직장생활, 출산, 육아, 이민 등 변화와 도전의 인생살이 속에서 이분들에 대한 그리움이 문득 찾아들 때마다 가슴이 촉촉해지곤 했는데 어느 날 인터넷의 힘을 빌려 이분들을 찾게 된 것이었다. 이 세상에 계실 때 찾아뵐 수 있었고 온가족의 나에 대한 변함없는 우정에 감사하며 다시 경비행기에 몸을 맡기고 떠나는 내 마음은 신기하게도 전혀 두려움 없이 커다란 일을 해낸 성취감과 행복감으로 가득 차 있었다.

시드니로 돌아온 후 버지니아에서 보낸 우편물이 도착하였다. 떠나기 전날 그 지역 신문기자가 취재를 해 갔는데 "한국 교환학생 37년 만에 밸리(Valley)의 가족에게 돌아오다"라는 타이틀과 함께 우리들의 훈훈한 이야기를 크게 소개한 것이다. 부모님과 함께 예전에 살던 집을 쳐다보는 사진과 캐롤과 내가 그 당시 한복을 입고 찍은 사진을 기자 앞에서 들고 있는 사진이 실려있다. 두 분께서는 이 신문이 나온 후 그 지역 유명인사가 되셨다며 기쁘게 전해 주셨다. 이제 추억의 길을 찾아 떠났던 타임머신은 나를 다시 복잡하고 바쁜 일상으로 데려다주었지만, 이따금 그 길로 되돌아가서 흐뭇한 정을 되살리며 미소 짓는다.

  삶의 어떤 시절은 먼 길을 돌아 다시 왔을 때 비로소 그 의미를 온전히 품게 된다. 오랜 시간이 흘렀지만 그 인연은 오늘의 나를 더욱 단단히 지탱해 준다.

  (2007)

PEOPLE | RENEWING OLD TIES

Young-Kyu Kwon Yasugi views a picture of the Morris homeplace, where she lived in 1968 with her host family (from right) Carrie and Elzie Morris and their daughter Carol Ann Chapman.

Home Again

Korean Exchange Student Visits Her Valley Family After 37 Years

By REBECCA MARTINEZ
Daily News-Record

GROTTOES — When the Morris family sat down to lunch in the sunroom of their Grottoes farmhouse last Tuesday, the table was filled with happy chatter. As they passed around plates of pork, tomato-and-pimento sandwiches, and Mrs. Morris's sweet pickles, they laughed, told stories and finished one another's sentences. If it weren't for Young-Kyu Kwon Yasugi's olive complexion and almond-shaped eyes, you'd never have guessed they weren't blood relations.

After 37 years and three homes across the Western Hemisphere, Young-Kyu has returned to visit the hosts who became her own family during her year as a foreign exchange student in Virginia.

A Growing Family

Elzie and Carrie Morris raised their children on a farm on the Shenandoah River in Elkton and emphasized family values.

"Our family had church, school, and working on the farm," says Carol Ann Chapman, the fourth child of the Morris family and closest to Young-Kyu in age. "If you ate, you worked."

Elzie and Carrie are well versed in hospitality. For years, the Morris family hosted live-in guests, including a mentally disabled uncle and several foster children, one of whom they adopted.

For 50 years, the family has attended Mill Creek Church of the Brethren, through which Carrie arranged to host numerous exchange students from around the world. All of them called Carrie and Elzie "Mama and Daddy".

"I don't remember living with Mama and Daddy and just us," Chapman recalls.

Carrie adds, "Not for a year at a time."

This kind of home life has made her children more sensitive to disabled and elderly people, as well as people from different cultures, Carrie said. Of all the exchange students, none has stayed on as long with the Morris family or become as close with them as Young-Kyu.

Seeing The Country Life

Young-Kyu was raised in Seoul, South Korea, the oldest daughter of a well-to-do family and self-proclaimed "city girl."

"Young-Kyu had people from county come to the city to clean [her home]," Carrie says.

Despite the dramatic difference between her

Carol Ann Chapman and Young-Kyu Kwon Yasugi hold a photo of themselves dressed for a party in 1968.

home in Seoul and the Morris farm, the family says Young-Kyu fit right in.

"She was very pleasant and had a wonderful disposition," Elzie says. "We bonded so well."

On her first day with them, she helped the youngest boys, twin eighth-graders, gather eggs from the family's 500 laying hens.

"She was never afraid to do anything," Chapman says.

Although she could read and write in English, Young-Kyu didn't speak or understand spoken English very well.

"Once, Uncle Jack, Mama's brother, told a joke at the dinner table and everybody got it except me," Young-Kyu said. "Mama had to write it down, and then I laughed."

While Young-Kyu and the Morris family managed well despite the language barrier, Carrie suspected that Young-Kyu felt homesick for the Korean language.

"Mama thought Young-Kyu was missing her language, so she brought her down to see a Korean professor at Virginia Tech," Chapman recalls. "He said it was the first time he'd heard Korean in a Southern drawl."

During her year abroad, Young-Kyu was a senior at Montevideo High School, where she attended football games and prom, and worked diligently on her studies.

Chapman and Young-Kyu shared a bedroom, went on double dates and agree that they developed the closest-knit relationship of all the siblings during the year.

"I couldn't take her to the bus [at the end of the year]," Chapman said. "We cried too much the night before."

See **EXCHANGE**, Page B6

3부

이 시대의 바벨탑

```
이때과거 식량하거나 음료
THIS TIME PAST FOOD OR DRINK
```

　쇼핑센터에 갔다가 벽에 붙어 있는 수수께끼 같은 문구에 눈이 끌렸다.
　'이때 과거 식량하거나 음료'
　훤히 들여다보이는 안쪽에서는 어린아이들이 놀고 있고 놀이기구도 보인다. 어른들이 쇼핑할 동안 아이들을 돌봐주는 곳인가 본데 나를 어리둥절하게 만든 이 문구는 영어, 중국어, 한국어 3개 국어로 되어 있다.
　맨 윗줄의 영어를 보고 나서야 무슨 말을 하려 했는지 알 수 있었다. 'No food or drink past this point(음식물이나 음료수 반입 금지)'를 인터넷의 번역 기능을 이용하여 그대로 베껴다 놓은 것이 분명했다. 아무리 새겨서 읽어봐도 전혀 감이 잡히지 않았다. 인터넷 번역이 이 정도로 엉터리 수준일 줄이야.
　아무리 세상이 기계화 되어가고 있다고 해도 이것만큼은 사람의 손을 거쳐야 되나 보다. 기계로 해서 마치 로보트가 하는 말처럼 들리는 것보다 사람 냄새가 나는 편이 훨씬 좋다. 언어 때문에 겪는 사람들의 실수는 기계로 인한 잘못됨과는 차원이 다르지만 우스운, 또는 웃지 못할 에피소드를 남기기도 한다.

나이 20대 후반에 도쿄에서 직장을 갖게 되었을 때 나의 일어 수준은 바닥이었다. 영어를 웬만큼 하면 일하기엔 지장이 없었는데 주위에서 들려오는 일본인 동료들의 대화를 알아들을 수 없어 날이 갈수록 군중 속에서 외로움을 느끼는 꼴이 되어갔다.

결국엔 저녁 시간에 학원으로 달려갔지만 학원에서 가르쳐 주지 않는 말들은 TV를 보며 내 나름 입체적으로 일어 공부에 몰입했다. 그런데 드라마에서 남자들이 쉽게 쓰던 '치xx(젠-장!)'이라는 좋지 않은 말을 제일 먼저 배우고도 가벼운 말('이런!')인줄 착각하고 회사에서 남발을 했으니 돌이키면 얼굴이 화끈 달아오른다.

말을 배우는 중이니까 이말 저말 자주 사용해 볼때였는데… 아무리 그네들이 남의 마음을 상하게 하거나 부끄럽게 하는 일은 미덕이 아니라고 어렸을 때부터 배운다지만 누구도 나를 정정해 주지 않았다. 시간이 지나 스스럼없는 사이가 된 동료가 내 기분을 살피며 말해 주었다. 내 입에서 나온 '치xx'는 뉘앙스가 다르게 들려 귀여운 데가 있었다나. 그때 나는 부끄러워서 쥐구멍이라도 있으면 들어가고 싶었다.

서울올림픽이 열리던 해에 나는 십 년 동안의 일본 생활에 종

지부를 찍고 가족과 함께 삶의 터전을 호주로 옮겼다. 시드니 공항에는 일본에 교환학생으로 일 년간 와 있었던 호주 친구가 부모님과 함께 우리를 마중 나와주었다.

무남독녀 외딸인 이 친구는 일본에서 지내는 동안 어려움을 겪을 때마다 우리 내외를 찾곤 했었다. 다른 문화권에서 교환학생으로 생활한 경험이 있는 남편과 나는 그녀의 고충을 이해하기에 늘 도움이 되어 주었다. 그런 친구가 부모님과 함께 시드니 공항에서 플래카드를 들고 우리 가족을 기다리고 있었다. 그런데 일어로 플래카드에 적힌 말이 '호주에 오신 것을 환영합니다'가 아닌 '호주로 돌아오신 것을 환영합니다'로 되어 있지 않은가.

나는 28년이 지난 지금도 그때를 생각하면 오직 그 친절과 배려에 감사할 뿐 그녀의 일어를 정정해서 무안하게 할 생각은 추호도 없다.

내가 호주에 온 지 며칠 후 이 친구의 어머니가 'Tea'를 하러 집으로 오라 했을 때 오후에 마시는 티로 생각하고 점심시간을 피해서 갔다. 어머니가 말한 'Tea'가 가벼운 식사를 의미하는 줄 알았을 때 얼마나 미안했는지 모른다.

그때 우리 가족은 임시로 아파트를 빌려 있었는데 핸드폰이 없던 시절이라 친구의 아버지를 전철역에서 오랫동안 기다리게 하는 촌극을 벌였다. 친구가 직장엘 가기 때문에 미리 그려준 약도를 보고 그 집을 찾아갈 참이었다. 우리들이 하도 나타나질 않아서 친구의 아버지는 걱정하며 전철역에서 기다리고 있었던 것이다.

우리는 사람이기에 실수를 한다. 하지만 대중을 상대로 쇼핑센터에 붙여 놓을 문구라면 마땅히 올바르게 구사해야 되지 않겠는가. 이 세상에 수없이 많은 언어가 존재하건만 인터넷에 의하여 또 다른 국적 불명의 언어들이 생성되는 요즈음이다. 이것이야말로 이 시대의 바벨탑*이라는 생각이 든다.

(2016)

---

* 바벨탑: 온 세상이 같은 말을 썼던 때에 사람들이 그들의 이름을 위하여 하늘에 닿게 탑을 쌓던 중에 하나님이 말을 뒤섞어 놓아 탑 쌓기를 그만두고 흩어졌다고 기독교 성경에 기록됨. 히브리어로 바벨은 '혼란'을 의미.

바야흐로 휴대폰 시대

얼마 전 카톡에 흥미로운 사진이 올라왔다. 1916년이라고 표시된 상단엔 마차가 있는 거리에서 긴 코트 차림에 중절모를 쓴 남자들이 길가에 나란히 서서 신문을 펼쳐 보고 있다. 다시 그 하단에는 2016년의 사진으로 자동차들이 주차된 길가 건물 앞에 티셔츠와 반바지 등 캐주얼차림의 젊은이들이 기대서서 휴대폰을 들여다보고 있다.

이렇듯 100년 동안의 변화를 보면서 나는 격세지감을 느꼈다. 손바닥만 한 휴대폰으로 뉴스를 볼 수 있는 현대의 젊은이들에겐 양팔로 넓은 종이신문을 펼쳐 들고 있는 사진 속의 남자들은 호랑이 담배 피우던 시절에 살았다고 생각할 터이다. 지금은 이 작은 휴대폰이 단순한 휴대전화가 아닌 컴퓨터의 온갖 기능이 들어 있는 소위 스마트폰으로서, 나에겐 마치 알라딘의 요술램프로 생각되기도 한다.

손안에 있는 휴대폰. 그 안에 온 세계가 있다. 첨단기술 변화의 속도가 하도 빨라 아날로그 시대를 살아온 나로서는 따라가기가 벅차다.

다이얼을 일일이 돌리던 전화기가 번호 버튼을 누르는 푸쉬폰으로 바뀌어졌을 때 전화를 많이 사용하는 직장인들이 더 이상 손가락이 아파 볼펜으로 다이얼을 돌릴 필요가 없어졌다고 좋아라 했던 것을 기억한다. 그때부터 푸쉬폰식 휴대폰이 나왔는데 값이 비싸고 귀할 때라 자동차에 두고 내렸다가는 차창 유리를 깨고 훔쳐 가는 일이 빈번히 발생해 나 자신도 당한 적이 있다.

그 후 등장한 것은 지금의 터치폰, 두께가 얇아진 데다가 손가락으로 번호 위를 터치 하는 휴대폰에 컴퓨터 기능이 들어있어서 바야흐로 우리는 스마트폰 시대에 와있다. 아니, 오히려 손바닥 크기의 휴대용 컴퓨터에 전화 기능이 있다고 해야 옳을 것이다. 초창기 컴퓨터가 20평 가까운 방만 한 크기에 무게가 30톤이나 나갔다는 것을 감안하면 과학자들의 비상한 두뇌에 절로 감탄사가 나온다.

휴대폰에 지각변동이 일어나더니 이제 스마트폰은 현대인의 생활필수품이 되어 버렸다. 아예 신체의 일부분인 양 집안에서도 호주머니에 넣어 몸에 지니거나 손에서 놓지 않고 사는 사람들이 하나도 이상할 게 없다. 문명의 이기에 맛들인 현대인은 이렇듯 휴대폰에 의지하며 살고 있다. 나는 이 편리한 생필품의 노예가 되어가는 자신을 발견하곤 솔직히 도망가고 싶을 때가 있다. 어쩌다 하루 종일 카톡에 매달린 날은 손끝이 전기가 오르듯 찌릿

찌릿해진다.

　건강에 좋을 리가 없다. 그리운 친구에게 손편지를 써서 봉투에 넣어 우표를 붙여 보내면 받는 친구는 얼마나 반가워할까. 지금은 그저 모든 안부나 하고 싶은 말들을 카톡으로 하고 있으니 손끝이 알알할 수밖에… 그렇다고 손편지는 생각일 뿐 어느새 이 작은 휴대폰에 손이 먼저 가고 만다.

　사고 방지와 안전을 위한 목적으로 한국에서는 유치원에 다니는 어린이들까지 휴대폰을 목에 걸고 다니는 세상이 되었다. 작년에 유치원 다니는 조카의 딸이 자그맣고 예쁜 모양의 휴대폰을 목에 걸고 있는 것을 보고 깜짝 놀랐다. 조카네는 집 전화가 아예 없고 온 가족이 각자 휴대폰을 소유하고 있다. 아이들이 행여나 스마트폰 중독에 걸릴까 봐 걱정하면서도 손바닥만 한 컴퓨터가 공부하는데 도움이 된다니 울며 겨자 먹기로 안 사줄 수도 없지 않은가.

　나는 이런 걱정 없을 때 아이들이 학교에 다녔지만 지금은 학교 다니는 학생을 자녀로 둔 부모들의 세대가 컴퓨터에 능통한 세대라 나는 때때로 닭 쫓던 개 지붕 쳐다보듯 아련히 바라만 보게 된다. 동서양을 막론하고 초등에서 고등학교까지 학생들이 교실에 휴대폰 반입을 금지하는 나라들이 많이 있다고 알고 있다. 어느 학교는 등교 시 사물함에 넣어두고 하교 시 꺼내 가도록 했더니 학생들의 수업 참여율이 높아졌다고 한다.

　스마트폰으로 인해서 일어나는 문제점들이 어디 이뿐이랴. 보이스 피싱 같은 것도 있으니 순진하게 당하지 말고 정신 바짝 차리고 대처해야만 한다. 스마트폰 세대를 신인류라 하고 폰(phone)과 사피엔스를 합해서 포노 사피엔스라는 새로운 합성어까지 탄생했다. 게다가 스마트폰에 인공지능을 탑재하는 연구가 진행되고 있다니 내 생애에 포노 사피엔스의 미래를 보게 될 가능성은 희박하지만 과연 미래는 어떤 세상이 펼쳐질지 자못 궁금해진다.

공상과학 영화에서나 보던 일들이 현실로 다가와 있는데 후세대들은 지금 우리의 상상을 초월하는 두뇌로 이 지구를 확 바꿔 놓을 게 뻔하니 말이다. 첨단기술의 발달로 인하여 따뜻한 정이 사라져 버린 마치 플라스틱 가슴을 가진 사람들이 모여 기계적인 삶을 살아가게 되지 않을까 우려의 상상을 해본다.

19세기에 다이너마이트라는 폭발 장치를 발명한 노벨은 이것을 단지 산업용으로 사용하기 위해서 개발했는데 전쟁에 사용되는 것을 보고 후회했다고 한다. 그래서 유산의 대부분을 바쳐 인류 문명의 발달에 기여한 사람들에게 주는 노벨상을 설립하도록 했다. 나는 이 스마트한 스마트폰이 결코 다이너마이트처럼 잘못 쓰이지 않기만을 간절히 바랄 뿐이다.

(2020)

문화의 힘

그 동영상은 처음 화면부터 나의 호기심을 끌어들이고 있었다.
 그동안 모국의 위상이 각 분야에서 세계인의 관심 속에 특히 K-Pop, K-Food 등 K로 시작되는 한국의 문화가 큰 호응을 받고 있는 것은 익히 알고 있었지만, 오늘 나는 동영상에서 그 실상을 목격하게 되어 퍽이나 감격하게 되었다. 모국이 선진국 대열에 들어서게 되니, 호주의 한 초등학교에서까지 '한국의 날'로 정해 어린 학생들에게 한국 문화 체험에 동참할 기회가 주어진 건 퍽이나 고무적이라 생각된다.
 동영상에서는 시드니의 한 초등학교에서 한국의 날 축제가 열리고 있었다. 전교생이 등교부터 하교 시간까지 학년별로 나뉘어 한국 문화를 체험하는 유익한 프로그램을 한국어를 가르치는 선생님이 주관하여 한국 학생들과 어울려 잘 해내고 있었다. 동영상 속에는 자원 봉사하는 한국 어머니들도 보이고, 한국문화원과 한국교육원 인사들도 보이는 것으로 보아 한국기관의 후원을 엿볼 수 있었다.

한 교실에서는 태극기를 그리는 체험을 하고 있었다. 학생들이 정성껏 그린 태극기에 손잡이 부분에는 연필을 놓고 돌돌 말아 쥐고 흔들면서 '해피 코리아 데이~'를 외치고 있다. 저학년의 한 여학생이 큰 눈을 반짝이며 인터뷰에서 "오늘은 코리안 데이라서 코리안 국기를 만들었어요."라고 야무지게 한마디 하는 모습이 사랑스럽다. 다른 한 교실에서는 한국 학생이 앞에 나와서 딱지 만드는 시범을 보이고 있었다. 잠시 후 모두 손수 만든 딱지로 치기에 열중하며 즐거운 모습들이다. 또 한편에서는 페이스 페인팅도 하고 있다. 얼굴이나 손등에 태극 문양, 아이러브 코리아 등 호주 남자 선생도 거들면서 서로 열심히들 그려주고 있다.

홀에 모인 학생들과 선생들이 무대에서 시범을 보이는 K-Pop 댄서를 따라서 신나게 춤을 춘다. 그 열기가 동영상을 보는 나에게까지 후끈하게 끼쳐오는 듯하다.

점심으로는 전교생에게 비빔밥을 제공하고 있었다. 우리네가 먹는 전형적인 비빔밥과는 조금 다르게 이곳 아이들 취향에 맞게 뷔페 스타일로 원하는 고기와 채소를 택해서 간장이나 고추장에 비벼 먹도록 했다. 불고기에 상추와 오이를 담고 고추장까지 넣어 비벼 먹으며 '으음~ 맛있어요.' 하는 모습이 정말 맛있어 보이는 표정들이었다. 나는 우리의 건강식 비빔밥을 외국아이들도 맛있게 먹는 걸 흐뭇하게 바라보고 있었다. 그런데 한 아이가 숟가락 대신 아예 일회용 비닐장갑을 낀 손으로 밥을 비벼대는 모습이 나타나자 어찌 보면 고정관념을 넘어 참신한 발상이란 생각을 하면서도 나는 그만 폭소를 터뜨리고 말았다.

　우리 가족이 호주에 정착한 것은 88 서울 올림픽이 열리던 해였다. 시드니에 도착한 지 5주 만에, 남편의 직장 문제로 당분간 멜번에서 살게 되었다. 그 당시 아들이 멜번 교외의 초등학교 2학년으로 들어갔는데 각 학년이 한 반밖에 없는 작은 학교였다. 마침, 6학년 학생들이 올림픽 개최국인 한국을 과제로 준비하던 중이었다. 지역도서관에서 자료를 수집하며 토끼 모양의 한반도 지형을 입체적으로 제작하기도 했다. 학생들이 빌려온 한국 관련 서적들은 종이마저 누렇게 변한 오래된 자료가 다였다. 6학년 담임선생님이 나에게 한국에 대하여 프리젠테이션을 해 줄 수 있겠느냐고 도움을 요청해 왔다. 마침 우리 가족은 남편의 직장 관계로 시드니 항구에 도착한 이삿짐을 갑자기 멜번으로 방향을 틀게 되어 막 짐을 받은 터였다. 나는 뒤범벅이 된 짐들 속에서 한복이 들어 있는 박스를 찾아내고, 일광식품이라는 유일한 한국 식품점에서 올림픽 전야제 비디오도 빌려왔다. 드디어 학생들 앞에 서게 되는 날 나는 한복을 차려입고 학교로 향했다. 마켓리서치 회사에서 10여 년간 일한 경험을 토대로 우선 칠판에 분필로 중국과 한반도와 일본과 호주를 그리고, 우리나라 역사부터 시작해서 올림픽을 개최할 만큼 발전한 이야기를 해주었다. 인터넷 세상이 되기 훨씬 전이었고, 주위에 도움을 청할 곳도 없었지만 그런대로 무난히 잘 마칠 수 있었다.

　그 후 우리 가족은 원래 계획에 따라 1990년 4월 대한항공 여객기가 시드니로 첫 취항한 역사적인 해에 시드니로 옮겨 살게 되었다. 비록 호주에서 소수민족 이민자로 살아가고 있지만, 모국의 위상에 따라 우리 교포들의 자긍심도 바뀐다는 것을 실감한다.

이민관의 말대로 무한한 기회의 나라에 개척 정신을 갖고 왔으나 현실은 그리 호락호락하지 않았다. 그러나 우리 가족은 호주 생활에 만족하며 지금까지 잘 살아왔다고 생각한다.

'오직 한없이 가지고 싶은 것은 높은 문화의 힘이다. 문화의 힘은 우리 자신을 행복하게 하고 나아가서 남에게 행복을 주기 때문이다.'

위에 백범 김구 선생이 말씀하신 그의 바람이 비단 그만의 염원이었을까. 오늘날까지 우리 온 국민의 한결같은 마음이 아니겠는가.

(2022)

제주도 해녀를 만나다

폭염이 예상되는 한여름에 제주도를 다녀왔다. 이번 여행은 애초에 계획한 건 아니었다. 이곳 시드니에서 학교 선생으로 일하는 딸이 한국문화원에 들렀던 게 계기가 되었다. 딸은 그날 문화원 도서실에서 해녀 사진이 표지에 나온 책을 집어 들고 책장을 넘기면서부터 해녀에 대한 호기심에 빠져들었단다. 같은 여자이면서 겁도 없이 그 검푸른 바닷속으로 자맥질하여 깊게는 20미터까지 내려가 전복을 비롯한 해산물들을 채취한다는 얘기며, 아무런 산소 장치 없이 일이 분 동안 무호흡으로 작업을 한다는 게 믿기지 않을 만큼 충격을 받은 것 같다. 더구나 딸은 제주도에 가서 직접 해녀를 만나보고 학생들에게 소개해 주고 싶은 직업의식이 발동했던 모양이다. 원래 계획했던 해외여행에 제주도를 추가하고 엄마도 가자는 바람에 나는 부랴부랴 짐을 꾸려 같이 나서게 되었다.

제주공항에 도착하자 공기부터가 달랐다. 섬 냄새라고 할까. 이국적인 느낌이 물씬 풍겼다. 숙소에 짐을 풀고, 이튿날 먼저 렌터카로 제주 해안을 한 바퀴 돌다가 해녀할망(할머니)들이 쭈그리고 앉아서 무언가 손질을 하는 곳에 차를 멈췄다. 아침에 자맥질하여 따온 성게를 갈라서 작은 숟가락으로 파내어 유리병에 담고 있는 손놀림이 빠르고 능숙하다. 딸기잼 병 크기의 용기를 성게 알로 조금씩 채워가는데 껍질이 수북이 쌓인다. 옆의 바위에 널려 있는 잠수복은 뙤약볕에 벌써 말라 있다. 오래 입어 바닷속에서 낡아진 고무옷이다. 성게 한 병 사기로 하고 한참을 기다리는 동안 한 사람은 귀가 안 들린다는 것을 알았다. 구십 가까이 된다고 옆의 할망이 알려준다. 오래 전엔 지금처럼 귀를 가리는 고무 모자 대신 광목천으로 만든 물수건을 사용하고 깊은 바다에 들어갔으니 청력을 잃고 만 것이리라.

해녀의 역사를 보면 처음부터 여자들이 바다에서 물질을 한 것은 아니었다. 조선 시대에는 원래 남자가 물질을 했다고 한다. 그러나 남자가 일하면 세금을 내야 했기에 생활이 되지 않자 그만둘 수밖에 없었다. 여자에게는 세금을 부과하지 않았다. 여자가 옷을 벗고 바다에 뛰어들어 일하는 것을 금하라는 명이 내렸지만 먹고 살기 위해서 이를 아랑곳 하지 않고 물질을 계속 이어 갔다. 여자들은 어려서부터 바다에 나가 헤엄을 배우고 자맥질 기술을 익혔다. 이들은 결혼을 하고도 강인한 생활력으로 가족의 생계를 꾸려나가게 되었다. 이쯤에 이르자 남편들은 요즘 말하는 '하우스 허즈번드'가 되어 집에서 아이들을 돌보고 집안일을 맡았다. 그러나 갓난아기가 배고파 울면 아내가 바다에서 나올 때까지 아기를 방치할 수밖에 없던 모진 세월을 견뎌내야 했다.

　해녀 박물관에는 직접 해녀들의 이야기를 들을 수 있는 동영상이 꽤 있었다. 예전엔 배고팠던 것보다 천대 당하는 게 더 싫었는데 지금은 떳떳하고 보람되게 생각한다고 말했다. 재미있는 표현으로, 바다는 나에게 입출금 전표가 필요 없는 은행, 노력한 만큼 주는 바다는 정확하다, 한없이 깊고 넓은 만큼 한없이 좋은 바다라며 자부심을 갖고 있었다. 더욱 깜짝 놀란 사실은 만삭의 몸으로 바다에 나갔다가 저녁에 들어와서 2시간 후 출산을 했다는 이야기며, 아기를 낳고 3일 만에 다시 바다로 나갔다는 이야기에는 입이 다물어지질 않았다. 소라가 많이 나오는 때에는 찬 겨울 바닷물에도 아랑곳하지 않고 일을 했다고 한다. 이렇게 벌어들인 돈으로 생활은 물론 집도 사고, 땅도 사고, 자녀들을 육지에 보내 공부도 시켰다. 그러나 이들은 딸들에게 고된 해녀 일을 물려주고 싶지 않아 교육을 시켰다고 한다. 이처럼 강인함을 넘어 경이적인 억척스러움은 대체 그 힘이 어디에서 나오는 것이었을까. 해녀들의 굵게 패인 주름진 얼굴이 참 아름다워 보였다. 그 숱한 인고의 세월을 바닷속에서 보낸 그들에게 바다는 또한 엄마이기도 했단다. 힘든 일을 겪을 땐 엄마 같은 바다에 나가 울었으니까.

　박물관에서는 공연을 하는 날도 있었다. 제주방언으로 해녀 노래를 부르며 해산물 캐는 광경을 보여 주기도 하고, 멸치 후리는 노래에 맞추어 그물망을 잡고 좌우로 흔들어 대는 장면은 관람객을 불러내어 함께 했다. 딸에게 등을 떠밀려 나도 한몫했는데 그물에 걸린 멸치들이 사탕으로 둔갑해 있어서 웃음을 자아내기도 했다.

가장 우리의 관심을 모은 건 해녀 체험을 하고 노래까지 배울 수 있었다는 사실이다. 현장 답습을 하느라 폭염 속을 뚫고 우리는 강행군을 했다. 딸이 해녀 할머니와 단둘이 한 시간가량 물질을 배우는 동안 나는 멀리서 사진과 비디오를 찍었다. 땡볕에 계속 서 있기 힘들어졌을 때 시원한 바닷물에 발을 담그려고 돌바닥에 맨발을 디뎠다가 기겁을 했다. 불볕에 달구어진 돌바닥은 마치 물이 펄펄 끓고 있는 가마솥 뚜껑같이 뜨거웠다. 그래도 딸이 멀리서 직접 캔 성게를 높이 들어 보여줬을 땐 정말 잘 왔다는 생각이 들었다. 박물관 공연에서 노래를 선창하던 분을 찾아가 장구 치며 해녀 노래도 배웠다. 딸의 취지를 듣고 노래를 가르쳐주마 하고 쾌히 승낙해 준 고마운 명창도 예전엔 해녀였다고 한다.

2016년에 제주 해녀는 유네스코 무형문화유산으로 등재되어 지금은 전 세계에 알려졌지만, 해녀의 평균연령이 70세가 넘고 숫자는 점점 줄어든다고 한다. 해녀 양성과 해녀 문화를 보존하기 위한 부단한 노력이 제주도의 커다란 과제이기도 하다.

시드니로 돌아온 딸이 제주 해녀 이야기를 앞으로 학생들에게 어떻게 구상하고 연출을 할 것인지 매우 궁금하다.

(2018년)

이 수필을 쓴 이후 딸과 나는 제주 해녀들에 영감을 받아 "해녀: 바다의 여인들"이라는 인형극을 제작하였다.

2018년 딸 케이가 해녀 체험을 하는 모습

딸이 크로셰 뜨기로 만든 해녀 퍼펫이 태왁 망사리 옆에 앉아있다.

문화유산 계승의 힘

공자 왈, '70세에는 마음이 내키는 대로 행동해도 법도에 어긋남이 없다.'라고 했다. 그래서 나이 70을 일명 종심(從心)의 나이라고도 한다. 내가 이 나이에 퍼펫쇼(puppet show)를 하겠다고 용기를 내어 그것도 이태리에서 대중 앞에 '첫 데뷔?'를 했으니, 나의 당돌한 용기는 공자의 설파와도 무관치 않다고 본다. 실은 한 가지가 더 있긴 하다. 십여 년 전, 칠십이 다 된 나이에 석사 모를 쓴 호주 부인이 있었다. 그녀는 나이와 무관하게 대학원에 진학하여 역사를 공부하고 훨훨 크루즈 여행을 떠났던 것이다. 아마도 가슴에 묻어두었던 버킷리스트에서 드디어 항목 하나를 지우지 않았을까 싶다. 나는 그런 리스트가 있었던 건 아니었지만 새삼스럽게 그녀를 떠올리며 용기를 내었다. 나도 뒤늦은 나이에 새로운 일을 시작하고 보니 마음속에 새싹이 움트는 듯 회춘을 느낀다.

중세의 흔적이 고스란히 남아있는 이태리의 소도시에서 올 여름에 열린 퍼펫 페스티벌에 초대되어 딸과 함께 다녀왔다. 초등학교 선생이자 퍼펫 경력 십오 년의 딸에게 배워서 우리 모녀가 함께 참가하게 된 공연 제목은 '해녀, 바다의 여인들'이었다. 소도구로는, 소라, 전복, 거북이, 문어 등 대부분의 퍼펫을 털실로 크로셰 짜기하여 만들었다. 이야기는 동화처럼 펼쳐진다. 할머니가 건네주는 태왁망사리(제주도 사투리. 물에 뜨게 하는 부표와 채취물들을 담는 그물 망태)를 거부하던 어린 손녀가 어느 날 플라스틱이 목에 걸린 거북이를 발견하게 된다. 플라스틱을 떼어주고 거북을 따라서 용궁에 다녀온 할머니가 흰 조개를 받아오는데 …. 마침내 손녀는 할머니와 함께 물에 들어가게 된다. 피날레에서는 공연 전에 미리 정한 관중 속의 어린이들이 앞에 나와서 바다를 연상케 하는 파란 실크 천을 양쪽에서 흔들고 그 위를 해녀와 손녀, 물고기와 문어 퍼펫이 유유히 헤엄을 치고 있다.

옛날 수도원이었던 장소에서 여덟 번 공연을 했다. 어린이들부터 어른들에게 사라져가는 한국의 해녀 문화를 소개하고 계승하려는 노력이 나름대로 잘 전해졌다고 생각한다. 공연 시작 전에 제주해녀에 대하여 이태리어로 번역한 것을 딸이 간단히 소개했다. 그리고 해녀 노래, 대금 등 음악을 배경으로 대화 없이 비주얼 효과를 노렸다. 대사는 없어도 간단한 한국어와 이태리어로 '아이구', '이리온~ 비에니' 등 몇 마디만 던질 정도였다. 공연이 끝나고 우리가 모녀라고 소개되었을 때 관중들의 박수 소리가 소나기 쏟아지듯 들렸다. 우리는 마치 한국 전통문화 홍보대사라도 되는 양 큰 보람으로 가슴이 벅차올랐다. 공연한 고장은 예로부터 어머니가 딸에게 전수하여 이어지고 있는 '보빈레이스' 짜기로 유명하기에 우리의 공연은 더 가까이 공감대를 형성할 수 있었다는 생각이 든다.

이 고장에서는 전통적으로 어머니에서 딸에게로 물 흐르듯 전수되어 오는 독특한 문화가 있다. 돌로 높이 쌓아 올린 성벽을 배경으로 세 사람이 앉아서 무언가 하고 있는 동상이 눈에 뜨였다. 호기심에 다가가 보니, 할머니, 딸, 손녀 3대가 앉아서 각자 받침대에 베개처럼 생긴 것을 얹고 그 위에 방망이를 축소한 모양의 작은 실패(보빈)가 여러 개 매달려 있는 기구 앞에서 보빈레이스 짜기를 하는 모습이었다. 바늘 대신 실패를 이용하는 레이스짜기는 올리브, 와인과 함께 이 고장의 3대 대표적인 유산으로 손꼽힌다. 안경을 코에 걸친 큰 몸집의 할머니와 엄마 옆에서 레이스 짜기를 하는 어린 손녀가 조각되어 있는 매우 인상적인 동상이었다. 옛날에는 흔하디흔한 모습이었겠지만 전수를 외면해 버린 현대인으로서는 조각으로 남긴 동상을 보는 현실이 되고 말았으니, 나는 해녀의 물질 역시 맥이 끊길 단계라 동병상련의 마음으로 한참을 그 앞에 서 있었다.

우리가 2주 동안 머문 숙소는 성벽 안 유적지가 그대로 남아 있는 곳이었는데 매일 보빈레이스 가게가 있는 골목길을 지나게 되었다. 가게 위층은 살림집인 듯 환갑이 넘어 보이는 여주인 피나 씨가 매일 가게 앞에 나와 앉아 딸그락거리며 레이스를 짜고 있는 게 아닌가. 창백한 얼굴에 깔끔하고 고상한 차림새의 그녀와 나는 말은 통하지 않지만 서로 '안녕하세요' 정도 인사를 나누는 사이가 되었다. 지인의 귀띔으로, 피나 씨의 외동아들이 젊은 나이에 사고로 세상을 떠났다고 한다. 나는 그 말을 듣고 나름대로 이런 상상을 했다. 그녀가 꿈꾸었을 아들의 결혼식, 넥타이를 맨 어린 아이가 반지를 올려놓은 피나 씨의 수제품 레이스 쿠션을 양손에 받쳐 들고 음악에 맞추어 걸어 들어오는 모습. 식탁보도 짜주고 손녀가 탄생하면 이 기술을 전수하리라 마음먹었을 터이지만 그 꿈이 유리 깨지듯 산산조각이 났으니 얼마나 가슴 저리고 슬플까. 딸이 있었다고 해도 레이스 짜기를 선뜻 배우고 싶어 했으리라 장담할 수는 없지만.

  제주도 해녀의 딸들과 이태리 소도시 Offida의 딸들이 언제까지 그들의 어머니의 길을 가게 될 것인지. 문명의 발달로 그 많은 수제품과 생활 방식은 아날로그 시대의 흔적으로 사라져가고 있다. 하루가 다르게 변화무쌍한 이 시대를 살고 있는 종심(從心)의 나는 뒤지지 않기 위해서 숨가쁘게 곡예 하듯 살아야 하는 건 아닐까.

  (2019년)

사진: Darren Gill (멜버른 인형극 축제, 2023)

떳떳할 수 없는 역사

거대한 호주 땅에서 육만 년 동안이나 기록된 법 없이 살아오던 애보리진 원주민의 세계에 시커먼 먹구름이 덮치기 시작한 것은 불과 이백삼십오 년 전의 일이었다. 영국을 해가 지지 않는 부자나라라고 한국이 가난했던 초등학교 때 배웠을 때만 해도, 남의 나라를 식민지로 삼은 결과라는 것을 알기엔 내가 너무 어린 나이였다. 사진으로 보기에도 멋진 제복, 흰 바지에 붉은색이나 검은색 상의와 위엄 있어 보이는 모자를 쓰고, 호주 땅에 닿은 개척자들의 눈에 원주민들은 검은 피부를 드러낸 벌거벗고 흉측한 모습으로 비쳤으니, 인간 이하의 존재로 취급되었으리라. 그러나 인간 세계에도 약육강식의 법칙은 존재했고, 그 덕분에 오늘날 내가 호주라는 나라의 체제 안에서 잘 먹고 잘살고 있다는 사실이 아이러니하다.

우리 가족이 호주에 이민 온 지도 어느덧 35년이 되어간다. 그 당시 나와 남편을 인터뷰하던 이민 담당 서기관은 비자를 내주며 '호주는 무궁무진한 기회의 나라'라고 말했다. 그 말을 들었을 때만 해도, 마치 개척자가 된 듯 이곳에서 무언가를 이뤄낼 수 있으리라는 기대감이 풍선처럼 부풀어 올랐다. 무지가 용감을 키운다고 했던가. 우리는 앞길에 놓인 일들을 헤쳐나가는 데만 집중했다. 그러다 보니 원주민에 대해서는 추상적으로만 알았을 뿐, 굳이 알려고도 하지 않았다. 그럴 여유조차 없었다. 매스컴에서 이슈가 될 때마다 그저 그런가 보다 하고 지나쳤고, 어린 두 아이를 데리고 온 우리는 정착과 학교 문제에 신경 쓰느라 내 방식대로 바쁘게 살아갈 뿐이었다. 그런데 최근에서야, 끝내 모르고 지날 뻔했던 원주민의 통한의 역사를 조금이나마 알게 되었고, 며칠 동안 바위처럼 무거워진 마음으로 그들을 떠올리며 지내야 했다.

딸이 교편을 잡고 있는 학교에 애보리진 교육관들이 와서 세 시간 동안 교사들에게 강의를 했다고 한다. 그 내용을 딸에게 듣고 세상에서 인간이 제일 잔인한 동물이라는 생각에 몸서리를 쳤다. 이제까지 내가 뿌리내리고 사는 이 나라의 역사를 백인의 입장에서만 알았으나 원주민의 입장에서도 보아야 한다는 너무나 당연한 사실을 간과할 수가 없게 되었다.

이 땅의 원주민에게 백인들이 저지른 만행들을 나는 여태 모르고 살았다. 아서 필립 제독이 이끈 첫 번째 함대는 11척으로 구성되어 있었고, 첫 번째 죄수선에는 남자들만 탔었다. 그러나 호주 땅에 도착하자 그들은 원주민 여성들을 희롱했다. 백인과 원주민의 혼혈을 1/2, 1/4, 1/8…로 융화시키려던 정책이었다니, 그 사실만으로도 아연실색하지 않을 수 없다. 평화롭게 삶을 살아가던 애보리진 여성들이 얼마나 끔찍하게 당했을지, 그리고 그들에게 얼마나 큰 공포였을지 상상조차 어렵다.

원주민 말살 작전의 하나로 그들이 마시는 물에 독을 넣고, 천연두 균이 묻은 담요를 건네기도 했다. 그들의 문화와 이름, 정체성을 빼앗고 언어 사용을 금지했으며, 수십 년에 걸쳐 학살을 자행했다. 이 진실들을 마주하고 앉아 있자니 마음이 견딜 수 없을 만큼 무겁게 짓눌려 왔고, 인간이 어찌하여 다른 인간에게 이토록 끔찍한 고통을 가할 수 있었을까 하는 물음을 피할 수가 없었다.

뉴카슬대학의 한 역사학자가 올해 새로이 발표한 내용에 의하면 가해자들은 원주민들의 목을 쇠사슬로 엮은 채로 땔감을 주워오게 했으며 나무에 등유를 부어 불을 붙인 다음 원주민들을 그대로 불 속으로 밀어 넣었다는 최악으로 잔혹한 만행도 저질렀으며, 가해자들은 점점 더 계획적이고 잔인해졌다고 한다.

과학적 증거에 의하면 이들이 겪은 트라우마는 여덟 세대에 걸쳐 DNA에 녹아 들어 있다고 한다. '빼앗긴 세대(Stolen Generations)'라든지 실화를 영화로 만든 '토끼막이 울타리' 등은 백인들이 약자인 애보리진 원주민들을 인간 이하로 취급했음을 여실히 알 수 있다. 문명화 교육을 목적으로 아이들을 마치 길바닥에서 어슬렁거리는 주인 없는 개들을 낚아채듯이 마구잡이로 데려가 입양이나 기숙사에 강제 수용해서 원주민 언어를 사용하지 못하게 했다. 이들은 신체적, 정신적, 성적 학대를 당하고 훗날에도 트라우마에 시달려 정상적인 생활을 하기가 어려웠다고 한다. 나의 어린 손주들이 거리에서 강제로 잡혀가 이런 일을 당했다고 감히 상상하니 할머니로서 내가 까무러쳐 죽을 것 같은데 그 아이들 부모들의 뼈아픈 고통을 어찌 상상인들 제대로 할 수 있으랴. 도저히 있을 수 없는 이런 일들이 백인들에 의해 자행 되었던 것이다.

유튜브에서 '1월 26일'이라는 노래를 들었다. 아서 필립 제독이 록스(The Rocks)에 영국 국기를 꽂은 날을 기념하는 호주의 날 1월 26일을 데이빗 베니욱이라는 울릉공 출신의 저널리스트이자 민요가수 겸 작곡가가 부르는 이 노래는 나에게 깨달음을 주기에 충분했다. 왜 비극의 날을 경축하느냐는 가사를 반복해 부르면서 배경에 나오는 동영상엔 애보리진 원주민 남자들이 목에 굵은 쇠사슬을 감고 옆 사람들과 같은 쇠사슬로 이어져 있는 사진과 '침략, 살인, 강간, 도둑질이 시작된 이날을 경축합시다'라고 비꼬아 만든 포스터가 나온다. 원주민들에게 침략의 이날을 구태여 호주의 날로 정하지 않아도 되지 않을까.

나는 이제 원주민들을 보는 시각을 달리하게 되었다. 한국말로 하면 호주 원주민, 애보리진 등으로 칭하지만 영어로 이들을 칭할 때는 딸의 학교에 왔던 강사에 의하면 애보리지널(Aboriginal)이라고 부르는 게 적합하다고 한다. 흔히 애보리지니(Aborigine)라고 부르기도 하는데 이것은 일제강점기 때 우리나라 사람들을 조센징이라고 비하해 부른 것처럼 비하하는 말이라고 한다.

2007년이 되어서야 연방정부 차원에서 '빼앗긴 세대'에 대한 사죄를 했다. 보수파들의 반발이 있었고 시행하는데 진통을 겪었지만 당시 케빈 러드 총리는 사과를 관철했다. 양파껍질 벗기듯 앞으로 당면한 커다란 문제를 논하기엔 내 깜냥으론 너무 부족하지만 적어도 관심을 가지고 마음으로나마 성원을 할 뿐이다. 인간의 탐욕과 잔혹함의 그 끝은 과연 어디까지일까, 치가 떨린다. 식민지 개척자들은 꼭 그런 방법으로 이 거대한 땅을 삼켜야 했을까.

(2022년)

천재(天災)와 인재(人災)

어제저녁 하늘이 무너져 내리듯 쏟아지는 장대비가 우리 집 부엌 밖의 시멘트 바닥을 뚫어지라 때리고 있을 때였다. 그 소리가 얼마나 컸던지 부엌 안 TV의 뉴스채널에서 시시각각 숨가쁘게 알려주는 NSW주와 퀸즈랜드주의 물폭탄으로 인한 치명적인 대홍수와 우크라이나 전쟁 뉴스가 잘 들리지 않아 볼륨을 크게 올려야 했다. 3월에 들어선 지금도 일기예보를 보면 일주일 내내 비 또는 천둥번개라고 나온다. NSW주에서는 북동부의 리스모어(Lismore)와 발리나(Ballina)에서 가장 피해가 크고 아직도 여기저기에서 엄청난 폭우가 진행중이다. 발리나만해도 육천여 가구가 물에 잠겼을 때 지도상에서 사라질지도 모른다는 말이 나올 정도였다. 리스모어에서 고령의 두 사람이 자신의 집이 침수되어 익사체로 발견되었다는 너무나 안타까운 뉴스며, 사방이 물바다가 된 지붕 위에서 수많은 사람들이 헬리콥터로 구조되는 광경을 떨리는 가슴으로 지켜보았다. 불어나는 물을 피해 소와 말들이 뒤섞여서 함께 달려가는 모습은 눈물 없이 볼 수 없었다. 가축들이 떼죽음을 당한 처참한 사실들은 너무나 가슴이 아프다. 우크라이나에서 일주일째 일어나고 있는 전쟁의 참상 또한 가슴을 미어지게 한다.

우크라이나 전쟁이 왜, 어떻게 일어나게 되었는가에 대해서는 매체를 통하여 보고 들을 수 있고 우리가 인터넷 세상에 사는 덕분에 전쟁의 진행상황도 실시간 속보로 알려진다. 수도 키예프를 비롯하여 10여 개의 도시에 러시아군의 폭격이 가해지며 18~60세 우크라이나 남성은 나라를 떠나는 것이 금지되고 전쟁에 가담하도록 했다. 그러나 이 징집명령이 떨어지기 전에 남녀노소 학생에서 교수, 반러 국회의원, 전직 대통령 등 직업을 막론하고 수많은 지원병이 조국을 지키기 위해 참여했다. 해외에서도 지원병이 돌아왔다. 결혼한 지 하루밖에 되지 않은 신혼부부도 방위병으로 나섰다. 주부들을 포함한 민간인들이 몰로토프 칵테일이라는 화염병 제조를 신속히 돕는 모습도 속보에 나왔다. 지하에 피신한 상태에서 호주의 매체에 상황을 전하는 용감한 젊은 여성도 있었다. 북새통 속에 기차로 떠나는 아내와 자녀들과 작별의 입맞춤을 하고 돌아서서 빠르게 발길을 옮기며 눈물을 훔치는 남자도 화면에 비춰졌다. 오늘 TV 뉴스에서는 미사일 폭격으로 아내를 잃은 한 남자, 머리에서 이마로 흘러내린 핏자국과 얼굴에 상처를 입은 이 남자는 사랑하는 아내를 잃은 처절함에 한 주먹을 번쩍 들더니 허탈한 듯 다른 손바닥에 내리치며 애써 딸과 부모가 살아 곁에 있다는 사실에 위안을 받는 듯했다. 그러나 그의 큰 두 눈에는 곧 터질 듯한 눈물로 가득한 것을 나는 놓치지 않았다. 주요 시설뿐만 아니라 민간 지역에도 미사일을 떨어뜨려 민간인 사망자가 속출하고 있다. 임산부가 지하에 피신해서 출산을 하다니 제왕절개 같은 수술이 필요하게 되면 얼마나 위험한가.

걷고 또 걸어서 이웃나라 폴란드로 피난을 가는 행렬을 보며 한국의 6·25 동란 당시 내 부모님의 절박했던 때를 상상해 보았다. 엄동설한의 1·4후퇴 때 어머니는 아기였던 나를 등에 업고 포대기 위를 담요로 덮은 채 아버지와 함께 서울을 떠나 남쪽으로 걷고 또 걸었다. 아버지가 이따금 담요를 들추어 내가 숨을 쉬고 있는지를 확인했다고 한다. 우크라이나 피난 행렬의 사람들은 푹신한 코트와 양털부츠 같은 걸 신고 있는데 비해 70년 전 가난한 한국에선 추운 겨울에 여자들은 버선발에 고무신을 신지 않았나 싶다. 얼마나 춥고 무섭고 불안했을까. 피난길 엄마의 손발에 동상이라도 걸리진 않았는지… 그때 엄마는 20대 중반의 아리따운 색시였다.

북대서양조약기구(NATO) 회원국 중 3월 초 현재 12개국이 우크라이나를 전면적으로 지원하고 있고 한국과 일본과 호주도 지원을 보낸다고 한다. 올해 44세인 젤렌스키 우크라이나 대통령은 본인이 대통령으로서 죽음을 두려워할 권리가 없다며 수도를 지키고 끝까지 싸울 것이라고 했다. 외신은 지하벙커에서 국제사회에 도움을 촉구하고 있는 그가 영웅으로 급부상하고 있다고 전한다.

한국의 6·25 동란 때, 전투 병력, 의료, 물자 지원, 지원 의사 표명국까지 전부 63개국에서 한국을 도왔다. 미국에서만 180만 가까운 병력이 한반도를 지원했다. 태국도 육해공군의 병력을 지원했고 필리핀도 파병을 했다. 이들 중 희생자 또한 얼마나 많았던가. 물자 지원국 리스트에 이란, 베트남, 캄보디아가 포함되었고 지금 최빈국이 된 아이티에서 미화 3천 불을 지원했다. 엘살바도르에서도 미화 500불을 보내왔다. 돈의 가치는 지금보다 훨씬 있었겠지만 십시일반 이렇게 한국을 도왔구나 생각하면 너무나 감사한 마음에 고개가 숙여진다. 한국동란은 3년이나 계속되었지만 우크라이나 전쟁이 하루빨리 종결되기를 바라는 마음 간절하다. 러시아의 푸틴은 3일 안에 우크라이나 수도를 함락하는 속전속결을 예상했으나 우크라이나 사람들의 단결력에 길어지고 있다한다.

우크라이나를 돕기 위한 모금 운동이 지구촌 곳곳에서 일어나고 있다. 타이완에서는 총통, 부총통 등이 한 달 치 월급을 기부했다고 한다. 국회 차원에서도 거액을 기부한다고 하는데 타이완을 호시탐탐 노리는 중국이 있기에 더욱 동병상련의 마음으로 총통이 나선 것이리라. 한국에서도 성금이 쇄도하고 있다고 한다. 호주에서는 우크라이나 어린이를 위한 모금, 여성을 위한 모금, 기타 등으로 나누어 기부할 수 있다. 호주는 지금 당면한 대홍수의 엄청난 피해를 돕기 위한 모금을 호소하고 있다. 정부의 도움과 십시일반 성금이 모아져서 모든 것을 잃은 수재민들의 삶이 정상으로 회복되고, 지구촌 곳곳에서 보내는 지원의 손길에 힘입어 우크라이나에도 하루속히 평화가 찾아들기를 바라는 마음이 결코 무리한 희망은 아닐 것이다.

가뜩이나 코로나로 인해 벌써 3년째 전 세계인을 공포 속에 몰아넣고 있는 이 마당에 난데없는 전쟁에다 설상가상으로 호주는 홍수와의 재난으로 불안에 떨고 지낸다. 천재(天災)와 인재(人災)가 다투어 세상을 휘젓고 있는 요즘이다. 최초의 인간 아담과 이브가 에덴동산에서 쫓겨난 이후 인간이 그처럼 염원하는 지상의 파라다이스는 정녕 신기루로 남을 것인가.

(2022년)

우리 아주 멀리서 왔어요

 가을 하늘이 유난히 청명한 5월 어느 날, 오페라하우스를 향해 걷는 우리 모녀의 발걸음은 마냥 가벼웠다. 정오의 산들바람은 우리들의 뺨을 부드럽게 스치고 지나는데 시드니 하버의 물결은 태양이 보석을 쏟아 놓은 듯 반짝거렸다. 주변은 화창한 날씨를 즐기러 나온 사람들로 붐볐고 길 한쪽에 일렬로 설치된 레스토랑들의 텐트 안에는 식탁보를 씌운 테이블에서 점심을 즐기는 사람들의 모습이 행복해 보였다. 우리들이 오페라하우스에서 관람한 연극은 이렇게 아름답고 평화스러운 시드니의 한낮 풍경이 무색하게도 몹시 무거운 주제의 실화극이었다.
 역사의 매운바람에 휩쓸린 사람들의 이야기, 보통사람들이 불행히도 그때 그곳에 있었던 탓에 겪어야 했던 엄청난 상황들을 주로 제작하는 이 극단은 노르웨이에 본거지를 두고 유럽 여러나라의 아티스트들과 연계하여 20여 년간 공연을 해왔다고 한다.

그날 본 연극의 제목은 We Come From Far, Far Away. '우리 아주 멀리서 왔어요'였다. 그저 멀리 가야 한다는 일념으로 온갖 위험과 죽음을 무릅쓰고 내전 중인 시리아에서 탈출해 노르웨이의 수도 오슬로까지 온 난민 청소년들과 대화를 통하여 제작되었다.

극 중에서 15살이 된 소년이 어머니가 마련해 준 돈을 모자 속에 넣어 꾹 눌러쓰고 친구와 함께 트럭에 숨겨져 도착한 곳은 해안가였다. 불법으로 지중해를 건너 그리스까지 태워주는 이들에게 큰돈을 지불하고 캄캄한 밤에 배가 떠났다. 정원을 무시하고 사람들을 너무 많이 태웠으니 도중에 배에 문제가 생겨 개인 소지품을 모조리 바다에 던져야 했고 어디인지도 모르는 캄캄한 바다에서 작은 배로 뛰어 내려야 했다. 절망하며 먼저 내리는 친구의 손을 잡아 주었는데 그는 차갑고 어두운 바닷속으로 떨어지고 말았다. 대개 이런 식으로 25,000명이나 수장되었다고 한다. 구명조끼라고 받은 것은 기능을 할 수 없는 모조품이었다.

소년은 그리스에서 자기에게 무서운 얼굴로 무어라고 소리치는 가게 주인으로부터 캠프용 작은 텐트를 구입했다. 얼마나 떨렸을까. 두려운 가슴을 조이며 이동할 때마다 소년은 공포를 극복하는 수단으로 마치 죽은 친구가 곁에 있는 것처럼 혼자 말로 주고받으면서 외로움과 두려움을 떨쳐냈다. 드디어 오슬로에 도착한 소년은 경찰서를 찾아가 난민 신청을 하면서 기어이 참았던 울음을 터뜨리고 만다. 그동안 살얼음판을 건너는 지독한 공포와 긴장이 풀리면서 자신의 온몸을 부여잡고 눈물을 쏟아내는 소년을 바라보는 나의 뺨에도 눈물이 흘러내렸다. 나뿐만이 아니라 훌쩍이는 소리가 관객석을 적시고 있었다. 무서운 바다, 잃은 친구, 엄마를 생각하며 15살의 소년이 구사일생으로 먼 북유럽까지 왔으니 그 끈질긴 생명력은 기적으로 밖에는 설명할 길이 없다. 소년은 청소년 난민센터로 보내지게 된다.

오페라하우스의 스튜디오, 그 큰 공간에 직경 8미터가 되는 몽골 유목민의 거주 텐트가 설치되어 있었다. 유목민들의 실제 거주 텐트보다 훨씬 더 크게 만들어서 보통은 문이 한 개인데 연극을 위하여 만든 문은 네 개나 된다. 연극 자체는 몽골과 아무런 관련이 없지만 관객들은 배우들의 안내에 따라 그 몽골 텐트 안으로 들어갔다. 네 명의 배우 중 두 명의 남자배우는 관객들이 모두 착석할 때까지 악기를 연주하고 있었다. 그 텐트 안에는 다른 세계가 있었다. 2/5가량이 무대로 사용되었고 무대에는 작은 캠프용 텐트가 한가운데 놓여 있다. 벽에는 구명조끼, 경찰 퍼펫 등 장치물이 걸려 있다. 관객들은 나머지 공간에 비교적 푹신하게 마련된 바닥에 앉는데 미리 신발을 밖에 벗어 놓게 되어있었다. 가장자리에는 벤치가 몇 개 놓여 있어서 우리는 벤치에 자리를 잡았다. 관객 수는 미리 예약한 시드니의 어느 하이스쿨 학생과 선생들 합해서 80명이었다고 한다. 60명가량이 비교적 편하게 채워지는 공간에 예상보다 훨씬 많은 인원수인 셈이다. 감히 비교도 안 되지만 극이 진행되는 동안 정원을 훨씬 넘은 배처럼 닫힌 공간에 모두 끼어 앉아 연극에 몰두할 때 머리를 스카프로 감싼 중동 여학생이 눈물을 닦으며 옆자리의 친구에게 속삭이는 모습이 보였다.

시리아 내전은 2011년에 발발하여 10년 이상 아직도 계속되고 있는데 그동안 민간인 40만 명 이상이 죽고 국민의 절반 이상인 1,200만 명의 난민이 발생했다고 한다. 호주에 살고 있는 여느 청소년들과 똑같은 보통 아이들이 시리아에서 태어났기에 삶터가 폭파되어 잿더미로 변하고 귀중한 생명들이 파리목숨처럼 죽어가는 가운데 탈출을 시도하는 사람들이 유럽으로 몰려드니 그 많은 사람들을 수용할 능력이 없는 유럽 국가들이 난처한 상황에 놓이게 되었지만 어쩔 것인가. 지금도 내전으로 고통받는 지역이 어디 시리아뿐인가. 아프리카와 중동 등에서 종교적, 민족 간의 갈등으로 피비린내 나는 내전이 멈출 줄을 모르니 무고한 아이들이며 민간인들의 삶이 언론에서 소개될 때마다 그 처참한 모습에 마음이 무너진다.

연극이 끝나자 몽골 텐트의 한 면을 바깥쪽에서 조금 풀어 올렸는데 금세 시원하게 통풍이 되니 모두 안도의 미소를 지었다. 배우들이 나란히 서서 인사를 한 뒤에 질문과 답하는 시간이 이어졌는데 또래의 하이스쿨 학생들의 적절한 질문에 산교육의 중요성을 절감했다. 이 이야기가 사실입니까? 왜 이런 연극을 만들었어요? 등. 주연배우가 답하기를 "사실은 함께 탈출했던 소년의 절친은 튀르키예 국경에서 총에 맞아 죽었습니다. 하지만 작은 배로 옮겨 내리다가 바다에 빠져 죽어간 사람들이 많이 있어서 친구로 표현했습니다." 마지막으로 이 연극을 보고 충격이나 상처를 받은 청소년들이 있을 경우에 대비해서 카운슬링 전문가가 앞에 나와 자신을 소개했다. 푸근한 아줌마 같은 인상을 주는 여성이었다.

이 작품은 노르웨이에서 가장 권위 있는 상을 수상했다고 하는데 연극을 통해서 상황을 알리고 인간애를 느끼게 하려는 그들의 목적은 달성했다고 할만했다. 이 복잡한 지구촌에서 과연 해답이 나오기는 할까. 오직 하늘의 큰 힘에 의지하며 희망을 가져볼 뿐이다. 우리 모녀는 정오에 지나갔던 하얀 텐트의 레스토랑에 자리 잡고 와인이 포함된 세트 메뉴를 골랐다. 압둘라라는 실제 인물을 떠올리며 지금쯤 성인이 되어 있을 그에게 건배를 올렸다. 하버브릿지를 배경으로 사진을 찍는 사람들, 즐거운 모습으로 우리들 곁을 지나는 사람들을 바라보면서 세상이 아무리 불공평하더라도 우리에게 주어진 삶을 살아내야 한다는 진실을 새삼 느꼈다. 씁쓸했다.

(2023)

4부

장인정신

주 5일 아침마다 교토의 한 작은 식당에 어김없이 배달되는 신선한 도미 일곱 마리. M 셰프가 지난 35년간 손질한 도미만 14만 마리쯤 된다고 한다. 그의 손과 하나된 칼이 칼질을 기억한다. 회를 뜰 때 미묘하게 들어 올리는 칼끝은 마치 오케스트라 지휘자를 따라 악기를 연주하듯 리듬감이 정교하여 보는 사람의 눈이 끌려 들어간다. 죽순을 다루는 그의 솜씨 또한 예술이다. 아침에 수확하여 배달된 10개의 죽순을 큰 들통 두 개에 번갈아 옮겨가며 끓여서 애벌로 조리한 후에 손님들 앞에서 빠르게 마무리하여 김이 모락모락 나는 요리를 내놓는다. 그의 손을 거친 다양한 요리는 한결같이 카운터에 앉은 10명의 고객을 감동케 한다. 보는 순간 침샘이 자극되어 입맛을 다시게 된다. 입에 넣어 허물어 버리기엔 너무 아까울 정도다. 그냥 오래도록 감상하고 싶어진다. 그가 오늘에 이르기까지 오랜 세월 쌓아온 과정에는 유명한 셰

프였던 그의 아버지와 할아버지가 있었다. 도미를 손질하고 회를 뜨는 일은 보통 이삼십 년 경험을 쌓은 고참이 한다는데 아버지는 3대째를 이어갈 새내기 아들에게 그 일을 시키며 혹독한 훈련을 거쳤다.

어느 분야에서나 성공하기까지는 쉬운 길이 없다. 나의 글 스승님은 반백이 훌쩍 넘어 수필문학에 입문한 나를 두고 '너무 늦게 시작했다'고 하신다. 내 스스로 생각해도 늦은 나이였다. 많이 읽고 많이 사색하고 많이 써야 하는데 이제는 그 속도마저 예전 같지 않으니 아쉬움에 그렇게 말씀하시는 게 아닐까. 그러나 어쩌겠는가. 사실 삼십 대에 호주에 이민 와서는 나 자신보다 가정과 자녀 교육이 우선이었다. 아이들을 위해서 우리 부부가 선택한 이민이었기에 나는 언제나 아이들 곁에서 대기하는 마음으로 있다가 아이들이 나를 필요로 할 때면 하던 일을 내던지고 달려갔으니 누구누구 엄마로 산 세월은 두 아이가 적어도 고등학교를 마칠 때까지 계속되었다. 아이들이 성장하며 드디어 나만의 시간을 온전히 갖게 되자 기껏 한다는 게 취직이었으니 틈틈이 독서는 했으나 글을 쓰게 되기까지 또 시간이 흐르고 말았다. 그러나 나는 스승님의 문예창작교실 수강 후에 문학을 하게 된 것이 내 인생에 제일 잘한 일 중에 하나로서 뽑는데 변함이 없다. 수십 년 동안 타국살이를 해오며 종국엔 호주 땅에 묻히게 될지라도 모국어로 글 쓰기를 계속한다는 것은 얼마나 보람 있고 가슴 벅찬 일인가.

보통 회갑에 이른 주부들이라면 가정사에서 놓여나게 된다. 수

명도 늘어나 팔구십까지 생존을 가정하더라도 앞으로 이삼십년의 기간은 마지막 보너스처럼 오롯이 나만을 위하여 사용할 수 있는 황금기를 낳게 된다. 나는 무엇을 하여 이 기간을 알차게 보낼 수 있을까를 고민하다가 글쓰기 모임에 발을 들여놓게 된 것은 내게는 적절한 선택이었다는 생각을 한다. 언감생심 저 M셰프처럼 장인까지는 바라지도 않는다. 다만 그의 장인정신은 배우고 싶다. 그는 자신이 20세기 피아노의 거장 호로비츠가 연주하는 모짜르트를 들을 때마다 감동하는 것처럼 요리도 감동을 주어야 한다는 철학을 갖고 연구를 거듭해 왔다는데 이것이 장인정신이 아닐까. 작품 한편을 써내기 위한 작업은 만만치가 않다. 일상에서 나의 관심은 글감을 찾아내기에 촉각을 세우고 컴퓨터 앞에서 한두 줄 써놓고 어휘 고르기에, 서두 쓰기에 시간가는 줄 모르고 몰입할 때가 많다. 비록 어설픈 작품일지라도 얼기설기 짜맞추어 가는 과정에서 형상화가 된 글로 완성되었을 때 느껴지는 기쁨은 그 어디에도 견줄 데가 없다. 행복의 비밀은 좋아하는 일을 하는 것이 아니라 자신이 하는 일을 좋아하는 것이라고 했던가. 그런 의미에서 나는 행복한 사람이 아닐까 한다.

 문우들과 월례회를 시작하기 전에 우리들은 클래식 음악을 감상한다. 음악에 조예가 깊은 회원이 매달 곡을 선정하여 정성 들여 곡의 배경과 해설을 곁들인 프린트까지 나눠 주고 있다. 정기 모임 시작 전에 마음을 가다듬고 음악을 듣는다. 18세기 작곡가가 살았던 시대와 개인의 삶이 음악에 묻어나오는 것을 들으며 글의 소재를 생각하게도 된다. 작년에 보스턴에서 열린 밴 클라

이번 피아노 콩쿠르에서 18세 최연소로 참가하여 금상을 수상한 한국의 임윤찬 피아니스트는 리스트의 초절기교를 연주하기 위하여 단테의 신곡을 열 번이나 읽었다고 한다. 문학과 음악, 미술, 요리까지 모든 예술은 연결되어 있음에 새삼스럽게 짜릿한 전율을 느낀다.

 아직 나의 갈 길은 마치 대학 시절 지리산 노고단을 향해 헉헉대며 등반했던 그 힘들고 벅찼던 기억을 떠올리게 한다. 과연 내가 선택한 이 길을 중도에 좌절하지 않고 봉우리 끝까지 등반할 수 있을까 하는 생각이 일 때가 없지 않다. 그러나 오랜 세월 함께해오며 동기간같이 가까운 사이가 된 문우들과 서로 격려하며 당근과 채찍을 나누고 있지 않은가. 한번 트인 물길이 마르게 되지는 않을 것이다. 여기에 희망을 걸어 본다.

 (2023)

새해를 맞으며

2022년이 시작되었다. 코로나 팬데믹으로 백신이다, 봉쇄령이다, 부스터다하며 시끌벅적하는 동안에도 무심한 세월은 줄기차게 흘러가 어김없이 새해는 도래했다. 정월 초하루부터 시작되는 일 년이라는 시간은 창조주가 정한 건 아닌데 기원전 로마의 줄리어스 시저가 달력를 만든 덕분에 올해 또 나이 한 살 더 먹게 되었다. 덧없이 나이만 먹고 있다는 생각이 드니 괜스레 시저 탓을 해본다. 어렸을 때나 젊은 시절에는 떡국을 먹고 나이 한 살 더 먹게 되는 새해가 마냥 즐겁고 희망에 차 있었다. 새해의 다짐을 하며 꿈을 꾸고 원대한 포부를 성취하기 위하여 계획을 세우기도 했다. 비록 작심삼일만에 삼천포로 빠진 적이 있기도 했었지만 시행착오를 거치며 지금에 이르렀다. 내가 살아온 날보다 살아갈 날이 점점 짧아져 가니 이제는 새해의 다짐이라기보다 희망사항이라고 해야 옳다.

사람들과의 만남을 더욱 소중하게 여기는 한 해가 되었으면 하는 바람이다. 새해까지 따라와 3년째로 계속되는 팬데믹이 사람들의 생활양식을 완전히 바꾸어 놓아 예전과 같은 일상으로 돌아가지 못할 것이라 하니 슬퍼진다. 봉쇄령이 내려 집콕하며 사람들과 만날 수 없었을 때 얼마나 답답했던가. 그야말로 사면초가 상태가 아니었던가. 2001년 전 세계를 경악하게 한 미국의 911 테러 사건으로 인하여 세상이 더 이상 예전 상태로 되돌아갈 수 없게 되었을 때도 사람들은 서로 끌어안고 위로하며 비극을 극복하도록 최선을 다할 수 있었건만 바이러스의 힘 앞에서는 그야말로 '뭉치면 죽고 흩어져야 산다'는 말이 나올 정도니 앞으로 어떤 세상이 펼쳐질지 마음이 편치 못하다.

지난 12월 초 뮤지컬 Come From Away(외지에서 오다) 공연을 관람했다. 미국의 911 테러 당시의 이야기로 일년 전에 보려다가 코로나 때문에 취소되었는데 다시 진행하게 되어 재빨리 티켓을 구입했다. NSW 정부에서 12월 15일부터 코로나 백신을 접종하지 않은 사람들도 밖에 나다닐 수 있도록 규제를 완화한다는 바람에 그 전에 서둘러 관람했던 것이다. 그러나 안타깝게도 뮤지컬이 성탄절 전에 다시 취소되었으니 우리 모녀는 운이 좋았다고 할까. 실화를 배경으로 등장인물도 실제 이름을 사용한 뮤지컬은 관객들에게 눈물과 웃음을 선사했다.

911 테러 사건 당일 미국으로 향하던 38대의 항공기에 93개 국적의 7,000명 가까운 사람들이 타고 있었다. 그 비행기들이 착륙할 예정이었던 공항이 폐쇄되었다고 조종석의 파일럿들에게 긴

박한 연락이 왔다. 그들은 캐나다 최동부 뉴펀들랜드섬에 있는 갠더(Gander)라는 작은 타운에 위치한 공항으로 방향을 돌리라는 지시를 받았다. 그 당시 인구 9,300명의 작은 타운에 갑자기 7,000명이 들이닥친 것이다. 그들은 수하물 없이 몸만 내렸다. 호텔방은 다 합해도 침대 500개뿐. 모든 학교, 체육관, 커뮤니티센터가 임시 숙소가 되었고 아이스하키장은 냉장고로 탈바꿈했다. 인근 타운을 포함하여 많은 자원봉사자들이 발 벗고 나서서 도왔다. 옷 가게 주인은 가게를 개방해서 맞는 옷을 마음대로 가져가게 했고 식사를 준비하는 사람들은 몸을 아끼지 않고 봉사에 나섰다. 떠나게 될 때까지 닷새를 지내는 동안 '첫날의 낯선 타인 칠천 명이 셋째 날은 칠천의 친구가 되었고 떠나는 다섯째 날은 칠천 명의 가족을 잃었다고 할 만큼 가까워졌다'고 한다. 주민들이 합심하여 사랑을 실천한 덕분에 전원 무사히 갠더를 떠날 수가 있었다. 지금은 뮤지컬을 통해서 그 당시 비극적인 상황에서도 갠더 사람들과의 아름답고 감동스러운 이야기가 전해진다.

하필이면 우리 식구들은 팬데믹으로 봉쇄령이 내려 모두 집에 갇혀 있으면서 식구 중 한 사람만 하루에 한 번 식거리 구입이나 의료 목적 등을 위하여 외출이 허용되던 때에 이사를 했다. 비가 억수같이 내리던 날이었다. 26년 살던 집을 떠나오며 우리도 데려가 달라는 듯 보이는 정든 식물들을 화분에 삽목하니 이삿짐 트럭에 겹겹이 쌓아 올릴 수가 없어 트럭 한 대를 더 빌려야 했다. 새 주소지로 힘들게 옮겨와 달랑 우리 세 식구가 박스 더미에 둘러싸여 있을 때까지도 가까이 사는 남동생마저 누나네를 들여다 볼 수 없었다.

한여름인데도 간밤에 억수로 쏟아붓던 폭우 때문인지 오늘은 초가을처럼 서늘하기까지 하다. 늦은 아침을 끝내자 나는 커피 한잔을 내려 들고 서재로 와 오늘 읽을 책을 뽑아 든다. 그동안 집콕으로 인한 내 생활 패턴 역시 많이 바뀌어져 버렸다.

911 테러 사건으로 뉴펀들랜드의 갠더에서는 뜨거운 인류애의 기적을 만들어 낸 사실을 뮤지컬을 통해서 많은 교훈을 얻을 수가 있었다. 개인사에서나 세계적인 인류 역사는 가혹한 소용돌이가 거쳐갈 때마다 그 절망 속에서도 희망적인 반전이 일어난다는 사실이 놀랍기만 하다. 아무런 변화가 없는 평화만이 지속된다면, 어쩌면 절실한 희망이나 발전은 고사하고, 무의미한 나태 속에서 지리멸렬 살다가 소멸할지도 모른다. 이제 21세기에 이르러서는 세계를 위협하는 팬데믹으로 또 어떤 놀라운 깨달음의 기적이 일어날지 지금은 숨죽여 지켜볼 뿐이다. 하지만 한번 크게 출렁이고 흔들어낸 후에는 통에 담은 물건들도 질서가 유지되기 마련인 것처럼, 금년 한 해 어떤 재앙이 위협 조로 다가온다 해도 지나간 후에 들어설 새로운 형태의 기적을 향한 희망을 기대해 보려 한다.

(2022)

이 또한 지나가리라

2021년 새해가 밝았다. 코로나 팬데믹도 따라와 함께 해를 넘겼다. 팬데믹과의 전쟁이 올해는 종식되리라는 희망을 갖고 있으나 정확히 언제가 될지 오리무중이다. 과학의 발달은 신의 영역까지 따라잡을 판이지만 코로나를 잡지 못하니 가히 그 위력의 대단함을 실감케 한다. 이런 와중에 전 세계인에서 내 개인에 이르기까지 모든 삶의 패턴은 올스톱 상태가 되어 버렸다.

정월 초하루. 어제와 다를 게 없는 하루의 해가 떴건만 지구가 태양을 한 바퀴 다시 회전하기 시작하는 날이니 똑같으나 다르다. 시드니를 시작으로 시차에 따라 지구촌 곳곳에서는 비록 예전처럼 몰려드는 인파는 없지만 TV 화면에 비친 불꽃놀이로 축하를 하며 새해를 맞았다. 그러나 코로나로 아직 록다운 상태에서 불꽃축제는커녕 자유롭게 다니지도 못할 정도로 규제가 강화된 곳도 많다. 일출을 보러 드라이브를 나갔던 때가 새삼스럽다. 새로운 다짐을 하고 계획을 세워야 하거늘 어떻게 하면 올 한 해를 잘 살아낼 것인가 하는 생각에 머문다. 작년엔 팬데믹으로 온 세계가 어려움을 겪으며 시계가 멈춘 듯 무너지기도 했다. 오죽하면 '올해는 나이에 한 살을 추가하지 않았다. 사용하지 않았거든.'이라는 아무것도 할 수 없던 시간들을 빗댄 풍자만화가 카톡으로 떠돌아다니기도 했다. 좋은 일만 가득하길 바란다는 새해 인사 대신에 아무 일도 일어나지 말기를 바란다는 인사말까지 나돈다.

어둡고 힘든 시간을 견디어 낼 수 있는 힘이란 무엇일까. 희망이란 붙들고 있으면 이루어지는 마술 같은 것인가. 내일 세상의 종말이 온다면 나는 과연 오늘 사과나무를 심을 수 있을까. 최근에 크리스마스 선물로 딸에게서 책 한 권을 받았다. 〈Phosphorescence〉- On awe, wonder & things that sustain you when the world goes dark. 〈인광(燐光)〉-경외와 경이, 세상이 어두워질 때 우리를 지탱하는 것들. 저자 Julia Baird. '인광'은 구글 해보니 물체가 빛을 발하는 현상 또는 그 발하는 빛을 의미하는데 이 책에서는 은유적으로 쓰였다. 저자는 언론인, 방송인, 작가, 역사학 박사, 크리스천이고 두 자녀의 엄마이기도 하다.

코로나 팬데믹과 우연히 때를 맞추어 호주에서 세상 빛을 본 이 책이 나에게 용기와 희망을 준다. 캄캄한 곳에서 빛을 발하는 반딧불이처럼 인간의 내면 깊숙한 곳에서 발하는 빛, 그것은 어떠한 상황에서도 잃지 않는 희망과 의지였다. 암의 재발로 수차례 수술을 받고 마치 상처에 화학물질을 들이부어 씻어내는 것 같은 견디기 힘든 통증에 시달렸다는 그녀. 농구공만 한 종양이

복부에 들어 있었다고 한다. 수술과 수술 사이 병원에서 하루에 단 한 시간이라도 썼고 회복하는 동안 이 책을 완성했다. 그 과정이 카타르시스가 되었는지 그녀는 지금 암에서 자유로워졌고 ABC TV에서 DRUM이라는 시사 프로그램의 진행을 맡고 있다. 큰 수술을 앞둔 그녀가 침착할 수 있도록 붙들어 준 것은 기도, 모든 부정적인 것들을 끊고, 가족과 그녀에게 진심으로 기꺼이 실질적인 도움을 주는 사람들을 가까이했으며, 의식적으로 살고자 하는 의지를 가졌기 때문이라고 한다. 죽음의 문턱까지 갔던 그녀는 사람들이 일상에서 늘어놓는 불평이나 불만에 대해서 그들이 살아 있고 고통 없이 몸을 움직일 수 있는 것 자체가 축복이라고 일깨워준다.

이 책에는 월남전에 참전했던 해군 제독이 포로가 되어 하노이 힐튼이라는 악명 높은 감옥에서 뼈가 부러진 채 지옥 같은 고통과 시련을 7년 동안이나 견디며 끝까지 희망과 의지를 잃지 않고 살아 남은 이야기도 실려 있다. 군복무 기간, 고대 그리스 스토아파 철학자 에픽테토스의 담화론을 항상 침대 곁에 두었던 그는 로마의 노예로 고문 때문에 절름발이가 된 이 의지의 철학자로부터 '극기와 강인한 정신력'을 배웠음을 짐작할 수 있다. 제독에겐 에픽테토스가 인광이 되었음에 틀림없다. 우주비행사의 눈에 비추인 지구의 존재가 극히 작은 것과는 비교도 안 되겠지만 이 책으로 인하여 나에게 작은 변화가 생겼다면 팬데믹 이전에는 눈에 뜨이지 않았던 작은 일들이 나에게 기쁘고 감사하는 마음을 갖게 한다. 조그만 화분에서 자라고 있는 다육식물이 귀엽고 사랑스럽다. 여름이면 몸통의 껍질을 한 켜 벗어 버려 우리 집 드라이브웨이를 폭탄 맞은 것처럼 어지럽히는 유칼립투스 나무에 더 이상 불평을 하지 않기로 했다. 나무가 건강을 유지하기 위해서라니 새들에게도 좋지 않겠는가. 자연을 바라보는 눈이 달라졌으니 피할 수 없으면 즐기라는 말을 생각나게 한다.

예전엔 새해를 맞이하며 새로운 다짐이나 결심을 하고 의욕적으로 한 해를 시작하곤 했다. 그러나 연말이면 실행하지 못해 자책하며 실망을 하기 일쑤였다. 내가 나와의 약속을 지키지 못한 이유가 항상 과욕으로 무리를 했던 탓이기도 했다. 올해는 팬데믹으로 하늘 문이 닫히는 바람에 역마살이 다분히 낀 나의 발목이 묶이고 말았기에 계획하기를 좋아하는 나로서는 이번이야말로 실행할 수 있는 계획을 짜보려고 한다. 일단 하루하루를 충실하게 살아야겠다는 생각을 한다. 작년에 팬데믹으로 불안한 나날이 계속되었을 때 매일 같은 날의 연속으로 생각했던 날들도 돌이켜보면 같은 날이 아니고 하루밖에 없는 귀한 날이 아니었겠는가.

양력설을 쇠는 우리 집은 초하룻날 떡국을 먹었다. 전날, 딸과 마주 앉아 만두도 빚고 갈비찜이며 몇 가지 음식을 준비했다. 아침 식사를 마칠 무렵 미국의 아들네가 페이스타임으로 새해 인사를 해왔다. 손주 넷이 아홉 살에서 세 살까지 차례대로 한 줄로 서서 '새해 복 많이 받으세요~'를 합창하더니 절을 하는게 아닌가. 어린이들은 희망이다. 아이들을 보니 뿌듯한 힘이 솟는다. 지구상의 모든 아이가 이렇게 어린 시절 영문도 모른 채 팬데믹 세상을 겪고 있어 안쓰럽기 그지없다. 내 손주들만 해도 거의 집에서 갇혀 살며 며느리가 홈스쿨을 하고 있다. 바로 옆집에서 양성 케이스가 나왔었다고 하는데 얼마나 마음 졸이며 살까 생각하니 멀리 있는 내 마음 역시도 편치가 않다. 더욱 각별히 주의를 하고 살겠거니 싶다.

코로나의 종식을 온 세계가 축하하는 날은 언제 올 것인가. 분명한 것은 '이 또한 지나가리라' 하는 진리에 의지해서 2021년 한해를 향해 기대와 희망을 다시 가져보는 것이다.

(2021)

영혼의 흔적은 어디에

옆집이 팔렸다. 석 달 동안 텅 비어 있던 그 집을 우리 뒤뜰에서 바라볼 적마다 오랜 세월 혼자 살았던 헤이즐이 자기 집 뒤뜰로 나올 것만 같다. 여느 때처럼 새 모이를 잔디에 휙~ 휙~ 뿌리고 모여드는 새들에게 '배고프지? 어서들 먹어라' 하는 소리가 들릴 것만 같다. 오늘도 새들은 밥 먹으러 왔다가 영문을 모른 채 나뭇가지에 앉아 그녀가 나오기만을 마냥 기다리고 있지 않은지… 그 집 담장 옆에서 자라는 동백나무는 담장 너머 우리 집 쪽으로 초록 커튼을 길게 드리우고 있다가 4월이면 핑크색 꽃을 가득히 수놓아 우리 가족에게 즐거움을 선사한다. 오십 년 가까이 그 집 주인이었던 헤이즐과 미리 약속이라도 한 듯 올해도 어김없이 꽃은 활짝 피었는데 헤이즐은 어디로 갔나.

작년 크리스마스 때 과자를 구워 예쁘게 포장해서 옆집엘 들렀다. 인기척이 없길래 곧 오시려니 하고 현관 앞에 두고 왔는데 다음 날 가보니 그대로 있었다. 딸네 집에 가셨나 보다 생각한 바로 그날, 병원으로 간 지 열흘 만에 다시는 집으로 돌아오지 못하고 만 그녀. 헤이즐은 92세 나이보다 훨씬 젊어 보이는 멋쟁이 할머니였다.

　호주의 날 경축일에 갖는 우리 동네 거리의 아침 식사 모임에 그녀는 매년 와인 두 병을 포장해서 작은 호주 국기를 꽂아 들고 왔다. 주소 번지수를 추첨해서 뽑힌 사람에게 주는 와인이었다. 올해부턴 다른 이웃이 전통을 잇고 있지만 작년의 모임이 그녀에게 마지막이 될 줄이야.

　반세기 간격을 두고 우리가 한때 같은 은행에서 일했다는 사실은 전형적인 호주할머니와 한국인 이민자 사이에 공통분모를 만들어 주었다. 세계 제2차 대전 후 청춘의 나이에 다녔던 직장에 대한 향수가 옆집의 나를 더 가깝게 생각되었던 건 아닐까. 마주칠 때마다 우리 아이들의 근황을 물으며 관심을 보여 주었던 친절한 분이었다. 처음 이웃이 되어 인사했을 때 헤이즐은 성대신 이름으로 불러 달라고 했다. 우리네는 이 연배라면 흔히 '할머니' 라는 이름 하나로 통하지만 이 호주 할머니는 Mrs 누구가 아닌 본인의 이름으로 불리우길 원했다. 아무리 호주라 해도 친정어머니보다 나이가 많은 사람을 이름으로 부르는데 익숙해지기까진 시간이 걸렸다.

　헤이즐은 아들과 딸을 두었지만 천수를 다할 때까지 온 가족이 함께 살았던 집을 떠나지 않았다. 90을 넘긴 나이에도 건강해 보였다. 걷는 자세도 바르고 나이들어 가며 내가 두려워하는 치매

나 중풍은 남의 일이었다. 비결이 무엇일까. 매주 만나는 친구들과의 모임도 한몫하지 않았을까. 수요일이면 어김없이 그 집 앞에 몇 대의 승용차가 세워져 있곤 했다. 그녀의 집은 친구들의 아지트가 되어 노년의 친구들이 정기적으로 모였다. 젊었을 때부터 즐겨온 테니스를 치기도 하며 오후 시간을 매주 함께 보냈다. 해 저물 무렵 그 집 뒤뜰에 장식된 색색의 전구에 불이 밝혀지면 영락없는 바비큐였다. 저 할머니 할아버지들은 매주 만나 도대체 무슨 이야기를 나누실까. 언젠가 크리스마스쯤에 우리 내외가 초대받아 갔을 때 항상 궁금했던 의문이 풀렸다. 이분들은 영화를 많이 보는 것 같았다. 영화 이야기가 한참 이어지더니 시사, 정치, 여행 등 어떤 주제라도 끊임없이 대화를 했다. 전혀 나이를 의식하지 않는 듯싶었다. 그날 평소와 달리 세련된 목걸이며 멋진 팔찌도 끼고 한껏 멋을 낸 헤이즐이 즐겁게 살고 있는 모습이 참 부러웠다. 집에 와서 친정어머니를 생각했다. 병석에 오래 누워있다 돌아가신 어머니의 못다 한 삶, 가여운 삶을 내가 어머니 몫까지 잘 살아서 기쁘게 해 드려야겠다고….

  잘 사는 것도 중요하나 잘 죽는 것이 얼마나 중요한지 어머니를 생각하며 뼈저리게 느끼지만 죽는 일이 우리 마음대로 되는 일인가. 건강하게 인생을 즐기며 살다가 며칠만 병원 신세를 지고 간 헤이즐의 죽음은 축복이었다. 그녀는 테니스코트와 수영장이 있는 큰 집을 살아있는 동안 정리해서 자손들에게 나누어 주지 않고 혼자 지냈다. 호주 사람들에겐 당연한 일이라 해도, 은퇴한 부모가 자식들에게 미리 재산을 넘겨주거나 자식의 사업을 위해서 집문서까지 내주고 비극적인 처지가 된 경우를 어쩌다 모국의 뉴스나 지인에게서 본 것과는 너무나 대조적이다.

  헤이즐의 딸은 어머니와 똑같이 생겼다. 초로의 그녀는 어머니가 가신 후 집을 정리한 다음 인테리어 효과를 위한 가구만 남긴 채 부동산 시장에 내놓았다. 집이 팔리자 카운슬(구청)에 연락하여 한 달에 한 번 있는 카운슬 픽업서비스를 신청 했다. 호주에서는 냉장고나 세탁기 등을 버리게 되면 문짝을 떼어서 집 앞에 내놓아야 한다. 그런데 헤이즐의 딸이 내놓은 두 개의 냉장고며 세탁기는 문짝을 떼지 않은 채 밖에 나와 있었다. 고장 난 게 아니고 아직 사용 가능하다는 뜻이었다. 아니나 다를까. 길가에 나와 있던 물건들은 거의 모두 용케도 짧은 시간 안에 누군가가 가져갔다. 나는 그 집 뒤 뜰에 놓여 있던 야외용 둥근 테이블에 왠지 마음이 끌려 집으로 옮겼다. 헤이즐의 마음을 이식받은 기분이 들었다. 연륜이 다분히 쌓여 보이는 튼튼한 이 테이블을 보며 '하이, 헤이즐!' 하고 그녀를 불러 보기도 한다. 가족, 친구들과 빙 둘러앉아 식사도 하고 차도 마시며 긴 세월을 보냈을 테이블. 이제는 옆집의 내가 사용하고 있는 것을 보면 기뻐할 것 같다.

  우주의 질서에 따라 살아 있는 모든 것은 죽음의 순간을 맞이하겠지만 영혼의 흔적은 어디에 있는 것일까.

  (2014)

인생의 황금기에서

　호주에서 소수민족 이민자로 뿌리내리며 살아온 지 삼십 년이 지났다. 삼십 대 후반에 단행한 이민인데, 철학자 김형석 교수에 따르면 나는 지금 '인생에서 가장 아름답고 좋은 시절(65세~75세)'의 한가운데에 와 있다. 백세를 살아낸 김 교수의 말을 진작 들었다면, 이 황금기의 전반을 조금 다르게 보낼 수 있었을까.
　얼마 전 시드니의 어느 신학교 졸업식에 갈 기회가 있었다. NSW주 교육부 장관이 졸업생들에게 전한 말 중 'Never stop learning' 배움을 멈추지 말라는 조언이 특히 마음에 남았다. 학위 증서를 받으러 무대에 올라가는 사람 중에 중장년의 졸업생들이 눈에 띄었다. 지팡이나 목발을 짚은 이들, 골다공증으로 허리가 많이 굽어진 여성까지 있었다. 공부는 머리로 하는 것이라 허리가 굽거나 백발일지라도 그게 배움의 장애물이 될 수 없다는 듯 당당한 모습들이었다. 졸업생 대표로 스피치를 한 여성은 세 자녀의 어머니로서 8년 만에 학위를 마쳤다고 자랑스럽게 말했을 때 박수가 터져 나왔다. 평생교육이라는 말이 실감 나는 순간이었다. 나 역시 '죽을 때까지'를 목표로 오래전부터 외국어 하나를 배우고 있다. 처음엔 그 나라에 관광 갈 목적으로 교실 문을 두드렸으나 점점 재미를 느낀 데다 치매 방지에도 좋다니 은근과 끈기로 도전해 왔다. 65세가 되던 해에 그 나라를 처음 방문하고 어린애처럼 좋아라 했으니 인생의 황금기에 들어선 나이였음을 이제 깨닫는다.

매우 힘들었지만 큰 보람을 느낀 일도 있었다. 이를 통해 귀한 인연들을 만나게 되었고 그 인연들이 최근까지도 이어지는 인연의 도미노 현상을 만들어 내고 있으니 이 또한 좋은 시절임이 틀림없다. 여고 동창회가 없었던 시드니에서 뉴욕동창회 주최로 모교의 창립 130주년 기념 음악회를 열게 되었을 때 이를 계기로 일곱 명이 모여 동창회를 발족시켰다. 시드니 곳곳에서 동창들을 찾아내고 모두 힘을 합하여 전석 초대권인 천 석의 콘서트홀을 메운 일은 기적이 아닐 수 없다. 서울, 미국, 일본에서 모인 동창들의 음악회는 대성공이었다. '왜 하필 그 먼 호주까지 가서 하느냐?'는 질타를 무색하게 할 정도로 격조 높은 공연이었다. 몇 년이 지난 지금도 그때를 떠올리면 가슴이 뛴다. 아마도 내 생애에서 가장 큰 성취감을 느꼈던 추억으로 남으리라.

식상한 표현이나 해외동포들은 다 애국자들이라고 해도 과언이 아니다. 2019년 올해는 한국사적으로 의미 있는 해였다. 2·8 독립선언 백주년, 3·1독립운동 백주년, 상하이 임시정부 수립 백주년을 맞은 해로 시드니에서도 성대한 기념식이 거행되었다. 내가 한국에 살고 있었더라면 텔레비전이나 신문 등을 통해서 기념식 관련 뉴스를 접하는 것으로 이 뜻깊은 날들을 맞이했으리라. 그러나 호주에서는 달랐다. 시드니한인회관에서 거행된 기념식에 참석하여 만세삼창하고 왔으니 내 인생의 황금기다운 행보가 아닐까.

선배의 말을 빌리면 여고 시절 교장선생님께서 '첫째도 건강, 둘째도 셋째도 건강, 넷째가 공부'라고 하셨다고 한다. 이제 이 나이가 되고 보니 넷째도 건강이 되어야 한다는 것을 깨닫는다. '좋은 시절'의 후반부를 길게 이어가고 싶다. 호주에 뿌리내린 우리 가족의 아름드리나무가 무성하게 자라는 그림을 마음속 캔버스에 그려본다. 아내로서 엄마로서 할머니로서 그리고 내 개인으로서의 그림을 그려본다. 이만하면 나도 슈퍼우먼 대열에 한 발 내디딘 게 아닐까 하고 스스로 위로하는 것이다.

(2019)

인생 소나타

 언제부터인가 친구들과의 모임에서 아픈 이야기가 나오기 시작하면 마치 정해진 대화의 주제인 듯 너도나도 끼어든다. 증상부터 치료 단계의 설명에 들어가면 병명과 약 이름이 반복되는 선율의 음표처럼 들려온다. 의사들 뺨치게 종합병원에 다녀온 듯한 기분마저 들 때가 있다. 헤어질 때의 인사는 '다음에 만날 때까지 아프지 말자'이다. 하긴 이 나이 되도록 사용하느라 혹사시킨 치아나 장기가 온전할 리가 있겠는가. 젊었을 땐 딱딱한 호두를 통째로 깨물어 두 동강 나게 하는 것은 너무나 자연스러웠다. 그 맛있는 음식들을 배불리 먹을 때마다 몸속의 아우성을 듣지 못하고 행복해했다. 나처럼 아날로그 시대에 태어난 사람이 인터넷으로 유튜브로 온갖 건강 정보를 넘쳐나게 얻게 된 것이 그리 오래되지 않았으니 몸의 적신호에 대한 핑계를 댄다 한들 무슨 소용이랴. 게다가 길을 갈 때도 예전엔 앞을 똑바로 보고 걸었는데 이젠 땅바닥도 내려다보며 걷는다. 넘어지면 큰일이라니 조심하게 된다. 멀쩡하던 허리며 무릎이 자칫 삐끗 결리기라도 하면 고생이 이만저만이 아니다. 그러니 몸의 상태를 잘 헤아려가며 다뤄야 할 때가 온 것이다.

어느 날 남편이 뒤뜰에서 일하다가 허리를 다쳤다. 삐져나온 디스크가 척추의 신경을 압박하여 통증 쓰나미가 발끝까지 내리 덮쳤다. 그는 혼비백산하여 고통의 소리를 집안이 떠나갈 듯 뱉어냈다. 지금 생각하면 구급차를 불러야 했는데 남편의 만류를 나는 어리석게도 그의 말을 따랐다. 대신 옆집 부인에게 전화를 했다. 우리 집에서 남편의 큰소리가 들리더라도 개의치 말아 달라고.

물리치료사가 여러 번 왕진을 왔으나 큰 진전이 없던 차에 한국에서 재활전문의였던 지인의 소개로 디스크를 원상복구 시키는 기구가 있는 물리치료 병원을 가게 되었다. 남편과 남편의 나이만큼이나 오래되어 보이는-딸친구의 할머니가 사용하셨던-휠체어를 차에 싣고 내가 운전대를 잡은 것까지는 순조로웠다. 그런데 길에 주차를 하고 휠체어에 남편을 앉히고 밀기 시작하자 갑자기 앞으로 미끄러져 내려가는게 아닌가. 내가 손만 놓으면 그대로 찻길로 돌진할 판이다. 내 심장이 멎을 듯한 상황이었다. 그제야 보도블록이 약간 경사져 있는 것을 알았으나 너무나 당황하여 브레이크는 생각도 못 하고 오로지 나는 온 힘으로 휠체어를 내 한쪽 무릎 안쪽에 대고 끌어당기는 데만 열중했다. 그 사건으로 인해 내 무릎 통증이 시작되었다.

일련의 도미노 현상이 그때부터 일어났다. 남편은 허리를 다친 김에 여러 가지 검사를 했는데 결과가 좋지 않았다. 전문의 예약을 하고 나니 머릿속이 복잡해졌다. 며칠 후면 우리 모녀가 제주도에 가서 해녀 인형극을 공연하기로 몇 달 전부터 예정이 되어 있건만 어떻게 해야하나. 접이식 테이블이며 스크린 등 공연을 위한 모든 채비를 마치고 공항에 갈 준비가 되어 있는데 혼자 일어서는 것도 힘든 남편을 혼자 두고 떠날 수는 없었다. 이제 와서 공연 취소를 통보해야 하다니 쉽지 않은 기회였는데 실없는 사람이 되었다는 생각에 몹시 실망스러웠다. 결국 딸이 한국행을 포기하고 아빠와 남기로 했다. 전문의를 만나는 일과 다른 검사를 할 때 아빠의 휠체어를 밀고 동행하기로 했다. 딸은 내가 제주도에 가서 프리젠테이션이라도 할 자료를 준비했다. 내가 아침 비행기로 떠나는 전날 밤 우리 모녀는 한숨도 눈을 붙이지 못하고 말았다.

　대수롭지 않게 생각했던 내 무릎에 기어이 이상이 오고 말았다. 예정했던 대로 한국과 일본, 다시 한국에 가 있는 동안 나는 다리를 절룩거리게 되었다. 탱탱하게 부어오른 무릎을 굽히지도 못하고 통증은 점점 심해졌다. 결국 정형외과에 가서 스테로이드 주사를 약하게 맞기도 했다. 시드니로 돌아와서 MRI 검사 결과 연골 파열에 인대도 조금 손상이 갔다는 것을 알게 되었다. 다친 후 물리치료를 시작하기까지 8주나 걸렸으니 병을 키운 셈이 되고 말았다. 소를 잃었는데 외양간이 고쳐지질 않는다. 결국 나는 지팡이 신세까지 지게 되었다.

　설상가상으로 남편이 또 사고를 쳤다. 이번엔 부엌 뒤뜰에서 넘어져 양쪽 무릎을 다쳤다. 골절되지 않아 천만다행이나 손바닥만 한 반창고를 양쪽 무릎 전체에 붙일 정도로 상처가 컸다. 그는 마침 집에 있던 등산용 지팡이를 꺼내 들었다. 부부가 갑자기 나란히 지팡이를 짚는 신세가 되다니 나이 들어가는 광고를 주위에 톡톡히 하는 처지가 되었다.

서양에서도 나쁜 일은 연거푸 세 번 일어난다는 속담이 있으니 세상의 이치는 참으로 묘하다는 생각이 든다. 이제 남편은 허리를 다친 김에 여러 검사까지 하고 몸 안의 적신호를 미리 발견할 수 있게 되어 치료를 겸하고 있어서 전화위복이 아닐 수 없다. 그의 회복은 빠른 편인데 내 무릎은 시간이 오래 걸리는 것 같다. 때마침 여고 친구들 카톡방에 '세상 힘들어도 웃고 살아가요'라는 카드가 올라왔다. 이제 이만큼 살아왔으면 세상살이에 의연해질 때도 되었건만 여전히 호들갑을 떨게 되니 나는 얼마나 더 살아야 미숙함에서 벗어나게 될 것인가. 나이 듦의 과정도 감사하는 마음으로 즐겨야 한다는 것은 어쩌면 나 스스로의 위안일지도 모른다. 이런 모든 과정이 인생살이인 것을… 희로애락을 오가며 이어가는 나의 인생 소나타는 여전히 연주 중이다. 세월이 흐르면서, 기쁨과 슬픔의 무게를 모두 지니며 음악은 느린 악장으로 옮겨가고 있다.

(2023)

단편 소설
아버지의 봄

아버지 유품을 정리하던 중에 낯익은 머리빗이 나의 관심을 끌었다. 촘촘하게 만들어진 작은 반달 모양의 나무 빗에는 아버지의 흰 머리카락이 두어 가닥 걸려 있다. 아버지가 이 머리빗을 가까이 두고 마치 사랑하는 이의 손을 쓸어 만지듯 그런 모습을 몇 번인가 본 적이 있다. 아니, 나에게 들킨 적이 있다고 해야 맞다.

"아버지 또 그 머리빗 가지고 노시네요." 놀리는 나에게 살짝 얼굴까지 붉히시며 "예끼, 그 무슨 소리냐. 백발이라도 숱이 제법 많았는데 이젠 머릿밑이 훤히 드러나는게 싫어서 빗으로 머리를 가지런히 펴는게지. 으흠…"

아버지의 목소리가 내 귓전을 맴돌고 기억의 편린들이 스멀스멀 가슴으로 밀려든다. 창문을 활짝 열어 젖히니 아직은 싸한 초봄의 공기가 얼굴을 덮는다. 베란다 턱에 언제 날아 왔는지 새 한 마리가 나를 향해 앉아 있는게 마치 나를 주시하고 있는 듯 묘한 느낌이 들었다. 혹시 저 새가 아버지의 전령이라도 되는 것일까 하는.

* * *

선산의 못자리에 어머니의 관을 내리고 그 옆에 묘지기가 사기 사발을 엎어 아버지의 자리를 표시하는 것을 보시며 '내 여기 올 때까지 잘 있게' 하셨던 아버지는 이후 술잔을 기울일 때마다 눈가를 적시며 빨리 어머니 곁으로 가고 싶다고 하셨다. 나는 '아버지 또 그러시네. 이 외동딸을 고아로 만드실 셈이세요? 저를 위해서라도 엄마 몫까지 사셔야 해요!' 그리고 벌써 몇 번의 겨울을 맞이하게 되었던가. 아버지 가까이에 살고 있던 나는 교편을 잡고 있어서 방학 때면 아버지 곁에서 어머니의 빈자리를 채워드리려고 부산을 떨었다. 며칠째 함박눈이 온 세상을 하얗게 덮고 있던 어느 날, 그날따라 아버지는 내가 점심 설거지를 끝내고 부엌 정리를 하고 있을 때까지도 말없이 창밖을 내다보고 계시더니 무언가 결심한 듯한 목소리로

"연주야 부엌일 그만하고 여기와 앉아봐라. 이야기 좀 하자. 아버지가 부탁이 있다." 하고 나를 부르셨다.

나는 웬일인가 하고 젖은 손을 행주치마에 문지르며 소파에 다가가 앉았다. 아버지는 오십이 넘은 딸에게 너무나 의외의 이야기를 꺼냈다. '뭐라구요? 첫사랑을 찾고 싶다고요? 그런 말도 안 되는 소리 하지 마세요. 그게 어떻게 가능해요? 아버지 팔십이 넘으셨어요. 정신차리세요. 돌아가신 어머니가 무덤에서 뛰쳐 나오시겠어요…' 이렇게 외쳐대고 싶었지만 나를 의지하는 아버지에게 상처가 되면 마음을 닫으실까 봐 일단 입을 악물고 참았다. 그

날 밤 이리 뒤척 저리 뒤척거리며 잠을 이루지 못하는 동안 어느새 커튼 사이로 희미하게 밝은 빛이 들어오고 있었다. 아버지가 앞으로 얼마나 더 사실 지 모를 연세에 이르러 도쿄에 한번 가고 싶으시다는데 못 들어드릴 이유는 없다. 더구나 아버지 인생의 봄날에 만났던 첫사랑을 무작정 일본에 간다고 해서 찾을 수 있다는 보장은 없다. 어쩌면 산에 올라 물고기를 찾는 격이지 싶었다. 복잡하게 생각하지 않고 그냥 아버지 모시고 여행이나 시켜 드리자라는 편한 마음으로 바뀌어 갔다. 비록 추운 겨울이긴 하지만 마침 학교 방학으로 시간도 있고 내가 아버지의 한을 들어드릴 수 있다면 날씨가 무슨 상관이 있겠는가. 나는 마음이 변하기 전에 서둘러 비행기표부터 끊어버렸다.

* * *

아버지 이상필은 일제강점기 이십 대 초반의 동경 유학생이었다. 그가 가끔 자취방에서 멀지 않은 곳에 있는 잡화상에 들를 때면 항상 상냥하고 친절하게 대해주던 아가씨가 있었는데 가게에서 앞치마를 입은 부인에게 '오까상'이라고 부르는 것을 듣고 그 집 딸이라는 것을 알 수 있었다. 아버지 말로는 그 당시 이 아가씨가 대학생 이상필에게 호감을 갖고 있음을 느꼈다고 했다. 어느 날, 하염없이 휘몰아치는 진눈깨비가 잠잠해지기를 기다리며 학교 도서관에 있던 상필은 창밖에 어둠이 깔리기 시작하자 얼른 책을 덮고는 외투 깃을 여미며 자췻집으로 향했다. 길이 미끄러워 조심하며 걷고 있는데 낯익은 아가씨가 우산을 가지고 그의 앞에 나타났다. 그녀는 수줍은 목소리로 "코트가 눈에 젖어 얼어 버리면 내일 학교 갈 때 못 입을 수도 있어요. 내일은 더 추울 거라는데…" 하며 우산을 내미는게 아닌가. 놀란 상필은 얼떨결에 그것을 받아들었다. "그럼, 안녕. 조심해서 가세요." 하고 돌아서서 발걸음을 옮기는 그녀에게 소리쳤다.

"고맙습니다! 당신 이름은…?"

"미에꼬. 모리 미에꼬데스. 아나따와(당신은)?"

"이.상.필."

"이 상피루 상. 하이(네). 아리가또(고마워요)."

그해 겨울엔 유난히 눈 오는 날이 많았다. 부모 곁을 떠나 도쿄까지 와서 오직 학업에만 전념하고 있던 상필에게 설경 따위는 관심 밖이었고 눈 온 뒤 질퍽거리거나 미끄러운 길이 짜증스럽기만 했던 그였다. 눈 덮인 오솔길을 미에꼬와 함께 걸으며 그는 마치 설경을 처음 보는 듯 황홀감에 빠져들었다. 청년 상필의 마음은 점점 그녀에게 끌려가고 있었다. 청순하고 상냥한 미에꼬가 그냥 마음에 들었다. 늦게까지 도서관에서 시간을 보내는 상필에게 그녀는 손수 정성스럽게 준비한 도시락을 예쁜 보자기에 싸서 건네 주기도 했다. 생활 반경이 학교와 도서관과 자취방으로 거의 제한되어 있던 상필은 그녀의 친절이 싫지 않았다. 어느 날, 흰 눈이 소복이 쌓인 눈숲을 둘이 걷다가 눈을 이고 있는 가지들이 무거워 보인다며 상필이 힘껏 나무를 흔들어 대니 눈사태가 난 것처럼 두 사람을 덮쳤다. 상필은 반사적으로 그녀를 끌어안았다. 둘은 서로를 포옹한 채 한동안 그 자리에 서 있었다.

미에꼬와 헤어지고 자취방으로 돌아올 때마다 상필은 자신의 마음속에서 일어나고 있는 변화에 괴로워했다. 부모님이 자신에게 큰 기대를 걸고 유학을 보내며 당부했던 말이 귓전을 때렸다. 공부를 마칠 때까지 절대 한눈팔지 말라는. 더욱이 그녀는 일본 여자가 아닌가. 상필이 자책할수록 가슴 속에서는 사랑의 불씨가 반란을 일으키고 있었다. 혼란스러웠다.

1944년 일본이 태평양전쟁 막바지에 이르자 상필에게 징집령이 떨어졌다. 그는 상황이 절박해지자 차라리 도망치다가 죽으면 죽으리라 결심했다. 밀항선에서 도망친 학생들의 이름이 나팔을 통해 쩌렁쩌렁 불려 나올 때마다 그의 입술은 타들어 가고 온몸이 바람 빠진 풍선처럼 쪼그라들었다. 우여곡절 끝에 밀항에 성공하여 부산에 도착했다. 그러나 며칠 후 가족이 있는 서울에 도착했을 때 기다리고 있던 형사에게 붙잡히고야 말았다. 그는 어느 공장으로 끌려가 중노동으로 온갖 고초를 겪다가 일본이 패망하자 집에 돌아올 수 있었다.

그가 집안의 중매로 결혼한 것은 삼십 가까이 되어서였다. 완고한 집안에서 감히 미에꼬라는 이름의 미 字도 입 밖에 내서는 안된다는 것을 알기에 그는 도쿄에서 있었던 일을 무덤까지 가져가기로 굳게 마음먹었다. 그녀가 생각날 때마다 자신을 닦달해 가며 미에꼬를 향한 감성의 스위치를 끄기 위하여 온갖 애를 썼다. 그리고 아내와의 사이에 외동딸이 태어나자 오로지 가정만을 위해 열심히 살아왔다. 탐스럽던 아내의 검은 머리가 희끗희

꿋 변하는게 안쓰럽다고 생각되던 즈음 돌연히 상처한 상필은 단번에 살아갈 의욕을 잃고 말았다. 집 안 구석구석 어디에도 아내의 흔적이 배이지 않은 데가 없었다. 베란다에 가지런히 놓인 화분마다 아내의 숨결이 살아있는 듯했고 꽃이라도 피면 아내가 더욱 그리워졌다. 아내는 부지런하고 성실하게 가정을 잘 가꾸어냈다. 가정을 위해서 한결같이 남아있을 것 같은 듬직한 아내였다. 그런 아내가 막상 기둥이 내려앉듯 떠나버리자 아내의 빈자리는 동굴만큼이나 공허하게 컸다. 살아있을 때 고마움을 표현하지 못한 것이 후회되었다. '여보, 고마웠소. 그리고 미안하오.' 상필은 집안을 둘러보며 빈 공간에 대고 실성한 사람처럼 중얼댔다. 집안에서 어찌할 바를 모르고 술잔만 앞에 놓으면 아내 곁으로 빨리 가고 싶다는 마음뿐이었다.

그러던 아버지의 마음에 이번 겨울 이변이 생긴 것이다. 어둠이 내려앉은 밤에 거실의 커튼을 열어젖힌 채 유리문 밖으로 소리 없이 쏟아지는 함박눈을 물끄러미 바라보다가 적막감에 몸서리를 치는 순간, 갑자기 미에꼬가 눈앞에 나타나는 것이었다. 꿈은 아니었다. 소스라치게 놀라며 눈을 비비고 기억 속의 그녀를 바라보았다. 이게 무슨 연고인가. 까마득한 옛일로 잊혀진 줄 알았던 그녀가 웬일로 갑자기 나타난 것일까. 그녀는 상필의 잠재의식 저편에서 수십 년간 묻혀 있다가 마치 마법의 주문이 풀리듯 휘리릭 그 앞에 모습을 드러냈다. 분명히 잊었었는데… 상필은 마음이 착잡해졌다. 사진 한 장 없이 헤어졌으나 젊은 날의 희고 갸름한 얼굴과 반짝이던 두 눈과 도톰하고 작은 입술에서 나오는 말은 늘 상냥했고 그녀와 같이 걷던 하얀 세상이 환영처럼 한꺼번에 눈앞에 다가왔다. 눈물을 흘리는 그녀를 뒤로하고 급작스럽게 떠나야 했던 상필. 그 후 현실과 맞서지 못하고 애써 밀쳐냈던 미에꼬가 아닌가.

그녀는 어찌 되었을까. 미국이 도쿄에 융단폭격으로 대공습을 감행했을 때 오롯이 살아 남아 있을 거라는 보장은 없다. 만일 살아 있다고 해도 나이가 팔십이 넘었을 텐데 잘 지내고 있을까. 60여 년 세월이 훌쩍 지났건만 갑자기 찾아보고 싶다는 엉뚱한 생각이 간절하게 밀려왔다. 자신이 마치 어떤 보이지 않는 힘에 끌리고 있는 것만 같았다.

나는 아버지와 함께 나리타 공항에 내렸다. 짙은 갈색의 모직 바지, 체크 남방에 베이지색 캐쉬미어 가디건, 베이지 모직코트와 체크무늬 목도리에 모자를 쓰니 20년은 젊고 멋있어 보인다고 아버지를 추켜세우며 딸과의 여행을 즐기시라고 호들갑을 떨었다. 사실 나는 미에꼬라는 사람에 대한 기대는 전혀 하지 않았기에 아버지가 실망하지 않도록 미리 연막을 치고 싶었다. 동서남북도 가늠할 수 없는 이 큰 도시에서 까마득한 세월이 흐른 뒤 옛날의 미에꼬를 찾는다는 건 해변 모래밭에서 바늘 찾기가 아닐까. 내 생각에는 아버지도 여행이나 하자고 하실 줄 알았다. 그러나 아버지의 생각은 달랐다. 호텔에 짐을 풀고 전화번호부와 지도부터 펼치시고는 옛날 그녀 가족이 운영하던 가게와 그 뒤편에 살림집이 있던 동네부터 가보길 원하셨다. 나는 따라 나서긴 했지만 남의 나라에 와서 전철을 바꿔 타면서까지 모험할 마음의 준비가 전혀 되어 있지 않았다. 옛 흔적은 사라지고 빌딩이 들어선 곳에서 결국 첫째 날엔 미로를 헤매는 기분이 들었고 미로의 출발점으로 다시 와서 호텔로 돌아왔다. 나는 이미 녹초가 되어 눕고만 싶었다. 그러나 아버지는 쉬지 않고 전화기 앞에 앉았다. 전화번호부에 있는 동명이인들을 호텔 전화기로 일일이 확인하는데 꼬박 하루를 소모했다. 단언컨대 저 힘은 분명히 사랑의 힘일 것이다.

결국 나는 혼자 외출하여 주위를 둘러보며 전화기 앞에서 헛수고를 하고 계실 아버지를 생각하니 한심한 생각도 들고 아버지에게 야속한 생각마저 들었다. 딸하고 관광이나 하시지 노인네가 웬 주책인가 싶기도 했다. 내가 다시 호텔로 돌아와 살그머니 문을 열고 보니 아버지는 전화기 옆에서 양손으로 얼굴을 감싸고 있었다.

"아버지…."

고개를 들어 나를 쳐다보는 아버지의 얼굴이 일그러져 있다. 이젠 일일이 전화한다는 자체가 뜬구름 잡는 일이라는 걸 깨달으셨나 보다. 지칠 때도 되셨다는 생각이 들었다. 위로의 말을 드리려던 순간, 내 귀를 의심하고 싶은 말이 아버지로부터 들려오는 게 아닌가.

"연주야. 애비가 미에꼬를 찾았다…. 혹시라도 내가 찾아올까 봐… 수십 년 동안 그 지역을 떠나지 않고 있었다네…. 결혼도 하지 않고… 전화번호부에 계속 이름을 올렸다는구나….”
 목이 메어 더 이상 말을 잇지 못하는 아버지를 바라보며 나는 꿈을 꾸고 있다는 생각이 들었다. 꿈이 아니고서야 멀쩡한 생시에 이런 변이….

 다음 날 아침, 머리가 희끗희끗한 내 또래의 여성이 호텔로 우리를 데리러 왔다. 고개 숙여 정중하게 인사할 때 흘낏 본 그녀의 얼굴이 왠지 낯설지 않다는 생각이 들었다. 택시 뒷좌석에서 나와 나란히 앉은 아버지는 무얼 생각하고 계실까. 착잡한 마음일까. 설레는 마음일까. 가슴이 뛰고 있을까. 그녀를 알아보기는 할까. 이런 엄청난 일이라니…. 차창 밖에 스치는 많은 인파. 그들이 우리 일에는 아랑곳없다는 듯이 무관심한 표정으로 걷고 있는 게 이상해 보인다. 말도 안 되는 당연한 일인데 내가 미치고 있는 건가. 택시에서 내려 여인을 따라 좁은 골목길로 들어섰다. 내 눈엔 자동차 한 대가 겨우 지나갈 듯 좁아 보이는 골목에는 깨끗하고 검소한 인상을 주는 잿빛 집들이 마주 보고 들어서 있었다. 앞서 안내하던 여인이 골목길 끝 집 앞에서 걸음을 멈춰 섰다. 대문 안을 들어서니 작은 뜰에 앙상한 나무 한 그루와 빈 화단과 벽돌색 화분 몇 개가 추위를 견뎌 내고 있는 듯 보였다. 나는 갑자기 아버지가 옛 연인과 상봉하는 장면을 보고 싶지 않다는 생각이 들었다. 돌아가신 어머니와 금슬 좋게 살았는데 이제 와서 왜 우리가 여기에 있단 말인가? 설마 그녀를 찾을 수 있으리라고 추호도 생각하지 못한 나 자신이 원망스러웠다. 그렇다고 지금 돌아서서 나 혼자 호텔로 갈 수도 없지 않은가.

그녀는 현관에서 휠체어에 앉은 채 우리를 맞았다.

"상피루상…."

"미에꼬…."

아버지는 백발의 그녀에게 다가가 허리를 낮추고 그녀를 끌어안았다. 그 장면은 마치 어제 만났던 연인들이 오늘 다시 만난 듯 자연스러워 보이기까지 했다. 어찌 그럴 수가 있을까. 두 사람은 할 말을 잃고 한동안 미동도 하지 않았다. 그렇게 하고 있는 동안 그 옛날 눈 덮인 나무를 흔들어 눈 폭탄 아래서 포옹하던 때를 서로 떠올리고 있는 것일까. 지금 이 순간의 당사자가 내 아버지가 아니라면 나도 감동의 눈물을 쏟았을지도 모른다. 그녀는 볼에 흘러내리는 눈물을 닦으며 우리에게, 아니, 아버지에게 우리를 데리고 온 여인을 소개했다.

"얘가 당신의 딸 미에입니다."

나는 아버지가 그처럼 놀라는 모습을 일찍이 본 일이 없었다. 형용키 어려운 그 표정은 차라리 측은함과 절망감을 느끼게 했다. 그러고 보니 그녀의 이마와 눈매, 코가 나와 많이 닮아 있었다. 예쁘장한 입은 미에꼬할머니를 빼닮았다. 아버지를 바라보고 나는 현기증을 느꼈다. 둔기로 머리를 맞은 듯한 충격을 받았다. 아버지의 딸이라고 소개받은 미에도, 아니 우리를 안내해 온 여인도 입을 딱벌리고 있다. 미에꼬는 자신의 딸에게 지금까지 출생의 비밀을 감추고 살아왔던 것이다. 1945년에 태어난 미에는 아버지가 전쟁에서 죽었다고만 알고 있었다. 그런데 생부가 한국인이라니 이 사실을 어떻게 받아들여야 하나. 어머니 미에꼬는 훗날 언제가 될지 몰라도 생부를 찾게 되기를 바라는 마음에서 딸의 이름도 자기 이름을 따서 지었던 것이다. 상필을 닮은 딸을 낳고 상필을 보듯이 딸과 함께 살아온 세월이 반세기를 훨씬 넘었다는 이 믿지 못한 사실. 아버지의 외동딸로 사랑받고 살아온 나에게 이복언니가 있었다니 나 역시도 혼란스럽기만 하다. 나는 다음 날도 그다음 날도 미에꼬에게 가시는 아버지를 따라나서지 않고 혼자서 시간을 보냈다. 이 엄청난 현실을 받아들일 시간이 내겐 필요했다. 지금까지 별 탈 없이 평범하게 살아온 우리 가족에게 웬 날벼락인가. 아버지는 배신자인가 아니면 의리의 남자인가. 내 마음도 뒤죽박죽이다.

한국으로 돌아온 후 제일 먼저 아버지와 나는 어머니 산소를 찾았다. 아버지가 어머니에게 도쿄에 다녀온 이야기를 꺼내실 때 나는 슬그머니 자리를 비켜드렸다. '당신 옆으로 갈 때까지 잘 있소' 인사를 하고 하산하여 집에 온 아버지는 무겁게 가라앉았던 집안의 공기를 보이지 않는 새로운 에너지와 교체하려는 듯 집안의 창문을 활짝 열어 놓았다. 아버지의 여행 가방을 정리하는데 낯선 물건들이 나왔다. 그중에 나무로 정교하게 깎아 만든 반달 모양의 자그마한 머리빗이 있었다. 한동안 사용하여 기름때 절은 그 빗은 미에꼬 할머니가 오랜 세월 자신의 머리를 위로 빗어 올려 고정하는 데 사용하던 빗이었다. 아버지는 그 빗이 마치 그녀의 분신이라도 되는 것처럼 아끼셨다.

　아버지는 매주 월요일 오전 10시가 되면 도쿄의 미에꼬와 통화를 하신다. 아침에 샤워를 하고 미에꼬의 빗으로 몇 올 남지 않은 머리를 정성스레 빗고 마치 미에꼬와 데이트하러 외출하는 옷차림으로 전화기 앞에 앉는다. 나는 방학 때만 아버지가 전화 데이트를 하는 모습을 볼 수 있었는데 알아들을 수는 없으나 그동안 살아온 이야기를 하는 것이리라 짐작한다. 목이 메기도 하고 즐거운 표정을 보이기도 하는 아버지를 보며, 인사는커녕 뒤도 돌아보지 않고 떠나온 미에꼬와 미에라는 모녀에게 슬그머니 미안한 마음이 들기도 했다. 미에는 나의 이복언니가 아닌가. 아버지와 미에꼬는 나와 미에에게 시간이 필요하다는 것을 이해하고 우리가 마음을 열 때를 기다리기로 했단다. 아버지는 가끔 전화 내용을 들려 주셨다. "당시 미에꼬 아버지는 징집령이 내려도 전쟁터에 가는 것을 피하려고 깡마른 체구로 만들기 위해 집을 떠나 숨어서 밥을 굶고 있었는데 어느 날 밤 아내와 딸이 너무 보고 싶어서 가게에 들렀다가 함께 지내던 외할머니가 '우리까지 위험에 빠뜨릴 생각인가! 당장 나가게!'라고 야단을 쳐서 쫓아냈다고 하더라. 미에꼬의 배가 불러오자 집안에서 한바탕 난리를 겪고는 주위의 눈을 피해 외할머니가 데리고 지방의 친척 집으로 가 있다가 해산을 해 도쿄 대공습 때 폭격을 피할 수 있었다네. 그때 미에꼬는 고아가 되었어."

　"연주야. 미에는 어쨌거나 너의 언니다. 제 에미와 고락을 같이

하며 여태 결혼도 안 하고 살아왔어. 한때는 유치원 선생을 했다더라. 전에 살던 지역에서 홀로 잡화상을 하며 살아온 제 에미를 돕다가 얼마 전부터는 가게를 임대하고 그 수입으로 살고 있다고 한다. 두 사람이 한국에 여행 온 적도 있다는구나. 미에꼬가 사고로 휠체어 신세를 지게 되기 전의 일이다만…. 미에는 서울의 거리를 걸으면서 왠지 낯설지 않았다고 하는구나. 참 이상도 하지. 아니 이상할 것도 없지. 한국 피가 흐르고 있으니 말이다. 지금 미에는 한국 드라마를 즐겨 보며 한국말을 배우고 있다고 한다. 앞으로 네게 좋은 언니가 될 것이야. 그러니 이 아비는 너도 마음을 열게 되길 바랄 뿐이다."

아버지와 미에꼬와의 전화 데이트는 5년가량 계속되었다. 그들은 일주일에 한 번 어김없이 전화에서 만났다. 모녀가 단풍 여행을 다녀왔다며 불타듯 화려한 빨간 단풍과 샛노란 단풍이 절정을 이루고 있는데 상피루상도 함께 했으면 얼마나 좋을까 딸과 이야기했다며 전하는 그녀의 목소리는 약간 홍분되어 있었다. 그렇게 아버지와 통화를 하고 난 뒤 그녀는 왼쪽 가슴을 붙들고 쓰러졌다. 나는 도쿄에 다녀와야 한다는 아버지를 극구 만류했다. 아버지의 건강이 염려되어 쌍초상이 날까 봐 두려워서 안 된다고 말렸다. 미에꼬는 사랑하는 옛 애인과 아름다운 단풍놀이를 하고 온 이야기 끝에 생을 마감했으니 그나마 복된 죽음이 아닐까.

미에꼬가 그렇게 떠나고 아버지는 한동안 슬퍼하시며 다시 술잔을 기울이셨다. 식욕이 없다고 식사를 잘 안 하시더니 나중엔 아예 곡기를 끊기로 작정한 것처럼 보이기도 했다. 그러던 어느 날, 도쿄에서 두툼한 소포가 도착했다. 미에가 아버지에게 보낸 것이었다.

"… 어머니 장례식은 잘 마쳤습니다. 평소에 어머니가 저에게 일러주신 대로 저는 어머니 사후에 늘 잠겨있던 캐비닛 서랍을 열었습니다. 서랍 안에는 겉면에 '이상필 상'이라고 쓴 오래된 편지뭉치가 있었습니다. 지난 세월 주소는커녕 생사조차 모르는 애인을 그리워하며 틈틈이 적은 독백이더군요. 이승에서 못 만나면 저승에서라도 만나야 할 것 같은 절실한 편지였습니다.

어머니는 전쟁 통에 나를 낳아 전후 폐허 속에서 키우며 간간이 '너는 아버지를 닮았어'라며 제 얼굴을 쓰다듬으셨습니다. 사진 한 장 없는 애인의 얼굴을 제 얼굴에서 찾으며 어머니는 쓸쓸한 미소를 짓곤 했습니다. 수십 년을 그렇게 보내면서 얼마나 간절히 애인을 그리워했길래 하늘이 도우셨는지 재회를 할 수 있었던 게 아닐까요. 5년 전 어머니를 찾아 주셔서 감사했습니다.

사실 그 당시 제가 받은 충격은 이만저만이 아니었어요. 어떻게 그 긴 세월 동안 하나밖에 없는 딸에게 진실을 숨기고 살아왔는지 어머니가 원망스럽기까지 했습니다. 그때까지 아버지는 일본 사람이고(너무나 자연스럽고 당연한 사실로 이것은 의문의 여지가 없었지요) 도쿄 대공습 때 죽었다고 잘못 알고 있었다니까요. 그러나 지금 저는 생부가 한국인이라는 사실을 받아들이고 있습니다. 돌아가신 부인께는 참 죄송하지만, 저세상에서 제 어머니를 너그러이 받아 주시길 두 손 모아 빕니다. 제 머리에 서리가 내려앉은 지금이라도 한국에 아버지와 연주라는 여동생이 있다는 사실은 홀로 남은 저의 마음에 위로가 됩니다.

이곳 도서관에 한국 관련 책이 많이 있더군요. 이제부터 본격적으로 내 아버지의 나라에 대한 공부를 해보려고 합니다. 내년 봄엔 한국을 방문할 계획을 세우고 있습니다. 연주와 대화를 할 수 있도록 한국말도 열심히 배우고는 있으나 나이 탓인지 쉽지 않군요. 아버지와 부녀지정도 나누고 싶습니다.

어머니의 편지꾸러미를 보내드립니다. 부디 건강하시길 빕니다.
모리 미에 올림"

아버지는 여기까지 미에의 편지 내용을 내게 말씀해 주시곤 여러 날 동안 두문불출하며 미에꼬의 편지에 푹 빠져 지냈다.
"연주야 부탁이다. 나 죽거든 네 언니와 연락하고 잘 지내며 살아라. 불쌍한 사람이야. 제 어미와 고생을 많이 했더구나." 유언처럼 이 말을 남기던 아버지는 봄이 오면 한국엘 오겠다던 미에를 만나지 못한 채 눈을 감으셨다. 미에꼬의 편지가 얼마나 절절했기에 저세상에서 빨리 만나고 싶어 서둘러 가셨는가. 아버지와 한세상을 함께하셨던 아내, 나의 어머니에게로 빨리 가고 싶다고 하시던 아버지가 아니었던가. 저승에서 세 사람이 만난다면 어떤 일이 벌어질까.

아버지 장례식에 나는 미에를 부르지 않았다. 어차피 돌아가셨는데 이제 와서 먼 길을 오게 하고 싶지 않았고 남편을 제외하고는 자식들이며 다른 사람들에게 설명할 마음의 여유가 아직은 없는 데다 이야깃거리가 되는 것을 피하고 싶었기 때문이다.

아버지의 유품을 정리하던 날 베란다 턱에 날라와 내 쪽을 바라보고 앉았던 그 새가 내 마음에 사진처럼 또렷이 남아 있다. 어쩌면 그 새는 이복 언니와 연락하며 잘 지내라는 아버지의 전령이었을지도 모른다. 아버지가 미에꼬와 매주 통화했던 것처럼 지금은 나도 주말이면 정해진 시간에 미에 언니에게 안부 전화를 한다. 언니는 서툰 한국말로 나는 서툰 일어로 몇 마디를 나누는 게 다이지만.

나는 이번 방학 때 이 세상에 홀로 남은 이복 언니 미에를 만나보려고 도쿄에 갈 예정이다. 그리고 여행 가방 안에 아버지가 그리도 아끼시던 미에꼬의 나무 빗을 챙겨 넣는 것도 잊지 않았다.

"아버지의 봄"은 프랑스와 독일 사이에 실제로 있었던 일에서 영감을 받아 처음으로 시도한 단편소설입니다.

Snow on a Summer's Day

A Migrant's Life in Sydney-Bilingual Essays in Korean and English

Preface

In 2006, an ad appeared in a Korean community newspaper in Sydney, announcing the launch of a creative writing class. That notice stirred something powerful in me, as I had long carried the dream of writing in my heart. Though I was a latecomer, the saying "There is no time like the present" gave me the courage to act. Meeting novelist Lee Hyojeong as our teacher at that time was very fortunate.

When I began writing, my initial goal was to leave behind a simple record of my life perhaps in the form of a memoir or autobiography. But by the time I completed the 10 week course, I had fallen deeply in love with the essay genre. Since then, I've continued writing essays, discovering the joy of turning everyday life into words.

It has now been nearly half a century since I left my motherland. From 1978, I spent ten intense years in Tokyo, working, giving birth, and raising children. Then, in 1988, the year of the Seoul Olympics, my family immigrated to Australia. Throughout this immigrant life, I've experienced a range of changes and challenges that have brought me to where I am today. Now, in the latter part of life with a little more time to pause and reflect, I'm delighted to present my first collection of essays in both Korean and English.

There's a personal reason behind this bilingual edition: my son and daughter, raised in Australia, cannot fully understand the Korean essays their mother writes. My daughter, who moved here at the age of three, struggles to grasp Korean sentences fluently. She's often wondered what kind of things I write about. With this book, I hope she'll be inspired to study Korean more seriously.

Instead of hiring a professional translator, which seemed

daunting in cost, I turned to those around me for help. I owe my deepest gratitude to my daughter Kay and her friends: Nancy Lee, Sunny Lee, Sue Hendroff, Philippa Russell, Kate Harris and Sungsin Ro who helped with translation, proofreading, and refinement. Recently, I also had help from AI for translation. Two years ago, it couldn't translate the word 'monyeo' (mother and daughter) so I decided to write the long first draft myself and get help from my daughter. Progress was a lot slower than I expected. But this time, when I tried AI again, it translated that word 'monyeo' correctly. I was amazed not only by the accuracy but also by how fast the work went. Still, the translation had to match the author's intent, and AI can make mistakes. So I checked every sentence myself and also got help from English experts.

This book includes 30 essays selected from pieces I had contributed over the years to Korean community newspapers in Sydney such as the Hanho Daily (which closed in 2023) and Sydney Korean Herald. The title of this book, 'Snow on a Summer's Day', comes from one of the essays within. On a sweltering summer day in Sydney where the seasons are opposite to my motherland, I was watching a show at The State Theatre. The climax was when a blizzard of paper-snow poured down over the audience. Beneath that spectacular scene lay my own longing as a migrant from the Northern Hemisphere, where December always meant real snowfall.

While I cherish the memories of my motherland, I am also deeply grateful for the warmth, the light, and the opportunities that Australia has given me. This book is not only for my children, but also a small testament to myself and to the many others who have lived as immigrants. The writings may be unpolished, but they reflect my thoughts and journey as a migrant. I hope they resonate with other immigrants and inspire them to share their own stories. Above all, I hope my writings may touch the hearts of English-speaking readers as well.

At the end of this essay collection, I have included my first short story. Different from essays, it is a fictional exploration of another person's life. Though still unpolished, it represents a careful step toward new literary expression.

June 2025, in the winter of Sydney

Youngkyu (Yong) Kwon

Table of Contents

Preface　　　　　　　　172
APPENDIX　　　　　　378

Part One

Calling Australia Home	180
Street Breakfast	186
Snow on a Summer's Day	192
A Guest Named Walter	197
Sheryl's 60th Birthday Party	202
The Grand Tree	207
Living Simply	213
Cockatoos and Apple Trees	219

Part Two

The Domino of Fate	228
The Changing Faces of Brides	232
A New Mother and Seaweed Soup	237
The Power of Love	244
The Final Farewell	250
Savings in My Heart	256
The Fragrance of Friendship	261
Ah, Virginia!	267

Part Three

The Tower of Babel in Our Time	278
The Age of the Smartphone	283
The Power of Culture	288
Meeting the Haenyeo	293
The Power of Cultural Inheritance	300
A History We Cannot Be Proud Of	306
Natural Disasters and Man-made Disasters	312
We Come From Far, Far Away	318

Part Four

The Spirit of Craftsmanship	327
Welcoming the New Year	332
This Too Shall Pass	337
Where Do Traces of the Soul Remain?	342
In the Golden Years of Life	348
Life Sonata	352

Short Story

- **Father's Spring**   357

Part One

Calling Australia Home

That day, after what felt like an endless season of rain, the sky finally cleared as if offering solace to a heart long submerged in gloom. Drawn by the allure of the fine weather, my daughter and I set out and made our way to the Museum of Sydney. Though I've lived in Australia for many years, I felt a hint of shame that I had never stepped inside, even knowing it stood not far from the Opera House. We had often visited the Australian Museum instead when my children were young. Since November last year, the Museum of Sydney had been hosting an exhibition titled *How to Move a Zoo*, and by sheer luck, we arrived on its very last day like a ball slipping into the net just before the final whistle blew.

From 1884, for over thirty years, Sydney's first zoo stood

in Moore Park. Today, that very site is home to Sydney Boys High School and Sydney Girls High School. When the zoo's owner decided to relocate the facility to what is now Taronga Zoo, it was still a time before the Opera House and Harbour Bridge had come into being. It reportedly took six months to move the zoo's entire collection; 228 mammals, 552 birds, and 64 reptiles. Most animals were placed in cages or enclosures, then transported by vehicle to the ferry dock, from which they crossed the harbour by boat. The elephant, which weighed nearly four tonnes, had to walk all the way from Moore Park to the waterfront where the Opera House now stands in order to board the ferry.

When I told an Australian friend about the fascinating exhibition, he commented, "All the animals once at Moore Park left, and new ones came in." At first, I was puzzled by the comment, then I caught the playful glint in his eye and cracked up laughing. He had attended Sydney Boys High School himself and was jokingly referring to the students as the 'new animals' that had taken over the old zoo grounds.

One section of the exhibition was entirely devoted to recreating the journey of the elephant who weighed four thousand kilograms and was a particular favourite at the time. The room featured a miniature reconstruction of the path she walked, complete with people, trees, and buildings that once lined the route. There was even a tiny scene of a startled horse rearing up as the elephant approached. Its reaction had caused the milk it was delivering by cart to spill onto the road.

On 24 September, 1916 at 5:30am, the elephant named Jessie began her ninety-minute journey. Accompanied by three handlers, she cautiously made her way down narrow streets, crossing tram tracks and watching her step with care. Onlookers noted that she appeared to be in pain from her feet. After passing through Macquarie Street and arriving at the waterfront, now the site of the Sydney Opera House, Jessie boarded the waiting ferry. Once aboard, she curled her trunk over the railing and stood motionless like a massive rock, as the ferry made its way across Sydney Harbour. The image stirs something tender in my heart. Elephants are known for their intelligence and remarkable memory-there are even stories of them recognising their keepers after three decades apart. I wonder, as Jessie stood on that ferry, did she think she was returning to the wilds of her Southeast Asian homeland? Or did she long to go back to the familiar grounds of Moore Park Zoo? Her story, having arrived in Australia at the age of eight and won the affection of so many people, reminds me of my own family's immigration in 1988, the year of the Seoul

Olympics. My son, too, was eight when we came.

I don't mean to draw a direct comparison between the life of an elephant and that of my son, simply because they both came to Australia at the age of eight. And yet, like Jessie the elephant who didn't come to this country by choice but was brought here by human hands, my son too arrived not of his own will, but through the decisions of his parents. Elephants are said to have a high emotional intelligence. One can only imagine the stress Jessie must have felt being separated from her herd and brought across the world to live in a foreign land, confined within the fences of a zoo. Still, she must have gradually grown accustomed to the care of her keepers. In time, she came to be dearly loved by the people of Sydney, living out her years at Taronga Zoo. When she passed away at the age of sixty-four, having lived what would be considered a full life for an elephant, the entire city mourned her.

About three weeks after we arrived in Sydney, the school holidays ended and a new term began. My then 8 year old son started Year 2. Even now, I cannot forget that first day. As we walked hand in hand and the school came into view in the distance, my son suddenly stopped. "Mum, put your hand on my chest," he said. His heart was pounding wildly. Seeing how much he dreaded going in, I felt so sorry for him that I even wondered if coming to this country had been a mistake. After completing the enrollment process, I took him to the restroom by the side of the playground. Pointing to the door marked *Boy*, I told him to go in there. I also explained what he should say to the teacher if he needed to use the restroom during class. All day long, I waited anxiously for school to finish. When I returned in the afternoon and saw him playing with his classmates on the playground, I breathed a sigh of relief. Though he didn't speak a word of English, he adapted remarkably well to his new environment. And what about my daughter? She was only three years old when we came to Australia. She started preschool the following year but for the first six months, she didn't utter a single word in class. Not even a simple hello, good morning, thank you, or sorry. I was deeply worried. Her teacher reassured me, saying, "She seems to understand everything, but she probably lacks confidence. I think one day she'll just start talking." And she was right. One day, like a dam breaking, my daughter suddenly began to speak in a rush of words, surprising both the teacher and us parents.

Had Jessie the elephant remained on the grassy plains of Southeast Asia, she might have fallen victim to poachers seeking ivory. Instead, she was protected in a Sydney zoo, spending her life under the care of devoted keepers and the affection of countless visitors. Is it selfish of me to think she was fortunate? I sometimes wonder what kind of life our family might have lived over the past three decades had we not immigrated to Australia. But life comes only once, and there is no turning back. My husband and I have never regretted our decision to settle here. On the contrary, we often feel grateful, perhaps because life in our second home, Australia, has naturally taken root in us and become a part of our daily life.

(2022)

Street Breakfast

Every year on 26th January, Australia Day, the residents of our neighbourhood gather in front of the house on No.11 of our street for breakfast. This street breakfast has been a tradition for nearly 20 years in our small community of just over 40 homes. Each year, the invitation, slipped into our letterbox by the family at No. 9, includes the names of their three sons and their beloved youngest 'daughter' Jodie the dog. On this fresh midsummer morning, neighbours can be seen heading eagerly toward No. 11, carrying baskets of food and folding chairs. The usually quiet street comes alive with energy on this one special day. In today's world, I feel grateful and touched by the warm tradition in our neighbourhood where neighbours still come together and share friendly conversations.

The enticing aroma of bacon and sausages sizzling on a roadside barbecue drifts through the neighbourhood, while the soft scent of coffee gently fills the air. On this day, one might meet couples occasionally seen during morning walks, neighbours who haven't crossed paths all year, or even those who've moved away but return for this event. Like long-lost relatives reuniting, everyone greets each other warmly, sharing stories and laughter. Having lived here for almost 15 years, I've watched children who once played ball or rode bicycles outside transform into young adults, one of whom was now helping with name tags. With everyone wearing stickers indicating their names and house street numbers, there's no need for lengthy introductions. A Chinese family who recently moved in seems particularly happy to see our family, as we share similar skin. The wife, whose English is limited, communicates with broad smiles.

This annual breakfast also serves as a networking event. My daughter, who was in primary school when we moved here, was nearing graduation after studying primary education at university. She received advice from a neighbour who happened to be a primary school principal. Another neighbour, touched by my daughter's passion for puppetry, later left a newspaper article on the topic in our letterbox. I also felt a certain sense of camaraderie when I discovered a common thread between the elderly lady next door, the woman from No. 9, and myself. It turned out that all three of us were connected to the same Australian bank – the lady next door right after World War II, myself several years ago, and the woman from No. 9, who still works there. Whenever I run into her on the street, she'll casually mention that she's been transferred to a different branch, or that she's thinking of switching to part-time, or even considering retirement. She always seems pleased to have a neighbour who listens and responds with knowing nods.

After breakfast, once the atmosphere has reached its peak, the principal stands to make announcements, sharing noteworthy local news such as the council's plan to replace street trees. Then comes the raffle draw, with one ticket per household, each numbered to match the house addresses. The winners, two households, receive a bottle of wine donated by a neighbour. Since a member of the Wine Society who used to donate wine passed away unexpectedly two years ago, the elderly lady next door has been donating two bottles each year. This year, one of the winning numbers drawn by a child was ours, house number 40! Amid the applause and cheers, I felt a surge of excitement, convinced that this year was off to a great start.

During a trip to Korea two years ago, I visited an old neighbourhood in Seoul that I had longed to see. It was where three of the five siblings in my family were born. A *'hanok'* (traditional Korean house) that featured prominently in my childhood memories and dreams. I wondered if it still stood. The street where my younger brother, now well past his fifties, once reigned as the leader of the little kids seemed vast when I was young, but it turned out to be a small, narrow neighbourhood. About 14-15 small *hanok* houses stood facing each other along a narrow street and I was glad that the neighbourhood had not yet been replaced by one of the many modern apartments so common these days. The narrow street seemed to hold countless untold stories. The house where a shaman once performed a ritual for a couple to conceive a son was now a parking lot. Although the house we lived in was still there, regrettably, its tightly shut gate prevented me from peeking inside. Our house was right next to Donam Market. The memories came flooding back - my mother chatting with her friends who, whenever they came shopping, would drop by and perch on the wooden porch by the entrance, relatives and my friends stopping by. And the image of my late father who used to sweep clean outside the front gate in the early morning, lingered in my mind. Standing there, I couldn't help but feel an ache of longing and nostalgia for the warmth of those days.

In those times, community bonds were strong. In the 1960s, when few households had telephones or televisions, neighbours shared generously, whether it was borrowing a phone, watching sports or dramas together, or sharing celebratory or mourning moments. Children played games in the streets until the calls of their mothers for dinner brought them running home. Though decades have passed and change is only natural, I left that familiar-looking neighbourhood with a wistful smile. Its appearance is seemingly the same, yet its time is long gone.

On the evening of Australia Day, I saw the elderly lady next door dressed up and heading out. When I asked where she was going, she replied that a couple down the street had invited her to dinner. It seemed to me that the morning's breakfast gathering had fostered a connection leading to this invitation. A Channel 10 crew came and filmed the scene. It made a brief appearance on the evening news. Perhaps it's not a common sight even in Australia.

As an immigrant and a minority in a foreign land, I find

myself missing my motherland more often as I grow older. I've often wondered how I would endure the loneliness and the sense of alienation. But small events like this street breakfast subtly ease those feelings, offering a gentle sense of belonging. Like the elderly lady next door, I don't think I could ever leave this neighbourhood.

In today's world where even the simple connections with neighbours have become rare, the shared breakfast on our neighborhood street under the open blue sky felt like a small miracle that revived the warmth of community. Perhaps life, after all, has a way of blooming anew in such unexpected encounters.

(2008)

This essay was written 17 years ago, when I believed I could never leave this neighbourhood as long as I lived. But life took us elsewhere, and the feelings from those days still remain within me as cherished memories.

Snow on a Summer's Day

Outside, the peak summer temperature hovers above 30 degrees Celsius, and yet, snow is falling indoors?

Here I am, seated inside Sydney's historic State Theatre, waiting with hundreds of others for the show to begin. The title alone, *Slava's Snow Show,* sounds refreshing in this sweltering heat, and it stirs both curiosity and anticipation. In front of me sits a young boy next to his mother, and two rows ahead, my daughter is helping an elderly Russian couple and their young grandson find their seats. Looking around, I see people of all ages, most of them here with their families, gathered to enjoy the performance together. Soon, a pre-show announcement begins: turn off your mobile phones, and photography or video recording is not allowed. Just as

I thought the show was about to start, the announcement continues, now in Chinese, then Korean, and finally in Russian. Only then does it strike me, this must be an internationally touring performance.

When I think about where the world stands today in the wake of the pandemic, it still feels astonishing.

Just a year ago, the doors of this very theatre were tightly shut, every seat empty. Now, as I look down from my seat, the stage is set like a barren wasteland. It's an image that seems to reflect the performing arts industry which stood still for nearly three years during the pandemic. This show, a clown performance created by a Russian artist named Slava some thirty years ago, has gained international acclaim. I hear that his son now carries on the legacy, performing the clown character himself. Without a single word spoken, the clowns use only costume, makeup, and movement to evoke both laughter and tears from the audience.

As the performance begins, the characters wander across the desolate stage, trying to find a way to connect with one another. Eventually, the lead clown realises that the long string draped around his neck is actually tied to the string held by another character. That simple discovery felt deeply symbolic, just as we, after being shut indoors and isolated during lockdown, are now slowly reconnecting with others, here together again, watching this very performance.

Just before intermission, an enormous spiderweb unfurls from the stage and cascades over the entire audience, tangling itself among them. From my seat in the mezzanine, I looked down on this dramatic scene and couldn't help but recall how not long ago we had all been caught in the vast web of lockdown.

During the height of the lockdown, our family home was sold and we had to move, but we lived like insects trapped in a sticky web-unable to go forward or back. Only one member of the household was permitted to leave each day for essentials, so it was my husband who would go out, while my daughter and I remained shut off from the outside world.

The show reached its climax with a spectacular finale. Suddenly, swirling white smoke burst from the stage, followed by a snowstorm of thousands of white confetti pieces that swept over the audience, even reaching the mezzanine level where I sat. A snowstorm in the middle of summer. What an astonishing idea, born from the imagination of the Russian artist Slava. To see this grand old theatre which was completed in 1929 blanketed in paper snow, what could be more delightfully surreal?

I felt a deep pang of longing, wishing I could have shared this moment with my young grandchildren who live overseas. They had visited us in early December and stayed for more than a month, leaving just ten days ago. We had missed each other dearly since their last visit, which was just before the pandemic began three years ago. During this reunion, we joyfully attended several children's performances together. All throughout this magical show, I couldn't help thinking how wonderful it would have been to enjoy it with them. What a precious memory it could have become.

To be honest, I didn't fully understand the storyline of this clown performance. Perhaps that's the intention to leave it open to the audience's interpretation. What mattered more were the expressions, gestures, and antics of the clown and the other characters, which sent children into giggling fits and had adults smiling and clapping along. When the performers lip-synced to Russian songs, the elderly Russian couple two rows ahead of us clapped and waved enthusiastically, while I found myself chuckling at the comically exaggerated movements of their round, white-painted lips. What more could I ask for?

This summer has felt like a proper summer. Last year around this time, unrelenting rain and floods left us with no summer to speak of. So this year's heat, reaching over 30 degrees Celsius, feels almost like compensation. COVID still lingers in our lives, but even mask-wearing has now become a matter of personal choice. At my age, past the so-called *jongshim* (the stage of following one's heart without conflict-70 years of age) to briefly return to a childlike state and enjoy Slava's Snow Show felt like a joy. Throughout the performance, I laughed freely and was startled in the most delightful ways. It had been so long since I experienced such unfiltered fun. It felt as though the weight in my chest, built up during the long pandemic, had finally burst free, leaving me with a sense of lightness and release.

"How was it, Mum?" My daughter asked as we stepped out of the theatre. "It felt like I'd completely forgotten myself and gone back to my childhood- then returned. Haha!" The summer heat began to wrap itself around my skin again, but inside me, the snow was still falling. Those delicate flakes seemed to melt the part of my heart that had been frozen by the weight of the pandemic and everyday life.

(2023)

A Guest Named Walter*

These days in Korea, it's not uncommon to see foreigners who speak Korean fluently. There are even popular TV dramas and programs featuring non-Korean cast members. When I meet foreigners who genuinely enjoy Korean culture and cuisine, I find myself naturally drawn to them. Living in Australia, I feel an even stronger sense of connection when I encounter Australians who have a deep knowledge of or keen interest in Korea. And then I ask myself: how much do we who live in Australia truly know about this country and how much do we really appreciate it?

---

* Walter is a pseudonym used for privacy.

This year, the Easter holiday overlapped with other public holidays, creating a rare five-day long weekend. For our family who usually avoids traveling during peak traffic seasons, it was the perfect golden opportunity to relax and unwind at home. As usual, we stocked the fridge with all sorts of groceries, preparing to spend the holidays comfortably indoors. But unexpectedly, we ended up hosting a guest for three days. A man named Walter, an Australian my husband and I had never met before, who appeared to be in his fifties.

Walter, along with his partner, is a master puppeteer based in Melbourne. He was returning from a solo trip to Brisbane some 1,600 kilometres away, where he had driven a small van packed with everything needed for a puppet show. Originally, he was planning to stay at a fellow puppeteer's home in Sydney, but due to an unexpected situation, he suddenly contacted our daughter. As parents who hope our daughter, a primary school teacher who incorporates puppetry into her teaching, will one day become a master puppeteer herself, we gladly welcomed this guest. It was also a chance to repay the kindness he and his partner had shown our daughter when she visited their home.

My first impression of him reminded me so much of the American actor Robin Williams that I asked if they might be related. With a laugh, he replied that he gets that question from time to time. He was a man of modest build, with soft features and greying hair tied back in a short ponytail. On this chilly, grey April day, he seemed to be feeling the cold, so we offered him one of my husband's sweaters and turned on the heater. Sitting cozily together, we shared a Korean dinner. We started with grilled sirloin on an electric hot plate, followed by *bulgogi* (marinated beef) and LA *galbi* (marinated beef rib), all wrapped in lettuce leaves. For the finale, I stir-fried *kimchi* (fermented Chinese cabbage) with rice right on the hot plate and served it in our rice bowls. His expression was one of genuine happiness. Walter, who single-handedly finished the *kimchi* served with the meal, said the *kimchi* fried rice gave him a warm, comforting feeling. Over the years, I've met many Australians who enjoy Korean food, but it was surprising to see a man in his fifties so visibly delighted by *kimchi* fried rice. Though he told us he had visited Korea before and was no stranger to Korean cuisine, it was still quite a surprise. When our daughter visited Melbourne and was invited to his home, Walter cooked bean sprout rice for her, using a Korean cookbook he had bought from a local Korean grocery store. In his household, he said, he handles all the cooking while his partner does the dishes. That alone was impressive but a middle-aged Australian man making bean sprout rice? That was even more astonishing.

Walter's partner, I learned, had once trained to become an opera singer. Listening to a recording of her voice on his iPod, I couldn't help but be moved. She was singing an excerpt from an opera translated into Korean. She had recorded it during a visit to Korea, but due to time constraints, she hadn't been able to fully master the pronunciation. As a result, I could only clearly make out a few words like *"na-neun"* ("I am") and "opera singer." Still, the song was powerful and deeply moving. Had I listened to it several more times, I might have understood more, but unfortunately, Walter played it for us just before leaving for Melbourne, leaving me with a feeling of regret. I was so touched by her desire to sing in Korean that I offered to help her with the pronunciation myself if the couple visits Sydney again in the future.

Having once pursued a career in architecture, Walter eventually fell under the spell of puppetry, pouring his heart into it alongside his partner. Unsurprisingly, his background as an architect is clearly reflected in his puppet productions. As he was leaving, he left us with a thought to ponder. Looking at his van, packed from floor to ceiling with puppets and props for his performances, I couldn't help but say, "That must be such hard work." To which he replied, "It's hard but that's why I love it."

If all guests were like Walter and his partner, I wouldn't mind leaving our front door open all the time. I believe that if I, too, take a deeper interest in Australia and all things Australian, hearts on both sides will open more freely. And when we begin to exchange parts of ourselves – our cultures, our values – our life as immigrants will no longer be just about settling in, but about something richer, something more abundant.

(2011)

Sheryl*'s 60th Birthday Party

Coming back from a friend's birthday party, I found myself thinking about something I hadn't thought about in a while. Even as the rings of age grow, I should still be able to say with confidence that my heart remains young. Though wrinkles deepen on my face, I want my spirit to resemble the soft pink azaleas that bloom afresh every spring. But I've learned that for azaleas to come alive so brightly in early spring, they must be pruned, tended, and nourished with care. Perhaps I, too, must not neglect the work of feeding and nurturing my own heart.

---

*   Sheryl is a pseudonym

I had assumed that Sheryl was about my age until I received an invitation to her 60th birthday party. She was four years younger than me. Sheryl is the leader of our Bible study group of ten women. For the past ten years, we've been meeting regularly. In our contact list, only the day and month of each birthday are noted, never the year. Knowing that asking a Western woman's age is considered impolite, I had simply guessed she was around my age.

Just because their culture differs from ours doesn't mean we can treat them according to our customs. In Korea, it's common to ask someone's age soon after getting to know them or for the person to volunteer it themselves. With advances in medicine and longer life expectancy, people often say that seventy is the new sixty. For this reason, it's rather common to skip the traditional 60th birthday celebrations, saving the festivities for their 70th instead. In contrast, Australians mark milestone birthdays for those ending in a zero beginning at age thirty, often with a special party. One of my daughter's high school friends, an Australian diplomat stationed in the Philippines, took leave and flew home just to celebrate her 30th birthday. The 60th birthday is often treated with even greater significance, with families going out of their way to make it memorable. Compared to this, I now regret having let my own 60th birthday slip by quietly. I missed the chance to share joy and laughter with my friends on such a special occasion.

Sheryl's birthday celebration was held at her home in the form of an afternoon tea party. The centre of the dining table was beautifully decorated with flowers, overflowing with lovingly prepared treats; warm, oven-baked savouries, sandwiches, petite cakes, and platters of fruits. It was clear how much care had gone into the preparations. Sure enough, during a brief welcome speech, Sheryl's daughter, who is not only married with a two-year-old son but also pursuing her studies, revealed that she had single-handedly prepared everything to honour her mother's special day. She invited all of us, her mother's friends. She told us to enjoy the food and have a good time. What a wonderful gift it was from the daughter to her mother. This display of affection and devotion, thoughtfully shown through food, hospitality, and effort. From the invitations to the final flourish, it was a tribute that only a loving daughter could have given.

As we raised our glasses of champagne and toasted our friend's sixtieth, the warmth in the room deepened. Gathered in the cozy living room were women who had known Sheryl since kindergarten, high school friends, and even one who had stood beside her as a bridesmaid. We moved from seat to seat, sharing stories with different people, and among them, I found myself drawn to Maria, a tall, slender woman whose face was lined with age but bright with curiosity. She had once attended the same church as Sheryl, and even though she had been retired for quite some time, I was deeply moved by her ongoing passion for learning and attending classes.

One wall of the living room was lined with photos tracing Sheryl's life from birth to her 60th birthday. As I stood before the display, her elderly mother quietly appeared beside me and began to explain each photo; where it was taken, how old Sheryl was, and who the people in the pictures were. It was fascinating. I learned that my friend had attended primary school in Lidcombe, which is now becoming a 'Korea town', and went to high school in Strathfield, already known as a hub for Korean immigrants.

I couldn't help but wonder how she might feel about the way these neighbourhoods of her childhood and youth have changed so dramatically due to Korean and other immigrant communities. Then again, weren't her ancestors also immigrants from England? I decided not to bring it up, sensing it might make her mother uncomfortable, and simply turned my attention to the next photo.

What struck me most was how, nearing ninety, Sheryl's mother mingled effortlessly with her daughter's friends, recounting the stories behind each photo with remarkable clarity and warmth. Her vibrant presence made her the envy of many in the room.

I recall a poem written by German-American poet Samuel Ullman at aged seventy-eight:

"Youth is not a time of life, but a state of mind. It is not a matter of rosy cheeks, red lips, or supple knees. It is a matter of the will, a quality of the imagination, and a vigour of the emotions.

Nobody grows old merely by a number of years; we grow old by deserting our ideals. As long as we hold our heads high and embrace hope, we remain young at heart, even at eighty."

-Samuel Ullman, "Youth," 1918

When I reach seventy in a few years, I hope to host a memorable tea party with friends. I wonder what I will be like then...

(2014)

The Grand Tree

Lately, I've developed a strange habit. Among the rows of trees lining my neighborhood, my gaze is especially drawn to those whose trunks have been partially cut away on one side but still stand tall and majestic. Whenever I spot such a tree, without fail, I stop walking or even pull over my car. Then, with admiring eyes, I observe the tree carefully and quietly give it my own little rating.

The eucalyptus tree in front of my house stands with one arm lost. From the first floor veranda, I can see a tree in the distance with its two arms spread wide, resembling a saint raising their arms. For years, I have looked toward that tree with a prayerful heart. I never imagined that the centre of the tree was deeply hollowed out, bearing a scar. Somehow, I felt drawn to it and often raised my own arms in the same shape, feeling blessed. Now that I look closely, I notice trees here and there offering us their freshness in shapes like the Korean letter 'ㄴ' (an L-shaped angle), or leaning to one side with arms stretched out. You can see such trees where power lines pass by. They become obstacles for the wires and are cut by human hands, leaving the tree with a maimed body. However, even though thick branches have been cut off, leaving it misshapen, the tree still spreads out lush green leaves without concern. This is likely because its roots run deep underground. Seeing trees that live so resolutely, I sometimes wish to live a life just as admirable.

One spring day in the 1970's, I boarded a plane bound for Japan, following my groom who came to pick me up. After a tearful farewell at Gimpo Airport with my parents, four siblings, and close friends, I cut off branches of my heart like pruning a thick tree and left my family behind. Far from being filled with dreams of newlywed bliss or future plans, my heart ached with a fresh wound. For over two hours en route to Haneda Airport, tears streamed down my face like digging a well. Beside me, my groom was restless, not knowing what to do.

When I was in elementary school in the late 1950s, we had

anti-Japanese education. I still remember the time when our school went to see the film Yu Gwan-sun*. All of us young students sobbed uncontrollably, clenching their fists and crying out, "The Japanese are such villains!" Even after more than half a century, that scene lingers in a corner of my mind. Later, when Yu Gwan-sun's alma mater became my own, I felt a deep sense of pride.

We first met at the 'International Youth Conference for World Peace, Justice, and Reconciliation.' After that, though I was someone with a strong sense of national pride like no other, I tried hard not to be swayed by the continuous flood of his letters over five years. In my distress, I even coldly sent him a message asking him to stop writing. At first, his letters were written in English, but gradually they became filled only with Korean. Especially painful were words like, "I was born in Japan, so I am just Japanese." With every letter, his sincerity and earnestness made me slowly realise that my heart was beginning to lean toward him, which caused me to feel anxious. When my mother said she wanted to meet the person who had been sending letters to her daughter for five years, I was secretly surprised. Perhaps she became interested

---

* Yu Gwan-sun, a high school student and Christian independence activist against Japanese rule, was tortured to death in prison at age 17.

because a few of her high school friends were in contact with a Japanese teacher who had warmly cared for students during the Japanese colonial period.

The day he came to our home for the first time to see my parents, his earnest effort to communicate in our language seemed very sincere. Before meeting him, my siblings who were adamant that marriage to a Japanese person was out of the question, and my parents were worried. However, they all liked him and my parents gave their approval. A month later, he returned to Seoul with his parents, and we held the wedding. From gaining family permission to the wedding day, I had to endure criticism from relatives for that whole month. My uncle did not attend the wedding, saying it was shameful to our ancestors. My father was heartbroken and my uncle too seemed far from at ease. Due to visa procedure, I couldn't leave with him. On the day the groom left, my aunt called to say that we may visit uncle on the way to the airport. Thinking of how happy my father was then, my heart aches. He suffered greatly because of his daughter.

Our family elder, my tall and imposing uncle who always gave a dignified impression, stood in the main room with his hands clasped behind his back. He received our traditional Korean style bows while standing and then asked the groom a few simple questions in English even though he is fluent in Japanese. The groom answered in Korean. "Hmm··· you're not the '*waynom*' (a derogatory term for Japanese) I imagined," he said. After a meal was served, he even suggested postponing the departure until the next day. This helped break down a difficult hurdle. A few months later, when I was leaving, an officer at the Gimpo Airport immigration desk openly told me, "What a pity." The 1970s in Korea was indeed like that.

Back then, out of Japan's population of 120 million, I followed just one man, my husband. Even now, I'm not sure where that courage came from. I'd like to believe that some greater force was guiding the course of my life. Through a decade in Tokyo filled with work, childbirth, and bringing up children, even though I had genuinely good friends, I could never feel completely free in spirit. As is still the case today, I often felt angered and wounded by the reckless remarks of Japanese politicians and bureaucrats. This was before the 1988 Seoul Olympics, before Korea's national stature had begun to soar. One day, I made a crucial decision-for the sake of my two children, I would uproot the tree of my life and replant it elsewhere.

It has been 26 years since we began putting down roots in Australia. At first, the children faced ups and downs adjusting to a new language and environment, but they have grown to embrace the cultures of Korea, Japan, and Australia with confidence, and are now deeply rooted in this land. Now, our family stands firmly like a grand tree with lush leaves, and looking back, all I feel is gratitude.

(2014)

Living Simply

We are preparing to move, having decided to downsize our home. I hope this will be the last house I live in during my lifetime. We had set two essential conditions: a single-story house that would be easy to maintain and within walking distance of the train station. Finding one wasn't easy, but when I finally did, it felt as though I had caught a big fish.

But now I find myself facing the emotional struggle of letting go, sorting through and discarding the mountain of belongings we've accumulated over the years.

According to census data, Australians move an average of seven times in their lifetime. Counting my own moves: a couple while living with my parents, perhaps another after becoming independent, the first small home after marriage, upsizing as the family grew, and now downsizing as the nest empties. For some, this is eventually followed by assisted living or even a nursing home. It all adds up. With every move, furniture, decorations, clothes, books, kitchenware- they must have expanded and contracted like a balloon. How do people find the resolve to part with their belongings? That's the puzzle I now face, standing at the downsizing stage of life. I've lost count of how many times I've packed items into donation boxes for the Red Cross or Salvation Army, only to pull them back out again and place them among the moving boxes. I often find myself exasperated with my own indecision. After all, these things were bought one by one with the money we earned through years of hard work. But if letting go is this hard, how could I ever hope to leave this world someday with a light and unburdened heart?

Through the real estate agent who handled the sale of our home, I was introduced to Lynn, a professional home organiser. I had only ever seen people like her on TV or in magazines, but when I heard that she not only helped with decluttering but also packed and even organised things in the new home, my ears perked up. Lately, my blood pressure had spiked, and I was afraid I might end up in the hospital from overexertion, so I decided to leave the heavy work to her. As she began sorting through the kitchen, she unearthed gadgets I'd never even taken out of their boxes, as well as items I once searched for in vain, not realising they were hidden away. It felt embarrassing to expose the entirety of my household to someone else, but in truth, I was more upset with myself. Lynn, however, was every bit the experienced professional. She had a gentle way of reading the mood and putting me at ease. When five potato peelers emerged from a single drawer and I looked flustered, she laughed and said she and her mother also each have their preferred peelers-so having three made sense if my daughter lived with me too. There were several graters, too many knives... and tucked away in one corner, a melamine bowl and a divided plate once used by my son when he was a baby-and now he is a father of four. I hesitated to throw away such old plastic dishes. Just as my daughter said gently, *"It's time to let it go,"* Lynn stepped in to take my side: *"It's okay to keep something if it holds meaning."* In that moment, I felt an invisible umbilical cord still connecting me to my son. To others, they might look like nothing more than worn-out children's tableware, but for me, they held the image of my first child eating from that bowl, and a few years later, my young daughter doing the same. How could I so easily part with something that brought those memories to life like an old film reel? Ah – how will I ever let go, if I keep clinging to everything like this?

It was only after a series of unsettling events that my husband and I slowly began to accept the idea that it might be time to leave the home we had lived in for over a quarter of a century. One day, my husband fell from a ladder while sawing branches in the front yard. Not long after, I lost my balance while trimming a tree in the backyard and fell backward, hitting my head hard against the brick pavement. The sharp crack of that impact still echoes in my mind—I felt, in that moment, the terrifying closeness of death. And that wasn't all. There are too many incidents to list; just thinking of them makes my head ache. Of course, hiring help after retirement is out of the question for my husband, and truthfully, I didn't want to either. But unlike before, our strength has diminished, and even the small tasks we once did for exercise are now more difficult or limited. We knew we had to make a decision before it became too late. So we resolved to simplify our lives–paring down our possessions and moving into a smaller, low-maintenance, single-story home. But the real challenge came not in moving, but in having to drastically reduce what we already owned.

From the piano to bulky furniture and miscellaneous odds

and ends, I now face the dilemma of letting them go. Many people say books should be the first to go, but I've refused. I brought with me to Australia the complete set of world literature classics that once stood on my father's bookshelf–a collection over fifty years old. My siblings have urged me to throw them out, but I won't. Had my father still been alive, he would have turned 99 this year. The thought of him still brings a lump to my throat. How could I possibly toss those books into a recycling bin, as if they were meaningless?

I once believed I would live a long life, and perhaps that's why I quietly passed both my 60th and 70th birthdays without holding any celebrations. Part of me felt too shy to announce my age to the world as if I were advertising that I was growing old. In the past, reaching seventy was rare enough to be called a *Hee-soo* (rare longevity), but here we are in the 21st century, the so-called age of living to one hundred. Even so, my thoughts have changed. Having recently experienced once again how death does not follow the order of age, I now know the end can come without warning. I don't know when my final moment will arrive, but when I move into this new house, I've made one quiet promise to myself: I will begin using the fine dishes I've long kept tucked away. It would feel like such a waste if I ended up having to discard them without ever enjoying them. Some of these dishes only saw the light on New Year's Day, and I would wash them myself as carefully as one would bathe a newborn, afraid they might chip or crack. Once, I told my daughter to take them when she ever got married, but she replied she'd only take the ones she liked. I mentioned to Lynn, now in her fifties, that I sometimes regretted spending so much money in my younger years collecting these dishes. But she, ever understanding, said something that comforted me deeply: "That's okay. You were happy when you bought them. That's what matters."

If moving from one home to another in this world is this exhausting and complicated, how much more will there be to sort through when I set out on the one journey from which I cannot return? My son lives overseas, so it is what it is. But I've made a promise to myself: I will try to live with less and stay organised along the way, so that my daughter is not left with too heavy a burden when the time comes.

(2021)

Cockatoos and Apple Trees

It was during the height of the COVID lockdowns that we happened to move to our new house. Already, two and a half years have passed. On the day of the move, the sky seemed to be in a sulky mood, alternating between pouring rain and pauses. Perched motionless on the front fence of our new house was a large sulphur crested cockatoo, watching the movers as if inspecting their every move. Known for their intelligence, the cockatoos eventually began gathering in small flocks, pacing about on the front porch roof and the concrete path below. Perhaps they were hoping the new owners would kindly offer them something to eat. But fearing they might come in droves, we resisted the urge to feed them. Sensing that they wouldn't get anything from us, the clever birds no longer loitered near the entrance and instead took up residence in the tall tree next door. That roof, fitted with solar panels, often ends up covered in cockatoo droppings. With the streets deserted due to lockdown, it was as though we first greeted our new neighborhood through the eyes of the birds.

Here, when people move into a new home, it's customary to knock on their neighbours' doors with something home-baked, like cookies or a cake, as a kind of friendly introduction. But this was during lockdown, a time when stepping outside was strictly limited. Even with masks on and social distancing in place, the idea of ringing someone's doorbell or knocking on a stranger's door felt almost unthinkable. Instead, we wrote a short note introducing our family, wrapped it neatly with a bag of chocolate, and placed them in the neighbours' mailboxes. The next day, with rain pouring down, there was a knock at our door. A woman stood there, masked, and said she lived on our street. She handed me a welcome card and a still-warm cake fresh from the oven. The card listed the names of every family member including the school grades of her four children, the name of their dog, and the professions of her husband and herself. She said she hoped we could meet properly once the lockdown was over, then hurried away into the rain. A few others had also left cards in our mailbox.

For the first time after 36 years of living in Australia, we have a Korean family living just over the fence. Though we now exchange only the occasional greeting, they once called out to my husband in the backyard and kindly offered him some lettuce seedlings. Every now and then, I hear their grown up daughter call out, *"Umma!"* (Mum) and, for a fleeting moment, I mistake it for my own daughter's voice. When by chance the breeze carries over the scent of sizzling *galbi* (marinated beef ribs) or the unmistakable aroma of *doenjang-jjigae* (soybean stew), I can't help but feel good. Isn't it only natural that a Korean heart should be drawn, like a magnet, to something so deeply and familiarly Korean?

After leaving the neighbourhood where we had lived and grown attached to for 26 years, I sometimes find myself driving back there out of nostalgia. In that small community of about forty houses, it was a tradition for neighbours to gather on the street and share breakfast every Australia Day. Over time, however, the faces have changed—some residents have passed away, others have moved into retirement villages or nursing homes, and the neighbourhood itself now looks a bit different. I notice more people of Asian background walking for exercise or strolling with their dogs along the streets. The family who bought our former home was of Chinese heritage. Though the house was still perfectly livable, the new owner decided to tear it down and build a grand new house. The land was completely turned over, and the azaleas and many other flowering trees we had planted, once so colourful and abundant, were all uprooted and vanished without a trace. Only a few towering eucalyptus trees, which cannot be cut down without special permission, still stand in their original spots, reaching skyward as they always have. That house now lives only in our memories and photographs. Whenever I drive past it, I glance up at the eucalyptus trees and quietly say, "Hello."

Having lived in this new house for over two years now, we've grown quite fond of it. Inside, the layout is compact and convenient, and it's within walking distance of the train station, along flat roads, too. We often tell each other how fortunate we were to have moved here before we got any older. When we first moved in, Sydney was under lockdown. Only one person per household was allowed to leave the house once a day for essentials like groceries. That duty fell to my husband. Restless and eager to glimpse the outside world, he frequently visited the nearest Korean grocery store just within the five-kilometre travel limit. My daughter and I stayed home, organising our belongings in what people jokingly called "house arrest."

Because of downsizing, we had to give up more than half of our possessions. But all donation centres like the Red Cross and Salvation Army were closed, and the waste depots had shut their gates. Even the local council had suspended their pick-up services. In the end, we had no choice but to bring along even the items we had meant to throw away, which meant hiring additional moving trucks. It took quite some time to get rid of all the unsightly mess that had been cluttering the house inside and out. Thankfully, our house is set back from the street and isn't visible from there. At least we had that small mercy.

There's an amusing coincidence that makes me feel as though it was destiny that brought us to this house. Our dog's name is Louie. As it happens, the woman who lives right in front of ours is named Louise, and the cat next door is Louis. We call our dog by his nickname, 'Lou', but were startled to learn that our neighbour goes by the same nickname. Needless to say, we no longer call out "Lou!" too loudly when we're outside. Adding to the mix, the Korean family next door has a dog named Leo. They've had it since it was a puppy, and they coo over it like a baby – "Leo, Leo" – just as we do when our nephew brings over his baby boy, also named Leo, born last year. To top it off, the local GP we began seeing after moving here? His name is Dr. Leo. At some point, it all feels like more than coincidence. It's as if some unseen thread of fate has pulled us toward this place. Perhaps it's not just by chance that we left our motherland and ended up here in Sydney, Australia, making our life over so many years. And maybe it's no ordinary thing that we've made a home in what could very well be the last house we live in. There are some things in life that can only be accepted as part of a higher order, a mysterious providence we'll never fully understand.

The lockdowns have long been lifted. Though the world is not yet completely free from the grip of COVID, people have largely returned to their daily routines, living with a renewed sense of freedom. The elderly couple who lived in this house before us had made it their home for 52 years. When this Caucasian couple of British heritage first made their nest here half a century ago, Australia was still waving the banner of White Australia. Now, with Koreans on one side and Chinese on the other, they must have seen extraordinary change. Before they left, they entrusted us with a folder titled *Garden File*. Inside were plant tags from every tree and shrub they had ever purchased, each one labeled with the year of planting and where it was placed in the garden. There were even handwritten notes on how to care for each one. I often wonder what they might think now, if they could see the patch where their agapanthus once bloomed now transformed into a bed of Korean sesame leaves and lettuce.

The philosopher Spinoza said, 'Even if the world were to end tomorrow, I would still plant my apple tree today.' I planted them because they are my favourite fruits. Two kinds, Royal Gala and Pink Lady, stand side by side near our front door, and I care for them tenderly, watering them with rinsed rice water. When the apples hang heavy, I may have to cover them with nets to keep the cockatoos (those same birds that hovered outside on our moving day) away. But I know I cannot be greedy enough to claim the fruit for humans alone. I often miss the warmth of my childhood neighbourhood, where families would share rice cakes with their neighbours whenever they made them. At times, I long for that uniquely Korean sense of *jeong* (the heartfelt bond that flows from mind to mind) making people feel close and at ease with one another.

Thinking of the day I'll share these apples with my neighbours, I step outside carrying a bowl of rinsed rice water.

(2023)

Part Two

The Domino of Fate

Not long ago, my daughter gave me a DVD of a French film titled *Le Battement d'Ailes du Papillon* ("The Flutter of the Butterfly's Wings", also known in the English version as "Happenstance", 2000). The movie carries a rather poetic idea that the flap of a butterfly's wings over the Atlantic can trigger a hurricane across the Pacific. It portrays how the tangled stories of ordinary people ripple outward like a chain of dominoes, unfolding with a sense of inevitability, as if led by fate.

A grandmother gives her grandson a biscuit and tells him not to tell his mother. But the boy does tell her, and the mother, taking the biscuit tin, pulls one out and pops it into her mouth, only to spit it out in disgust and hurl it out the car window. A pigeon swoops down and pecks at the biscuit crumbs scattered on the pavement, then flutters away and lands on the roof above a photo shop. Just then, a Russian tourist exits the shop, examining a photo in her hand, when, PLOP! The pigeon's droppings fall right onto the photo. She hurries back inside and asks the female clerk to clean it for her. As the woman wipes the photograph, she is stunned to see, in the photo, her ex-boyfriend who she had lost touch with ten years ago over a misunderstanding.

Although the film's series of coincidences felt far removed from reality, the way those chance encounters led to what seemed like inevitable outcomes reminded me of a friend. In the early 1970s, I attended an international youth conference where I taught a Japanese university student how to sing a Korean song called *Saranghae* ('I Love You'), which was very popular at the time. I accompanied her on the guitar as she learned the lyrics. Years later, after graduating, she began working for an airline. At her company's Christmas party, she happened to meet a man, someone she had never seen before, as the company was so large that many employees didn't know one another. As the party reached its peak, a male colleague stepped forward and began to sing. To her surprise, it was *Saranghae*, the very song she had learned from me years before. She instinctively stood up, walked over, and sang along with the man she was meeting for the first time. He explained that he had learned the song while working at the company's Seoul office. The two eventually fell in love and got married. Later, she sent me a letter to thank me, saying that their marriage had come about thanks to me. The idea that I had played a role, however small, in their union brought me a sense of joy that was both surprising and deeply moving.

My own domino of fate also began to fall, as if it had been destined. In high school, I spent a year abroad as an exchange student, and during my university years, I traveled to Tokyo to attend an international youth conference. Not long after I returned home, I received a thick bundle of mail from H, a Japanese university student who had also studied abroad through the same exchange program. He had served as the conference's official photographer. Through his telephoto lens, he had captured images of me, and he sent those photographs along with a letter.

H's interest in Korea had begun back in the early 1970s. The letters he sent me over the course of five years started in English but gradually began to include Korean phrases. Eventually, they were written entirely in Korean. It wasn't until after we got married that I realised how genuine his interest in Korea had been. He used to sing popular Korean songs of the time with great fondness and read numerous Korea-related books as if he were studying for an exam. I later learned that he had taught himself Korean almost entirely on his own, filling dozens of notebooks with tiny, meticulous handwriting. It was because I attended that particular high school that I had the chance to become an exchange student, and perhaps that was the beginning of everything. Meeting H and eventually immigrating to Australia. Strangely enough, he also happened to be an alumnus of the university my father once attended during Japanese rule. Every now and then, I find myself thinking that our meeting nearly 40 years ago was something close to fate.

In the French film, the protagonist unexpectedly encounters a man late at night, sitting on a bench outside a hospital. It's the very same man who had been sitting across from her on the subway that morning. After a chain of seemingly trivial, yet interconnected events throughout the day, the film ends with a subtle suggestion: perhaps these two were always meant to meet. It makes me wonder – could it be that our everyday lives are quietly flowing along some unseen domino trail, each moment nudging the next without us even knowing? Fate works in such mysterious ways.

(2011)

The Changing Faces of Brides

During the long periods spent at home due to the coronavirus, I found myself sorting through piles of photos and videos. Among them, I came across a video of my niece's wedding once again. The bride, dressed elegantly in a refined white wedding gown, entered the venue with a constant smile, leisurely exchanging glances with the guests. At the exit, she beamed brightly, returning their greetings warmly. At that moment, I couldn't help but recall the image from a painting of a Joseon Dynasty wedding procession, where the bride rode in a flower palanquin with a stiff, expressionless face. Reflecting also on my own wedding back in the 1970s, I felt a profound sense of how times have changed.

A blue-eyed, unmarried British woman visited Joseon

(Korea) over a span of twenty years beginning in 1920, creating woodblock prints and watercolors. Her name was Elizabeth Keith, an artist and writer. Her book *"Korea-1920-1940"* was translated by a Korean-American translator, and it was not until 2006 that these previously little-known works came to light. The paintings vividly capture the customs and landscapes of Joseon during that era. Given the vast cultural differences between Britain and Joseon as stark as night and day, one can only imagine how fascinating and enchanting Korea must have appeared through her blue eyes.

Elizabeth painted with genuine affection for "this poor country," portraying wedding processions, children studying in village schools, and roadside taverns-scenes completely unlike those of her own homeland. Arriving in this small Eastern nation, long known as the "Land of the Morning Calm," she was captivated by its mysterious charm. She did not view the Koreans who had lost their country solely with pity; she also recounted visiting imprisoned female students of the March 1st Movement alongside Principal Appenzeller of Ewha School. In one humble tavern, the sign above the door read, "The best house to gaze at the moon." Through her descriptions, we sense the warmth of the owner's humour, attracting guests with such poetic phrasing despite poverty.

Perhaps the owner offered a traveling guest, gazing at the moon while sipping a cup of *makgeolli* (rice alcohol), a piece of *buchimgae* (savoury pancake).

Especially moving to me was the painting and description titled "Korean Bride," depicting a bride dressed in *wonsam* (traditional ceremonial robe) and *jokduri* (traditional bridal headpiece). Her face, adorned with red dots on her lips, cheeks and forehead (*yeonji* and *gonji*), was slightly bowed, eyes closed, and her expression was stiff and subdued. She looked exhausted. The artist's explanation of the painting goes as follows: "The most tragic figure in Korea! On her wedding day, the bride must sit all day without eating or even opening her eyes. In the past, paper was even glued over her eyes. Meanwhile, the groom spends the whole day happily eating, drinking, and socialising with his friends." Following the customs deeply rooted in male dominance and Confucian patriarchy, the bride silently endured, sitting with a face as stiff as plaster. Yet, how pitiful her situation must have seemed to the artist, who described the bride on what should be her happiest day as the most tragic figure, utterly unimaginable in England at the time.

Looking back, my own wedding in the 1970's fell somewhere in between; a delicate balance between solemn restraint and a frozen expression. I was too intimidated by the formal atmosphere to smile, yet my face wasn't entirely stiff either. My wedding dress, made at a local dressmaker's from plain white silk, reflected my personal taste at the time: extremely simple. It was a long, one-piece gown with a modest neckline, completely unadorned. During the height of the Saemaul Movement* exchanging wedding gifts at the ceremony was prohibited, and guests were not allowed any favours or tokens. In contrast, the British artist's painting of a "country wedding feast" shows women bustling about, preparing food and decorations. In my case, even the celebratory feast was skipped entirely.

The once-impenetrable wall of Confucian tradition has gradually crumbled, ushering us into the present day. Alongside rapid economic growth, wedding customs have undergone a complete transformation and have done so for quite some time. Specialised wedding planners now oversee every aspect of the ceremony, and with international travel readily accessible, most newlyweds opt for overseas honeymoons. Although the skies have temporarily closed due to the coronavirus pandemic, it was not long ago that couples

---

* New village movement, a political initiative launched to modernise the economy.

from Korea, easily spotted in matching outfits, were a familiar sight here in Sydney. Today's women enjoy unprecedented freedom and comfort. Husbands often assist with household chores, and parenting has become a shared responsibility. The rise of women's rights is something to celebrate wholeheartedly. Yet sometimes I wonder if this freedom has become so unbounded that a measure of restraint might now be necessary.

On a woman's wedding day, a major milestone in her life, the expressions on brides' faces have changed remarkably over the past century. The spirit of each era has clearly left its mark. I am grateful that I was not born in the Joseon era. That said, the thought of strolling around in matching couple outfits with my husband would still be enough to make me blush. And suddenly, I find myself wondering: how will brides of future generations look? What expressions will they wear, and what customs will shape their special day?

(2020)

A New Mother and Seaweed Soup

As my daughter-in-law's due date drew near, I resolved to care for her myself after childbirth, instead of leaving the task once again to her mother, who had already done it three times before. So I packed my bags and flew to the U.S., where my son's family lives. Long flights are always a physical ordeal for me, and this one was no exception. I requested an aisle seat so I could stand up often, walk to the back of the plane, and stretch. I was especially careful to conserve my strength during the flight. Because a similar journey five years ago when I sat still the entire time had taken a serious toll on my health. I flew with Korean Air and chose the Korean meal for dinner on the flight, and it came with a packet of instant *miyeokguk* (seaweed soup), just adding hot water. The instant *miyeokguk* served on the plane felt ironically poignant, as I was on my way to cook the real thing for my daughter-in-law. It stirred memories of my own childbirth, and thoughts of my mother suddenly came rushing back.

After I got married, I lived in Tokyo, and in 1980, I gave birth to my first child in the middle of the night at the Red Cross hospital. The next morning, from behind the curtain separating my bed from the next, a warm, savory smell of seaweed soup drifted over to me. The familiar scent tickled my salivary glands and my tear ducts. I had learned that the woman in the next bed was affiliated with the pro-North Korean organisation *Jochongryon*, so I couldn't even strike up a conversation. Instead, I swallowed the bland hospital breakfast in silence, tears streaming down my cheeks. When I was in primary school, my mother gave birth to both my younger sister and baby brother. I remember how she emptied a large bowl of seaweed soup with such deep satisfaction, as if it were a rare and precious delicacy. No one else was allowed to have that special soup. So, even as a child, I told myself, "One day, when I'm married and have a baby of my own, I'll have a big bowl of seaweed soup too just like Mum did." The rich, nutty aroma of sesame oil from the seaweed soup that my grandmother had lovingly prepared for my mother used to fill the entire room.

Lying in a foreign bed, eating unfamiliar food in a distant land, I found myself missing that soup so dearly that day.

When I gave birth to both of my children, my mother couldn't come to me because my father was gravely ill. Now that I look back, I realise just how much her heart must have ached for me, her eldest daughter. How much she must have longed to drop everything and rush to see her first grandchild. Instead, she taught my younger sister (who had just graduated from high school) how to make that special seaweed soup, and sent her to me on a flight. I'm sure she cried many silent tears. My sister arrived just two days after I had given birth, carrying a pot of soup and looking sheepish as she handed it to me, softly calling, "*Unni* (big sister)..."

She said she had made the broth using beef my husband had bought, but the soup turned out way too salty, so she made another batch, only this time, it was nothing but floating seaweed in tasteless water. Seaweed back then wasn't like what we have today. Mum had told her to scrub it well and rinse it seven times to get rid of the saltiness. But after two washes, my sister thought it looked clean enough and just went ahead. The soup came out salty again, and she had to throw it away more than once. Still, what could I do? To me, my sister was nothing short of an angel. Even now, I smile as I recall the bland soup she had struggled to make for me. Though it lacked seasoning, it was filled with sisterly love and that made it more nourishing than any perfectly prepared meal.

My son had gone to work, so it was my daughter-in-law, very pregnant and accompanied by her three little ones under the age of six, who came to the airport to greet me. As soon as I arrived at their home, I rolled up my sleeves and headed straight for the kitchen. Not long after my arrival, she unexpectedly went into labor, earlier than her due date. She was rushed to the hospital and gave birth in just 90 minutes. The very next day, she was discharged and came home. In an increasingly aging society, when more and more young couples hesitate to have children or choose to have just one, my daughter-in-law gave birth to four. I couldn't help but admire her deeply. As I held the newborn in my arms, marveling at how the baby so closely resembled its siblings, a sense of wonder filled me. I felt a rush of joy so overwhelming, it was as if my heart were floating. I could no longer hide the fact that I was, through and through, a grandmother. Though my hands grew busier caring for a household of six, my heart was simply full of happiness.

It was a quiet regret that I couldn't offer my daughter-in-law the same seaweed soup my grandmother had prepared for my mother. In the early months of her pregnancy, she had developed a thyroid condition and was advised not to eat seaweed due to its high iodine content. Instead, I simmered a hearty *doenjang-guk* (soybean paste soup) with Chinese cabbage and rich beef broth, ladling it into a large bowl to take the place of seaweed soup. My daughter-in-law gratefully accepted it and ate with genuine enjoyment. I also made other broths like radish soup with anchovy stock, spinach soup, and bean sprout soup. For dishes I wasn't confident about, I looked up recipes online and followed them carefully. Seeing the whole family enjoy my cooking made me think that perhaps I had inherited my mother's culinary touch after all.

Back in the early 1960s, my mother took cooking classes at Wang Jun-Yeon's cooking school, a well-known culinary institute at the time. Since there were no printers in those days, mum had handwritten all the recipes herself in a notebook that's now stained with soy sauce and oil. I still treasure it deeply. If she were alive today, I imagine we would chat like friends, sending messages on KakaoTalk and sharing cooking tips. But she passed away too soon, struck by a stroke that left her speechless and bedridden until the end. To this day, I feel a deep sense of sorrow and longing. She had prepared the *doljanchi* (first birthday celebration) for my son, her very first grandson in Korea. That very child has now grown into a dependable adult, married a wonderful wife, and is raising his own children in happiness. If she had seen this happy family, I could picture her face glowing with pride. My siblings often say that the way I speak and the way I go about my work are just like our mother's. Even I find myself startled at times when I catch glimpses of her in my own actions. Is she truly gone? Or is she right here with me? Before coming to the U.S., I stopped in Korea and visited her grave. I told her that I was on my way to take care of my daughter-in-law who is due soon. Now, as I go about my day here with my son's family, I can't help but feel that my mother's spirit has followed me, quietly watching over us.

After returning home in Sydney, I bought some *miyeok* (seaweed) from a Korean grocery and cooked *miyeokguk* (seaweed soup), just like my mother used to make. As I stirred the pot, a curious thought crossed my mind. When did this tradition of Korean mothers eating seaweed soup after childbirth actually begin? I looked it up online and found that during the Goryeo Dynasty (918-1392), people observed whales eating seaweed after giving birth to help heal their wounds, and they began to serve it to new mothers.

Later, in the Joseon era, it became customary to first offer a bowl of white rice and *miyeokguk* to the *Samsin* goddess of childbirth, before allowing the mother to eat. More recently, in Korean postpartum care centres, the meal plan often includes *miyeokguk* three times a day, every day for an entire week. However, medical sources say that seaweed soup may not be ideal for every new mother. In these fast-changing times, I wonder how much longer will this cultural practice of *miyeokguk* for mothers be passed down? Perhaps in the distant future, descendants will sit beside new mothers and share our stories like legends from the past.

(2018)

1980 –
After giving birth to my son in Tokyo

2017 –
Me and my son with his newborn (his 4th child)

The Power of Love

The train carriage was quiet. Next to me sat a sweet little girl with golden hair, chattering cheerfully to her mother who was standing in front of her. The child looked about three or four years old. Beside the young mother stood a young father, his hand resting on the handle of a stroller. Though there was an empty seat next to her daughter, the mother remained standing, frequently leaning over to check on the baby in the stroller. The stroller's cover extended from the handle forward, hiding most of the inside from view, but it was quiet, so I assumed the baby was asleep. As I stared ahead, I found myself thinking of my son's family, who left Australia over a decade ago. Back then, they used to take my eldest grandson, just five months old at the time, around in a stroller like this.

I suddenly noticed something that caught me off guard. The young father's actions startled me, and I had an urge to speak to him. The top of the stroller cover had a small flap, roughly the size of an outstretched hand, which could be lifted to reveal a transparent vinyl window just underneath. Through it, he was peeking in to check on the baby. What a clever idea! That sight instantly brought back a story my mother had told me about my young parents' evacuation from Seoul to the south during the Korean War in January 1951. My mother had carried me on her back, wrapped in a cloth carrier, with a blanket pulled over the top to shield me from the bitter cold. As our family fled southward among lines of evacuees, my father kept lifting the blanket from time to time to check whether I was still breathing.

I turned to the young father and asked,

"Were you just lifting that flap to check on your baby?"

"Yes," he replied with a smile.

"Wow! What a great idea. I've never seen anything like that before. Things are getting more convenient these days!"

Before I knew it, I had turned into a chatty *ajumma* (auntie), sharing the story of my parents – how they were a young couple in their twenties during the January 1951 evacuation in the Korean War. The young man smiled and said, "That's an amazing story. I'm glad you made it through and are here." Just then, the train reached its destination. I thanked him quickly and got off in a bit of a hurry. As I walked out through the ticket gates and down the street, the image of that young father lifting the palm-sized flap to peek at his baby replayed in my mind like YouTube shorts on a loop. Suddenly, an odd thought crossed my mind: maybe this young man, too, would someday learn to read his child's heart the way I once did. When my son was a child, I often felt I could understand exactly what he was thinking. Or perhaps I simply believed I could. Maybe it was because young children are still so simple in their emotions but there were many times when I would say something at the exact same moment he did, as if in chorus. Moments like that made me think I really knew what was in his mind. I suppose all parents raising little ones feel the same.

When my son was in middle school, he spent six months at his school's outdoor campus program in regional New South Wales. Fortunately, the school encouraged students to write letters to their families regularly, and through those handwritten notes, our family kept in touch and shared our hearts with one another. His letters described his life in the dormitory, his studies, friends, the surrounding nature, and even a kangaroo that had become a kind of pet. He wrote with such detail that I could picture everything vividly in my mind. Then, one day, he wrote something unexpected. He said that after the six-month program was over and he returned home, he wanted to start going to church and asked me to take him. In that moment, I sensed a shift, a quiet transformation in my son's heart. How could I possibly understand all that was going on inside a child who, in the midst of adolescence, suddenly seemed to be growing up before my eyes? I was reminded of something my own mother once said long ago. Speaking of her children, she had murmured, "I wish I could just step into their hearts for a moment just to see inside." Time has passed, and now that once-young boy is in his forties and serves as an elder at his church. Perhaps because they live far away, I may be idealising their lives but still, I feel a sense of joy watching the way my son and daughter-in-law live. They seem to understand each other so deeply, connected heart to heart. I'm glad she is my son's partner in life. They appear to live without ever needing to say things, like a Korean proverb, 'You may fathom the depth of water, but not the depth of a person's heart.' And what about me? How many times have I failed to understand the minds of those close to me? How often have I unknowingly disappointed or hurt someone? I wonder...

Recently, due to an unexpected injury, I've found myself needing to use a walking stick for a while. I decided to prepare two: one for use at home and another for going out. The indoor cane was an inexpensive purchase from a variety store, which has branches all over town. I also bought a small accessory to prevent it from tipping over when I lean it against something. With this add-on, I can neatly hook the stick onto the edge of a table or desk in an L-shape. It stays put and looks tidy too. For outdoor use, I found one at a pharmacy. I was drawn to its floral pattern, and though it cost several times more than the indoor one, it felt sturdy and reliable – the handle is wider and the shaft thicker, offering better stability when I put my weight on it. But there's a problem: I have to be constantly mindful not to let it fall over when I set it down. It's especially unsettling in places like restaurants, where it could topple with a loud clatter at any moment. The thought alone makes me nervous. Whenever I recall the moment I injured my knee, I feel a chill pass through me. I should have been more careful… But what's done is done. There's no use crying over spilled milk. These days, I've also been bedridden with a severe cold and body aches. It feels like I need a walking stick for my heart, too. What kind of inner stick could keep me steady and upright, no matter what? As these thoughts drifted through my mind, a message arrived from my son. It was nighttime where he was, and here, a new morning had just begun.

"Are you feeling better today? We're all praying for you."

My heart brightened as I read my son's message. I once watched all four of my grandchildren ranging in age from five to twelve eagerly take turns saying grace before each meal. Knowing they were now praying for me filled me with light. Prayer, I realised, is the power of love that binds a family together. Yes, the cane that holds me steady in my heart is love itself – the boundless love of heaven, the devoted love of my family, and the kindness and comfort offered by those around me. These are what move me, what lift me up and keep me going. 'Love your neighbour as yourself.' How can we, as imperfect humans, ever truly live out such a commandment? Perhaps it begins simply by not hating those around us. That alone would be a good start.

(2023)

The Final Farewell

Every farewell leaves behind a wound or a scar that is hard to heal. But the most painful goodbyes are those shared with family, your own flesh and blood, or with dear friends with whom you've shared life and heart. The final farewell I experienced left me in a world that suddenly felt hollow and desolate, as if I had fallen into an abyss of emptiness.

It was in the late 1970s. Out of nowhere, illness struck my father. He was suddenly paralyzed on his right side and lost his ability to speak. The diagnosis, *a stroke*, was something none of us had even heard of at the time. He was only 57 years old. I, the eldest daughter, had been living in Tokyo for a year after getting married, while three of my four younger siblings were still students. Later, I moved to Sydney to begin a new chapter of life, while my mother stayed behind, quietly suppressing her longing to visit her married daughter. For thirteen long years without missing a single day, she remained by my father's side.

After being admitted to the intensive care unit, there were several times in those first few years when I would receive an urgent call about my father's critical condition, and immediately board a plane. I once saw him convulsing before my eyes, his entire body turning a deep purple, as though bruised all over. At one point, my father refused to eat or drink, as if he had decided to leave this world. But my mother, determined to keep him alive, did everything in her power to bring him back. She pursued every option available, combining both traditional Korean and Western medicine. A native of Seoul with no family or connections in the countryside, she nonetheless tracked down practitioners reputed to have healing hands. Whenever she heard of a skilled acupuncturist in some remote town, she would take my father there, even against his will. He resisted, but she insisted. Perhaps her devotion moved heaven itself.

At some point, the seizures stopped, and gradually, the paralysis in his legs began to ease. We hoped he would begin writing with his left hand, to express himself to the family but instead, he used only hand gestures. My mother became his sole interpreter. Was it pride that made him hide his true feelings from us? He had once been a man of many words, but now, not a single sound passed his lips. So he swallowed his sorrow in silence. Even at mealtimes, he had to be fed by my mother. He must have felt such deep remorse for the burden he placed on her. Yet for my mother and for all of us his children, what mattered most was not how limited he had become. We simply wanted him to live.

My father was the youngest son of six siblings. When he suddenly fell ill, his older brothers and sisters were devastated. My great-aunt, the eldest among them, was already quite old, but whenever she saw me, she would tear up and quietly ask, "How is your father doing?" Even though she knew his condition, she would gaze at me with eyes full of hope, as if longing for the slightest hint of good news. That look of quiet desperation still lingers vividly in my memory. The two uncles who had worried so deeply about their youngest brother both passed away after barely reaching their seventies. So when my father turned seventy, I found myself quietly bracing for the worst. But fortunately, he had improved significantly. Though he still couldn't speak or use his right hand, he had regained enough strength to visit the barbershop in his apartment complex on his own. This was all thanks to my mother. He could even enjoy a glass of his favourite beer again. If we told him he couldn't, he would become upset and we feared that frustration might undo all the progress he had made, so we let him have it. Eventually, the whole family adjusted to this new way of life. There was even laughter in the house again. And seeing that, I found the courage to propose bringing my parents to Australia.

My father waved his hand firmly and with a gesture of his left hand, insisted, "Not me. Just take your mother with you." All my siblings agreed that it was time for our mother to take a much-needed break. They assured her that our father had recovered well and that they would take good care of him, urging her not to worry and to enjoy her trip to Australia. Ah… what a long-awaited, precious opportunity it was. And yet, from her point of view, she still believed it was her duty, not her children's, to remain by her ailing husband's side. However, having long envied her friends who freely came and went from their married daughters' homes, my mother at last resolved to make her first visit to her own daughter's home. The day we left for Australia, our entire family gathered at Gimpo Airport. The fact that father came to the airport to see mother off was newsworthy among our relatives. It was going to be a 60-day separation after all. In a Western setting, a couple might have embraced each other at such a farewell. But we all simply bowed deeply, then waved goodbye.

After arriving in Sydney, my mother and I talked endlessly, making up for the time we had been apart. As we stood in front of the Opera House, she gazed out at the blue waves of Sydney Harbour, shimmering under the sunlight, and quietly said, "I feel so relieved inside." But fate would not allow her to simply enjoy that brief moment of happiness with her daughter. On the 51st day of her visit, just ten days before she was due to return to Korea, I received a phone call in the middle of the night from my younger brother. The news hit like a bolt out of the blue: Father had passed away. Fearing that the shock might be too much for my mother, who had a heart condition, we told her only that Father had been taken to the hospital. Her firm voice, filled with conviction, still rings in my ears: "I've cared for him every single day for 13 years. Nothing must happen to him while I'm away." In the end, I had no choice but to tell her about Father's passing while we were still in the car, on our way home from the airport. Words cannot capture how it felt.

Mother grieved for Father as if she were bidding him farewell with her whole body, though he had already passed.

Looking back, that parting at Gimpo Airport fifty days earlier must have been the hardest of all, especially if Father had somehow sensed that it would be his final goodbye. As for me, I choose to see our irrevocable separation not just as a loss, but as a send-off for a long journey he was meant to take. And I hold on to the hope that we will one day meet again.

(2023)

Savings in My Heart

When travelling, I often find myself lost in unfamiliar places or unsure of which way to go in a busy subway station. Even with a guidebook and map in hand, I sometimes end up heading in the wrong direction, moving further away from my destination and feeling increasingly frustrated. During this trip, such moments occurred more than once, not just in new places like France and Switzerland, but even in my home country. Without the help of others, my travels would have been far more difficult. Although I don't remember their faces, I hold their kindness close to my heart like a treasure, wanting never to forget it.

When I boarded the flight from Incheon to Paris, I struck up a conversation with the passenger seated next to me. She was about my daughter's age and worked as an agricultural engineer on a French island in the South Pacific. Her father, who had come to pick her up at the airport, was kind enough to drive me all the way to my accommodation. I had planned to take a taxi into the city, but he skilfully navigated the back roads during rush hour to make my journey easier. Who says Parisians are high-nosed?

On my second day in Paris, after taking a boat ride on the Seine to see iconic landmarks like the Arc de Triomphe and the Eiffel Tower, I became so absorbed in the experience that I lost my way back to my accommodation. Holding the map, I realised I'd been walking in the wrong direction for some time. My feet, plagued by plantar fasciitis, were burning, and my legs ached to the point where I almost wanted to collapse on the pavement.

At a pedestrian crossing, I asked a young man for directions. He kindly walked me to a familiar landmark, ensuring I could confidently find my way from there. Despite my assurances that I'd be fine, he looked at me with concern, as if I were a lost child. With a polite bow, he wished me well and turned back. Watching him leave, I recalled a similar experience 40 years ago in Tokyo. Back then, when I couldn't speak the language at all, a kind young man not only bought me the right ticket but also escorted me through the ticket gates.

France was leaving a strong impression on me. Was it that French people were especially kind to women? But I'd also been helped by women, so perhaps it wasn't about gender after all. On a train to Provence, as I struggled to lift my heavy luggage, a young woman sprang from her seat and cheerfully hoisted it onto the rack for me. Were French people all this kind, or was I just lucky?

In Lyon, I experienced more of this kindness. Lyon, known as the culinary capital of France, stimulates my appetite even at the thought of it. During a week-long stay, I indulged in three-course lunches and dinners daily. One day, friends and I visited 'Les Halles de Lyon-Paul Bocuse,' a market named after one of France's top chefs. The variety of high-quality produce on display was stunning. Worried about my poor sense of direction, one friend asked a passerby for help before we parted ways. The well-dressed young man happened to be heading in the same direction I needed to go. With my limited French, I explained that it was my first time in France and that I was returning from a summer school held in a picturesque old monastery in Provence. This young man encountered some acquaintances approaching from the opposite direction, and since they assumed I was part of this young man's group, they held out their hands and before I knew it, I found myself shaking hands with them. Feeling out of place, I quietly lagged behind the group walking alone, when after a while he ran up to me and apologised. Such genuine effort to help a stranger amazed me. When he finally needed to turn off, he carefully explained that I should continue straight and then turn left, wishing me a pleasant trip. His politeness and gentlemanly manner left me wondering: does such grace stem from a French sense of national pride or from their education?

On my way back home, I stopped in Korea for the first time in five years. At Gangnam Station, I took the driverless Sinbundang Line. At Jeongja Station, I needed to transfer to the Bundang Line but found myself disoriented despite following the signs. A student I asked for directions was joined by a middle-aged woman, who kindly explained that I needed to take an elevator, climb some stairs, turn left, and then descend again. I had followed her instructions exactly, yet I ended up going in circles. Without realising it, I had rushed onto the train in front of me. "Why did you get on this one?" It was the surprised voice of the middle-aged woman sitting near the train door. Startled, I quickly jumped off just before the doors closed. Thinking of the woman sitting on the train, laughing at my little farce, I felt a bit embarrassed. But if it hadn't been for her, I would probably have kept heading in the wrong direction and ended up quite late for lunch with friends. Even now, it feels almost miraculous. That middle-aged woman, who had kindly shown me the way just moments ago, must have been startled to see me pacing back and forth. When I later told my friends the whole story, they couldn't stop laughing at my Aussie bumpkin moment.

When someone shows me pure, human kindness, I feel truly grateful. Those who offer kindness may quickly forget their actions, but the recipient treasures the memory for years to come, drawing strength from it even after time has passed. It reminds me of a poem titled Savings by Shibata Toyo, a Japanese woman who published her first poetry collection at the age of 99:

"When someone is kind to me, I deposit it in my heart. When I'm feeling lonely, I withdraw it to give me strength. You should start saving now. It's better than a pension."

(2016)

The Fragrance of Friendship

'I envy those who have someone they miss so deeply it aches.' When a woman said this during a casual gathering, there was a quiet loneliness in her face that made her seem, to my eyes, like a dried flower. She wasn't yet old enough for such sadness to be blamed on age alone, so why did she appear this way? Hearing her words made me reflect on myself. My husband and I immigrated to Australia with our two young children, and until they grew into adults, we lived an endlessly busy life. Perhaps for me, even the luxury of longing for anything beyond survival was too much to afford during those years. Now, with our youth behind us and a sense of peace finally finding its place in our lives, I felt it was time to reclaim some space just for myself. Isn't there a saying that with each stage of life, a new lifestyle becomes possible?

Looking back, I had a warm-hearted friend I could never forget. She came into my life like an angel when our family was living in Tokyo. An open-hearted Westerner from across the sea, her name was Ariane. She now is a civil servant in the field of architecture. During her university days, while studying architecture, she would travel to Japan on holidays to learn the art of flower arrangement. At the request of a mutual friend, she used to stay at our home during her time in Japan. I was working full-time then and always busy, and she kindly helped me in many ways – something I am still grateful for to this day.

Two summers ago, during a sweltering heatwave, I traveled with my daughter by train from Paris to a quiet rural town in southeast France to visit her. As I stepped out of the station, a wave of heat rose from the sun-scorched asphalt and hit my face like a wall. The village streets were hushed, almost deserted, the glaring sun the only thing in motion. I looked around and then I saw a woman running toward me with urgency in her steps. It was Ariane. I rushed to her as well, and we threw our arms around each other.

She gave me warm kisses on the cheeks again and again, and though her hair had turned partly silver, to me she looked exactly the same as she had in her twenties. She said I hadn't changed at all either, her eyes wide with amazement as she looked me up and down like a curious child. Though it had been thirty years since we last met, we saw each other with such unwavering affection that the wrinkles on our faces didn't seem to matter at all. Because she insisted so strongly, we stayed at her home for ten days both in France and in Geneva Switzerland, and during that time, we talked endlessly, catching up on everything we had missed in each other's lives.

Ariane's home reflected her warm heart in every corner. Each room was thoughtfully arranged, filled with little touches that were unmistakably hers. She and her husband had adopted two children from Nepal - her son, now fifteen, and her daughter, ten. Both had come as infants, and I believe she had kept their Nepali names to honour their roots . All around the house, I noticed drapes, paintings, and ornaments that reflected Nepalese culture. I was deeply moved by how she and her husband were raising their children with thoughtful care, helping them stay close to the country where they were born. I still remember how, thirty years ago, when I had my daughter, Ariane hand-knitted the softest baby wrap and an adorable little bonnet from soft, warm yarn, and sent them to me. I've kept them carefully all these years, thinking

I might pass them down to my future granddaughter one day. Not only that, when our son was three years old, she took a photograph of him, printed it large like a painting, and mounted it on cardboard along with a 1984 calendar and sent it to us. We hung it on our wall for years, admiring it as if it were a piece of fine art, regardless of the date. Ariane is a warm-hearted friend who can understand both adults and children, and I hold her truly dear.

Even now, there are moments when thoughts of Ariane suddenly come over me, like a breeze carrying the scent of memory. I find myself longing for her and for Switzerland, where she lives, still wrapped in the fragrance of her home and our ten days together. I remember how we could see the famous Mont Blanc, the highest peak in the Alps, from her living room window, far off in the distance. We took a train together to a mountain village called Zermatt, then boarded another train, the cogwheel railway, that took us right up close to the Matterhorn. I still recall how the three of us, my daughter, Ariane and I sat together, eating simple sandwiches that tasted like honey as we gazed at that majestic mountain. Even now, when I think of those moments, I can almost feel the spirit of the mountain wrapping around me, as if its energy never left.

They say having a good friend is like gaining another life. I will never allow myself to become a dried flower. Instead, though I have never smelled the fragrance of the wind orchid, I am drawn to it by name alone. Like that flower, I dream of spending the rest of my days with friends whose presence fills the air with gentle fragrance.

(2017)

1983 Me and my son Shinji with Ariane in Tokyo

2015 Me with Ariane and my daughter Kay in Switzerland

My daughter Kay made this card for Ariane before we left her home. She captured the time we shared in drawings.

Snow on a Summer's Day

Ah, Virginia!

It took a little over three hours after a domestic transfer to reach a small regional airport in the state of Virginia. The light aircraft, carrying about twenty passengers, trembled through the air currents as it crossed the sky. I clutched both armrests tightly the entire time, silently praying for a safe landing. Ah, Virginia! I was on my way back to the place I call the home of my heart, returning to Virginia after thirty-seven long years.

As I picked up my luggage and stepped through the door leading to the terminal, the small rural airport looked quiet, with only a few people standing around waiting to meet someone. Among them, I noticed a woman holding up a large sign with both arms outstretched. I assumed she was a travel agent greeting tourists. But the moment my eyes moved from the sign to her face, she dropped the sign she was holding, and I let go of my suitcase and cried out, "Ahhh!" as we ran toward each other. We fell into each other's arms, and the long years between us melted away in a heartbeat. Time that had drifted so far away suddenly returned to the present. It was Carol, my American sister and dear old friend, who had come to meet me. Tears and laughter blurred our faces as we clung to each other, again and again. It wasn't until a moment later that I realised someone nearby was filming our reunion. It was her husband, Raymond. Back in the day, he was a college student, but now with his hair turned white and thinned, he seemed like another person. And so began a ten-day journey: this couple would carry me in their time machine, back to 1968 and 1969, and then return me to 2006. Together, we were setting off down memory lane.

After World War II, in an effort to mend strained diplomatic ties between the United States and Germany, a student exchange initiative was launched, known as the International Christian Youth Exchange Program (ICYE). Through this program, I, a student at a Christian girls' high school in Seoul Korea, was given the rare opportunity to spend a year in Virginia. Back then, obtaining a visa to the U.S.-let alone securing a passport from Korea's Ministry of Foreign Affairs-was no simple task for a high school student. Wanting me to represent our country's culture well, my mother had me take intensive lessons in *gayageum* (traditional musical instrument) and traditional Korean dance. She even prepared several beautiful *hanbok* (traditional Korean dresses), just as she might for a daughter getting married. Had there been DVDs or videos back then, sharing our culture would have been much easier. But with only a surface-level grasp of the instruments and dances, I often had to bluff my way through mistakes, especially when I forgot a dance step. Thinking back now, those moments make me break into a cold sweat.

The American parents who cared for me like their own daughter during my one-year stay had a large family with five sons and two daughters. Even with two sons already married and the eldest daughter away at college, the household was still quite full. Through their church, they welcomed me, their first international exchange student, and treated me as their third daughter. Reuniting with their second daughter Carol, with whom I had shared a room for a year, was a truly emotional moment. "Oh, Youngkyu, you finally made it!" she exclaimed as we embraced at the airport. At home, my American parents, now much older, greeted me with tears of joy. One wall of their home was filled edge to edge with family photographs, capturing the history of this happy household. To my astonishment, among them was my own senior photo from the American high school I had graduated from. A welcome party was held that weekend in my honour. More than 70 people gathered—seven siblings and their families, the parents' brothers and sisters, cousins, and even some of my old high school friends. With a trembling voice full of emotion, my American father prayed, "Lord, thank you. Youngkyu has come home." My American parents had always lived lives grounded in service. I believe their decision to host me came from that same spirit. Even while raising their large family, my American mother regularly volunteered at a local hospital. I sometimes accompanied her, watching with admiration as she gently spoke with lonely elderly patients and offered them comfort and care. Their acts of service never ceased. In recent years, they had gone to Africa to help build a school, and travelled to hurricane-stricken New Orleans to help with carpentry and cook meals. Their unwavering passion for helping those in need made me reflect on my own life.

I returned to the high school where I had spent my senior year. From the outside, the building looked unchanged. But I soon learned that all the doors into the school, except one, were now locked. This has been the policy ever since the tragic Columbine High School shooting in 1999, a sobering reality of today's world. The three of us-me, Carol and Ray -visiting that day were all alumni of the school. Still, we had to sign in at the office and be accompanied by a teacher to tour the premises. Some areas had changed slightly, but the gymnasium and cafeteria remained just as I remembered them, stirring up a flood of memories. I had arrived in America the day before the new school year began, and not long after, a local newspaper journalist came to do an interview. The article read something like this: "This girl from faraway Korea asked the photographer to wait a moment before taking her picture so she could take off her glasses and put in her contact lenses. Clearly, the desire to look pretty is universal, whether in the East or the West." At that time, I wasn't just the only Asian student at the school, I was the only international student altogether. My history teacher, who had trouble pronouncing my unfamiliar name, took to calling me simply "the girl from Korea" during roll call. Four decades have passed since then, long enough for the world to have changed many times over. I can't help but wonder now: how do today's teachers call the names of the many Asian students who fill their classrooms?

During the ten days I stayed at my American parents' home,

we never ran out of stories. Memories from the past, tales of the years in between, the joys and hardships we had each lived through. They were overjoyed to see me blending in so effortlessly, as if I were a daughter who had only stepped out yesterday and returned today. Thanks to the kindness of the current owners, we were able to revisit the house where I once lived. It looked like something out of *Gone with the Wind*, a stately home built in the early 1800s. The couple living there were lovingly restoring it to its original character. I was stunned to find that the upstairs room I had once occupied nearly 40 years ago remained almost exactly as I remembered it. The house sits in the Shenandoah Valley, with the Shenandoah River flowing shallow and gentle just beside it, like a stream. I used to go fishing along that river with the twin boys of the family, who were then in middle school. One of them, the one who always said grace at the dinner table, is now in his fifties and a pastor.

When the time to say goodbye finally came, we stood hand in hand, giving thanks for the time we had shared. My American father offered a heartfelt prayer, asking for my safe journey home and for all of us to remain in good health until we meet again. Over the long years through marriage, career, childbirth, parenting, and immigration, all begun far from my own parents and siblings, I had often found myself missing this family with a quiet ache in my heart. Then one day, with the help of the internet, I was able to find them again. How grateful I am that I could visit them while they are still in this world, and that I could witness the unwavering affection they and their family have continued to hold for me. As I boarded the small plane once more, my heart was not filled with fear as it had been on my way in. Instead, I felt a profound sense of fulfillment and joy, grateful for a reunion that mended time and distance.

Not long after returning to Sydney, a package arrived from Virginia. Before I left, a local newspaper journalist had come to interview me, and now, the feature article had arrived: *"Korean Exchange Student Returns to Her Valley Family After 37 Years."* The article included a photo of me standing with my American parents in front of the house we had once shared, and another of Carol and me holding a picture of us in hanbok from years ago. My American parents happily told me that, thanks to the article, they had become something of a local celebrity. Though the time machine of memory has since brought me back to the rush of daily life, I often return to that journey in my mind, revisiting its warmth and smiling quietly at the bond that time could not break.

Some chapters of life reveal their full meaning only when we return to them after a long journey. Though many years have passed, the bond endures quietly, but firmly supporting the person I am today.

(2007)

Family, Student Stay In Touch Over Nearly Four Decades

Exchange FROM PAGE B5

Finding A New Home

Young-Kyu hoped to study library science at Madison College, now James Madison University, but the exchange program required students to go home for two years before returning abroad. She enrolled in a Methodist missionary college in Seoul.

In her first year, she traveled with nine other Korean students to a youth conference in Tokyo, where she met her Japanese husband Haruo Yasugi.

They exchanged letters for five years. When Young-Kyu finished her bachelor's degree in biology, Haruo paid a visit to her family in Seoul.

Young-Kyu Kwon Yasugi with her 1968 Montevideo High School yearbook picture.

sugis moved to Sydney 18 years ago, and call Australia home.

Renewing Family Ties

Back in the United States for her son's wedding last week, Young-Kyu made a side trip to the Valley to visit her host family.

To celebrate her return, the Morrises threw a party for Young-Kyu in a pavilion on their property in Grottoes. Even after 37 years, she recognized each of the Morris children.

"There have been a lot of tears," Young Kyu said. "We've been going down memory lane."

The Morrises don't intend to let Young-Kyu become a stranger.

"She's our sister," said E.J.

PEOPLE | RENEWING OLD TIES

Young-Kyu Kwon Yasugi views a picture of the Morris homeplace, where she lived in 1968 with her host family (from right) Carrie and Elzie Morris and their daughter Carol Ann Chapman.

Home Again

Korean Exchange Student Visits Her Valley Family After 37 Years

By REBECCA MARTINEZ
Daily News-Record

GROTTOES — When the Morris family sat down to lunch in the sunroom of their Grottoes farmhouse last Tuesday, the table was filled with happy chatter. As they passed around plates of pork, tomato-and-pimento sandwiches, and Mrs. Morris's sweet pickles, they laughed, told stories and finished one another's sentences. If it weren't for Young-Kyu Kwon Yasugi's olive complexion and almond-shaped eyes, you'd never have guessed they weren't blood relations.

After 37 years and three homes across the Western Hemisphere, Young-Kyu has returned to visit the hosts who became her own family during her year as a foreign exchange student in Virginia.

A Growing Family

Elzie and Carrie Morris raised their children on a farm on the Shenandoah River in Elkton and emphasized family values.

"Our family had church, school, and working on the farm," says Carol Ann Chapman, the fourth child of the Morris family and closest to Young-Kyu in age. "If you ate, you worked."

Elzie and Carrie are well versed in hospitality. For years, the Morris family hosted live-in guests, including a mentally disabled uncle and several foster children, one of whom they adopted.

For 50 years, the family has attended Mill Creek Church of the Brethren, through which Carrie arranged to host numerous exchange students from around the world. All of them called Carrie and Elzie "Mama and Daddy."

"I don't remember living with Mama and Daddy and just us," Chapman recalls.

Carrie adds, "Not for a year at a time."

This kind of home life has made her children more sensitive to disabled and elderly people, as well as people from different cultures, Carrie said.

Of all the exchange students, none has stayed on as long with the Morris family or become as close with them as Young-Kyu.

Seeing The Country Life

Young-Kyu was raised in Seoul, South Korea, the oldest daughter of a well-to-do family and self-proclaimed "city girl."

"Young-Kyu had people from county come to the city to clean [her home]," Carrie says.

Despite the dramatic difference between her

Carol Ann Chapman and Young-Kyu Kwon Yasugi hold a photo of themselves dressed for a party in 1968.

home in Seoul and the Morris farm, the family says Young-Kyu fit right in.

"She was very pleasant and had a wonderful disposition," Elzie says. "We bonded so well."

On her first day with them, she helped the youngest boys, twin eighth-graders, gather eggs from the family's 500 laying hens.

"She was never afraid to do anything," Chapman says.

Although she could read and write in English, Young-Kyu didn't speak or understand spoken English very well.

"Once, Uncle Jack, Mama's brother, told a joke at the dinner table and everybody got it except me," Young-Kyu said. "Mama had to write it down, and then I laughed."

While Young-Kyu and the Morris family managed well despite the language barrier, Carrie suspected that Young-Kyu felt homesick for the Korean language.

"Mama thought Young-Kyu was missing her language, so she brought her down to see a Korean professor at Virginia Tech," Chapman recalls. "He said it was the first time he'd heard Korean in a Southern drawl."

During her year abroad, Young-Kyu was a senior at Montevideo High School, where she attended football games and prom, and worked diligently on her studies.

Chapman and Young-Kyu shared a bedroom, went on double dates and agree that they developed the closest-knit relationship of all the siblings during the year.

"I couldn't take her to the bus [at the end of the year]," Chapman said. "We cried too much the night before."

See **EXCHANGE**, Page B6

Part Three

The Tower of Babel in Our Time

> 이때과거 식량하거나 음료
> THIS TIME PAST FOOD OR DRINK

At a local shopping centre, a puzzling sign in Korean on the wall caught my eye: "이때 과거 식량하거나 음료" ("This time past food or drink")

Through the glass behind the sign, I could see children playing on various play equipment. It looked like a space where kids could be cared for while their parents shopped. Yet this strange phrase displayed in English, Chinese, and Korean, left me completely baffled. It wasn't until I looked at the top line in English that I understood the intended meaning: *"No food or drink past this point."*

Clearly, the Korean version had been copied directly from an online translation tool, without the slightest correction or review. No matter how hard I tried to make sense of it, the phrase was meaningless. I had not realised just how misleading online translations could be. No matter how automated our world becomes, some things still require a human touch. A human voice, warm and nuanced, is far preferable to something that sounds robotic. Mistakes in language may not always be as disruptive as mechanical errors, but they can be just as confusing-and often leave moments that are either amusing or strangely unforgettable.

When I first started working in Tokyo in my late twenties, my Japanese was practically nonexistent. My English was adequate for work, but I couldn't understand the casual conversations my Japanese colleagues had around me. As the days went by, I began to feel increasingly isolated; a lonely face in the crowd. Eventually, I started attending language school in the evenings. Yet many expressions I needed weren't taught in class, so I immersed myself in Japanese through television dramas, trying to pick up words and phrases in context. One of the first expressions I learned, unfortunately, was often blurted out by male characters in dramas: *"Chikushō!"* It's a curse, roughly equivalent to "Damn it!" but I had misunderstood it to be a light, harmless exclamation, like "Oh no!" or "Oops!". To my horror, I began using it casually at work. Looking back, I cringe at the memory. At that stage of learning, experimenting with new expressions was normal but even so, I had unwittingly broken social norms. In Japanese culture, children are taught from an early age to avoid causing others hurt or embarrassment-yet at first, no one corrected me. Later, after I became closer with some colleagues, one kindly pointed out that when I said *"Chikushō,"* it sounded rather cute-coming from me. At that moment, I wanted to vanish into the nearest hole.

In the year of the Seoul Olympics, I brought a decade in Japan to a close and moved with my family to Australia. At Sydney Airport, we were met by an Australian friend who had spent a year in Japan as an exchange student. She had brought her parents along to welcome us. As an only child, she often turned to my husband and me for help during her stay in Japan whenever she faced difficulties. Since my husband and I had both experienced life in a foreign culture, we understood her struggles and tried to support her as best we could. Now, there she was at the airport, standing with her parents and holding a welcome placard written in Japanese. But instead of saying *'Yokoso'* (Welcome), it read: *'Okaerinasai'* (Welcome back). Even 28 years later, I remember that moment with nothing but gratitude for her thoughtfulness. I never even considered correcting her

Japanese or causing embarrassment. Her sincerity was all that mattered. Or, maybe I was wrong. Japanese is not my mother tongue afterall.

A few days after we arrived in Australia, my friend's mother invited us over for "tea." Assuming she meant the typical afternoon cup of tea, we made sure to avoid lunchtime and arrived later in the day. Only when we got there did I realise that what she had meant by "tea" was actually a light meal. I felt terribly sorry once I understood. At the time, our family was staying in a temporary apartment, and since mobile phones were not yet common, we had no way to contact anyone. We ended up creating a bit of a comedy of errors by unintentionally leaving my friend's father waiting at the train station for quite a while. Because my friend was at work that day, she had drawn us a map so we could find their house on our own. But when we didn't show up as expected, her father began to worry and kept waiting anxiously at the station.

We are human, and humans make mistakes. But when it comes to something displayed for the public, like a sign in a shopping centre, it should at least be correct. In a world of countless languages, online translations have created a new kind of language-one without a clear nationality or origin. But because these translations can be inaccurate or awkward, they sometimes confuse more than a human translator ever would. To me, it feels like a modern-day 'Tower of Babel'.

(Note: According to the Bible, the Tower of Babel was built at a time when the world spoke a single language. As people tried to build a tower reaching up to the heavens "to make a name for themselves," God confused their language, causing them to stop building and scatter. In Hebrew, "Babel" means confusion.)

(2016)

The Age of the Smartphone

Not long ago, I saw an intriguing photo shared on KakaoTalk. At the top of the image, labeled *1916*, men in long overcoats and fedoras are standing in a row by the side of a street filled with horse-drawn carriages, reading newspapers. Below it, labeled *2016*, a second photo shows casually dressed young people in T-shirts and shorts leaning against a building lined with parked cars, all staring into their smartphones. The contrast over a hundred years left me marveling at how much the world has changed. To young people today, who can access news in the palm of their hands, the men holding up large paper newspapers might seem like relics from an ancient, almost mythical time. Today's smartphone is no longer just a phone, it's a handheld computer packed with features. To me, it feels like Aladdin's magic lamp. Within this little device in my hand lies the entire world. The speed of technological advancement is so fast that, having lived most of my life in the analog era, I sometimes find it hard to keep up.

I remember the excitement when dial phones were replaced by push-button phones. Office workers who used the phone frequently were thrilled. They no longer had to wear out their fingers dialing or use a pen to turn the dial. Not long after that, push-button mobile phones appeared. But back then, they were so expensive and rare that if you left one in your car, thieves would often break the window to steal it. I was a victim of that myself. Then came today's touchscreen phones. Sleeker and thinner, these devices allowed you to dial simply by tapping your finger. On top of that, they came with computer functions. We had truly entered the age of the smartphone. Or rather, it would be more accurate to say that we now have handheld computers that just happen to include a phone function. When I think about how the earliest computers once took up a room of nearly 70 square meters and weighed 30 tonnes, I can't help but marvel at the brilliance of the scientists who made this possible. After a seismic shift in mobile technology, smartphones have now become essential to modern life. It's no surprise that people keep them in their pockets at home or carry them around in their hands like a part of their body. Modern people, having grown accustomed to these marvels of civilization, rely on their phones in almost every aspect of daily life. As for me, I sometimes catch myself becoming a slave to this convenient little necessity. To be honest, there are days I want to run away from it. On days when I spend hours glued to KakaoTalk, my fingertips start to feel a strange tingling, as if an electric current were running through them. That can't be good for my health. I wonder how delighted an old friend would be if I wrote a letter by hand, placed it in an envelope, and sent it with a stamp. But now, all the messages, not just greetings, go through KakaoTalk. It's no wonder my fingertips ache. Still, the idea of writing a letter stays just as an idea because before I know it, my hand reaches once again for this little phone.

In Korea, even kindergarten children now walk around with mobile phones hanging from their necks, apparently for safety and accident prevention. I was stunned last year when I saw my cousin's daughter, a preschooler, wearing a tiny, cute phone around her neck. My cousin's family doesn't even have a landline anymore; every member owns a mobile phone. They worry, of course, about the risk of smartphone addiction in children, but what can they do? These palm-sized computers are said to help with learning, so they reluctantly give in. When my own children were in school a long time ago, I didn't have to worry about such things. Now I often find myself speechless like a dog chasing the chicken staring up at the rooftop. While parents of school-aged children, fluent in all things digital, seem to navigate this new world with ease. I've heard that many countries, both in the East and the West, have banned students from bringing mobile phones into classrooms. Some schools require students to store their phones in lockers upon arrival and only retrieve them at the end of the day. This, it turns out, has led to higher classroom participation. But the problems caused by smartphones don't stop there. Think of phone scams like voice phishing. One must stay alert and cautious not to fall victim. We now even have a name for this new species shaped by the smartphone era: *phono sapiens*, a coined term that combines phone and homo sapiens. And now that artificial intelligence is being integrated into smartphones, I may not live long enough to witness the full future of the *phono sapiens*, but I can't help but wonder what kind of world awaits us. The kinds of things we once saw only in sci-fi films are becoming real. It seems inevitable that future generations, with minds far beyond our imagination, will reshape the world entirely. At the same time, I can't help but worry: will people, shaped by such high technology, one day live machine-like lives, devoid of warmth, as if they had hearts made of plastic?

In the 19th century, Alfred Nobel invented dynamite as a tool intended solely for industrial use. But when he saw it being used in warfare, he was filled with regret. This is why he left most of his fortune to establish the Nobel Prizes to honour those who contribute to the advancement of human civilisation. I can only hope, with all my heart, that these "smart" smartphones will never be misused like dynamite was.

(2020)

The Power of Culture

The video drew me in from the very first frame. I've long known that Korea's global standing has risen significantly in recent years, with growing international interest in various fields, particularly the immense popularity of Korean culture, often signaled by the "K-" prefix: K-Pop, K-Food, and more.

But today, I was deeply moved as I witnessed the real impact of that cultural wave through this video. Seeing Korea join the ranks of developed nations, I found it especially encouraging that even a primary school in Australia had designated a "Korea Day," giving young students the chance to experience Korean culture firsthand. The video featured a Korea Day celebration held at a primary school in Sydney. Throughout the school day from morning to dismissal, students rotated through activities by grade level to participate in a rich and engaging program. It was organised by a dedicated Korean language teacher at the school, who guided the events alongside Korean students with great success. I also spotted Korean mothers volunteering in the background, as well as representatives from the Korean Cultural Centre and the Korean Education Centre, hinting at support from official Korean institutions.

In one classroom, students were taking part in a hands-on activity where they drew the Korean flag, the *Taegeukgi*. After carefully colouring their flags, they wrapped the ends around pencils to make handheld versions, waving them proudly while chanting, "Happy Korea Day!" One young girl, eyes wide and sparkling, confidently said in an interview, "Today is Korea Day, so we made the Korean flag!" Her sweet and earnest tone was utterly endearing. In another classroom, a Korean student stood at the front demonstrating how to make *ttakji*, traditional paper game tiles. Soon, everyone was fully absorbed in making and flipping their handmade *ttakji*, smiling and laughing as they played.

Off to the side, students were getting face paintings. On their cheeks or the backs of their hands appeared designs like the *taegeuk* symbol or "I ♥ Korea." Even an Australian male teacher joined in, helping the students draw with enthusiasm and joy.

In the school hall, students and teachers gathered together, dancing joyfully as they followed the moves of a K-Pop dancer performing on stage. Even through the screen, I could feel the infectious energy radiating from the scene. For lunch, bibimbap was served to all the students. Unlike the traditional version we eat in Korea, it was offered in a buffet-style arrangement, tailored to local tastes. The children could choose their preferred meat and vegetables and mix them with soy sauce or *gochujang* (chili pepper paste).

One student piled *bulgogi* (marinated beef), lettuce, and cucumber into a bowl, added a touch of *gochujang*, mixed well and ate. She exclaimed "Mmm, delicious!" with such genuine delight. I couldn't help but smile at their enthusiastic enjoyment of our healthy Korean dish. But then came a moment that truly made me laugh: one student, skipping the spoon altogether, put on a disposable glove and mixed the rice and other meat and veggies with her hand. It was unexpected but in a way, it felt fresh and creative, as if breaking free from fixed ideas.

Our family settled in Australia in the year of the Seoul Olympics in 1988. Just five weeks after arriving in Sydney, we had to move to Melbourne for a while due to my husband's work. At that time, my 8 year old son entered Year 2 at a small suburban school in Melbourne where there was only one class per Year group. Coincidentally, the Year 6 students had just been assigned a project on Korea, the Olympic host nation. They were gathering information from the local library and had even created a 3D model of the Korean peninsula, shaped like a rabbit. But the Korean books they managed to borrow from the local library were old and yellow, clearly outdated. The Year 6 teacher approached me and asked if I could give a presentation about Korea. As it happened, due to my husband's job transfer, our family had just rerouted our household shipment from Sydney Harbour to Melbourne and they had just been delivered. In the chaos of half-unpacked boxes, I searched until I found one that held my *hanbok* (traditional Korean dress). I also managed to borrow a VHS tape of the Olympic Eve celebration from Ilkwang Foods, the only Korean grocery store in the area at the time. When the day finally arrived, I put on my hanbok and headed to the school. Drawing from my over ten years of experience working in a market research company, I began by sketching the map of China, Korea, Japan, and Australia on the chalkboard. Then, I shared with the students the history of our country and how it had grown to the point of hosting the Olympics. This was long before the internet era, and there was no one nearby to ask for help but somehow, I managed to deliver the presentation smoothly.

Later, our family moved to Sydney as originally planned in April 1990. That is the year Korean Air made its historic first passenger flight to Sydney.

Though we live in Australia as immigrants from a minority background, I've come to feel that the rising global status of Korea has also lifted the pride of Korean-Australians like us. As the Immigration Attaché at the Australian Embassy in Tokyo had once said, we came with a pioneering spirit to a land full of opportunity, but the reality wasn't always easy. Still, I believe our family has adjusted well and lived a fulfilling life in Australia.

"What I desire above all else is the power of high culture. The power of culture brings happiness to ourselves and, ultimately, spreads happiness to others."

These are the words of Baekbeom Kim Gu*, whose vision for Korea was grounded not in power or wealth, but in the strength of culture. Was this wish his alone? Surely, it reflects the enduring hope and spirit of our entire nation even to this day.

(2022)

---

* He was a leader of the Korean independence movement against the empire of Japan.

Meeting the Haenyeo

I visited Jeju Island in the middle of summer, when a heatwave was expected. The trip hadn't been planned in advance. The reason we ended up going was because of my daughter, who works as a school teacher in Sydney. One day, while stopping by the Korean Cultural Centre, she picked up a book in the library with a *haenyeo* (female diver) pictured on the cover. As she flipped through the pages, she found herself drawn deeper and deeper into curiosity about these women. The more she read, the more astonished she became. It was hard to believe that these women, without fear, would dive into the deep, dark ocean-sometimes as deep as 20 metres -to harvest seafood like abalone, all without any oxygen equipment. They would hold their breath for up to a minute or two while working underwater. As a fellow woman, my daughter was deeply moved and shocked by their courage. What's more, she felt a surge of professional interest-she wanted to go to Jeju Island herself, meet the *haenyeo* in person, and tell her students about them. That's how Jeju was added to her originally planned overseas trip. And since she asked me to come along, I hastily packed my bags and joined her on this unexpected journey.

When we arrived at Jeju Airport, even the air that greeted us felt different. Was it the scent of the island? It carried a distinctly exotic touch, something unfamiliar yet strangely inviting. After settling into our accommodation, we set out the next day to drive along the island's coastline. We soon came upon a group of elderly *haenyeo* crouched down, their hands busily at work. We stopped the car and watched for a while. They had just returned from their morning dives and were now splitting open sea urchins, scooping out the roe with small spoons, and carefully packing them into glass jars. Their hands moved with speed and precision, revealing a lifetime of practice. One by one, they filled the small jars-about the size of jam containers-while the sea urchin shells piled up beside them. Nearby, wetsuits lay spread across the rocks, already dried under the blazing sun. The suits, worn and weathered from years of use beneath the sea, told their own stories. We decided to buy one jar of sea urchin roe and waited patiently as they worked. It was during that wait that we learned one of the women was nearly deaf. Another grandmother beside her explained that she was close to ninety. In the old days, before rubber hoods covered their ears, the *haenyeo* had used cloth towels made of coarse cotton to tie back their hair. Diving deep into the sea with little protection must have taken its toll –and in her case, it had cost her hearing.

Looking into the history of *haenyeo*, we learn that it wasn't always women who dove into the sea. In the Joseon Dynasty, it was originally men who did the diving. However, once the government began taxing male divers, it became too difficult to sustain a livelihood, and they were forced to give it up. Women, on the other hand, were not subject to such taxes. Despite royal decrees prohibiting women from undressing and diving into the sea, they continued to do so–driven by the need to make a living. From a young age, girls were taught how to swim in the ocean and trained in the art of free diving. Even after marriage, they remained the breadwinners of the household, their fierce resilience supporting entire families. Eventually, husbands stayed home to care for the children and manage the household–what we might call "house husbands" today. But life was harsh. When a hungry infant cried, there was no choice but to wait until the mother emerged from the sea. These families endured times of unimaginable hardship.

At the Jeju Haenyeo Museum, there were numerous video clips where real *haenyeo* shared their stories. One woman said that, in the past, it wasn't the hunger that hurt the most-it was the social stigma and discrimination. But now she feels proud and fulfilled in her identity as a haenyeo. Some of their expressions were striking: *"The sea is my bank-I don't need deposit or withdrawal slips," "The ocean gives back exactly what you put in,"* and *"The sea is as generous as it is vast and deep."* These women spoke with pride and dignity. One testimony in particular made my jaw drop: *a haenyeo once went diving while nine months pregnant, returned home in the evening, and gave birth two hours later.* Another resumed diving just three days after childbirth. During peak conch season, they worked tirelessly-even in the frigid winter water. With their hard-earned income, they supported their families, bought homes and land, and sent their children to schools on the mainland. Yet many of them discouraged their daughters from following in their footsteps, choosing instead to invest in their education. Such strength-beyond resilience, almost miraculous in its persistence-leaves one wondering where that power could possibly come from. Their deeply lined, weathered faces struck me as truly beautiful. For these women, who spent a lifetime submerged in hardship and saltwater, the sea had become something more than a workplace-it had become a mother. *"When I was overwhelmed,"* one said, *"I would go to the sea and cry, just as I would in my mother's arms."*

At the museum, there were also days when performances took place. Former *haenyeo* divers would sing *haenyeo* songs in the Jeju dialect while demonstrating the harvesting of seafood. During the song about catching anchovies, they would hold the fishing nets and shake them side to side, inviting the audience to join in. Encouraged by my daughter, I even took part, which brought laughter as the anchovies caught in the net were actually candy disguised as fish. What captured our greatest interest was that visitors could experience being haenyeo and even learn the songs. Braving the intense heat, we pushed through a field trip full of activity. While my daughter spent about an hour learning how to dive and gather seafood from a *haenyeo* grandmother, I took photos and videos from a distance. When I tried to cool my feet in the sea by stepping barefoot onto the stone floor, I was shocked-the stones heated by the blazing sun were as hot as a boiling cauldron lid. Still, when my daughter proudly raised the sea urchin she had caught herself, I truly felt the trip was worthwhile. At the museum performance, we found the person who had been leading the songs and learned haenyeo songs while playing the *janggu* drum. Upon hearing my daughter's intention, the gracious master singer readily agreed to teach us and mentioned that she herself had been a *haenyeo* in the past.

In 2016, Jeju *haenyeo* were inscribed on UNESCO's Intangible Cultural Heritage list, bringing global recognition. However, the average age of the *haenyeo* exceeds 70, and their numbers continue to decline. The ongoing efforts to train new *haenyeo* and preserve this unique culture remain a significant challenge for Jeju Island.

I am very curious to see how my daughter, now back in Sydney, will plan and present the story of the Jeju haenyeo to her students in the future.

(2018)

Since writing this essay, my daughter and I created a puppet show called "Haenyeo: Women of the Sea", inspired by Jeju Haenyeo women divers.

2018 – My daughter Kay learning how to dive with a Haenyeo in Jeju Island, South Korea.

2018 – My daughter Kay crocheted this Haenyeo puppet to take to Jeju Island. It is sitting next to a Haenyeo's tewak mangsari (buoy and net).

The Power of Cultural Inheritance

Confucius once said, "At seventy, I could follow my heart's desire without transgressing what was right." That's why the age of seventy is often referred to as *jongshim*-a time when one is free to act according to one's heart. At that age, I summoned the courage to perform a puppet show. Yes, my first-ever public debut and that too in Italy. I dare say my boldness owes something to Confucius's declaration. Yet another inspiration comes to mind. Over a decade ago, an Aussie woman donned a master's cap at nearly seventy. Age did not deter her from enrolling in graduate school to study history, then setting sail on a grand cruise. I imagine she was finally checking off a long-held item on her bucket list. While I had no such list myself, thinking of her gave me the courage to try something new. Now, having embarked on this adventure later in life, I feel as though a new sprout has broken through in my heart, a sense of renewal, and even a touch of youthfulness.

In a small Italian town where traces of the medieval era remain beautifully intact, I was invited this summer to participate in a puppet festival with my daughter. The performance, titled *"Haenyeo: Women of the Sea,"* was the fruit of our collaboration. My daughter, a primary school teacher with fifteen years of puppetry experience, patiently taught me everything I needed to know. Most of the puppets- conch shells, abalone, a turtle, an octopus - were handmade from crocheted yarn. The story unfolds like a folk tale: a young girl initially refuses the *taewak-mangsari* (a floating buoy and net basket used by traditional haenyeo women divers) passed down to her by her grandmother. One day, she encounters a turtle with plastic tangled around its neck. After freeing the turtle, the grandmother follows it to the Dragon Palace under the sea and returns with a white seashell. Eventually, the girl joins her grandmother in the water. For the grand finale, children from the audience come to the front and wave a long blue silk cloth to mimic the sea. Across it swim the puppets of the *haenyeo*, her granddaughter, fish, and octopus, gliding gracefully to the delight of the crowd.

We gave eight performances in a venue that had once been an old monastery. I believe our effort to introduce and preserve the disappearing *haenyeo* (women divers) culture of Jeju Island, Korea, was conveyed meaningfully to both children and adults. Before each show, my daughter briefly introduced the haenyeo in Italian using a translated script. We aimed for strong visual storytelling with minimal spoken dialogue, set against a musical background that included haenyeo songs and *daegeum* (Korean bamboo flute) melodies. There were only a few brief expressions, simple Korean and Italian phrases like *"Aigo!"* (which can be a cry of surprise, frustration or pain in Korean) and *"iri-on/ vieni!"* ('come here')-just enough to add a playful human touch. After the performance, when it was revealed that we were a mother-daughter team, the applause poured down like a sudden summer shower. We felt as if we had become unofficial ambassadors for traditional Korean culture, and our hearts swelled with pride and fulfillment. Coincidentally, the town where we performed is also renowned for its traditional bobbin lace-making *(Merletto a tombolo)*, a craft passed down from mothers to daughters for generations. This shared tradition of intergenerational heritage made our performance resonate even more deeply with the local audience.

In this town, a unique tradition has been passed down seamlessly from mothers to daughters, like a flowing stream. While walking along the stone-paved streets, I came across a striking statue set against the backdrop of towering stone walls. Curiosity drew me closer, and I saw three women—a grandmother, mother, and granddaughter—each seated before a peculiar device resembling a small pillow atop a stand, with several miniature spools dangling like tiny rolling pins. They were engaged in the craft of bobbin lace-making, using spools instead of needles. This lacework, along with olives and wine, is considered one of the three major cultural heritages of the region. The sculpture, depicting a large-framed grandmother with glasses perched on her nose, a mother, and a young granddaughter all deeply focused on their lace-making, was profoundly moving. What was once a common sight has now become a scene preserved only in stone. As someone from a generation that has largely turned away from passing down traditional practices, I stood there for a long while, reflecting. I couldn't help but feel a kinship between this fading art and Korea's haenyeo diving tradition, which now teeters on the brink of disappearance.

The place we stayed for two weeks was nestled within the

old city walls, where remnants of history still stood intact. Each day, we would pass through a narrow alleyway where a small bobbin lace shop was tucked away. Above the shop was what seemed to be the owner's residence, and seated just outside was Ms. Pina, a woman in her sixties. With her pale face, neat attire, and graceful demeanor, she sat there each day, working diligently on her lace, the rhythmic clicking of the bobbins filling the quiet alley. Though we couldn't speak each other's language, we eventually began exchanging simple greetings, like *"Ciao/*Hello." Through a mutual acquaintance, I learned that Ms. Pina had lost her only son in an accident when he was still young. The moment I heard this, I couldn't help but imagine the dreams she might once have held-perhaps she envisioned her son's wedding day, a young boy in a necktie walking down the aisle, carrying one of her handmade lace ring cushions with both hands. Perhaps she planned to craft a lace tablecloth for the occasion, and dreamed of one day teaching her granddaughter the art of lace-making. But those dreams must have shattered like glass. I can only imagine the depth of her grief. And even if she had a daughter, there would have been no certainty that the tradition of lace-making would be willingly carried on.

How long will the daughters of Jeju's *haenyeo* and the

daughters of Offida in Italy continue to follow in their mothers' footsteps? With the advance of civilisation, many handcrafted traditions and ways of life are fading, leaving behind only faint traces of the analog era. Living in such a rapidly changing world, I, now at the age Confucius described as the time when one may follow the heart without straying from what is right, find myself wondering: must I live like a tightrope walker, breathless, just to keep from falling behind?

(2019)

"Haenyeo: Women of the Sea" Puppet show created by my daughter Kay Yasugi (Pupperoos), which we perform together. This photo was taken at the Melbourne Festival of Puppetry in 2023 (Photo by Darren Gill).

A History One Cannot Be Proud Of

It was only 235 years ago that a dark cloud began to loom over the world of the Aboriginal peoples, who had lived on the vast land of Australia for over 60,000 years without written laws. When I was a child in primary school in Korea, we were taught that Britain was a rich nation where the sun never set. At the time, I was too young to realise that this wealth had been built on the colonisation of other lands. When the colonisers arrived on Australian soil in striking uniforms—white trousers, crimson or black jackets, and imposing hats—they cast the Indigenous people, with their dark skin and unclothed bodies, as savage and indecent. It's easy to imagine that they were treated as less than human. But the law of the jungle applies not only in the animal world, but also among humans.

And here lies the irony: it is precisely because of such a brutal history that I now find myself living comfortably within the system of modern-day Australia.

It has now been nearly 35 years since our family immigrated to Australia. Back then, the immigration officer in Tokyo who handed us our visas said, "Australia is a land of limitless opportunity." Hearing that, we felt a swelling sense of possibility, as though we were destined to accomplish something here, a kind of pioneer spirit rising within us. Some say ignorance makes us bold. With our minds fixed only on the challenges ahead, we had only the vaguest notion of the Aboriginal people and made no real effort to learn more. There was simply no room for it in our lives. Whenever issues about Indigenous Australians appeared in the media, I received them passively, without much interest or attention. After all, we had arrived with two young children, and the urgency of settling down and getting them into school consumed all our energy. I simply lived my own way, absorbed in the busyness of daily life. Only recently, though belatedly, I was given the chance to learn more deeply about the tragic history of the Indigenous people, something I might otherwise have passed over in ignorance. For several days afterward, I carried a heart as heavy as stone; weighed down by thoughts of what they had endured.

At the school where my daughter teaches, Aboriginal educators came and conducted a three-hour seminar for the staff; sharing their stories and truths. When my daughter told me about the session, I was shaken to the core, overwhelmed by the realisation that, in this world, human beings may be the cruelest creatures of all. Until then, I had known the history of this country I now call home only through the lens of white settlers. But I can no longer ignore the obvious truth: that history must also be seen through the eyes of the Indigenous people.

So many horrific acts against the Indigenous peoples of this land seemed to have gone untold or overlooked. I learned that the First Fleet, led by Admiral Arthur Phillip, arrived with eleven ships, the first convict ship carrying only men. To think that, upon landing, they simply took Aboriginal women as they pleased–I could hardly bear the thought. Even more devastating was the discovery that there had once been an official policy of 'racial dilution': encouraging intermarriage until Aboriginal identity was reduced to fractions–one-half, one-quarter, one-eighth. The idea alone filled me with sorrow and dread. How terrifying it must have been for Aboriginal women, seeking only to live in peace, to endure such violations. The cruelty did not end there. Poisoned waterholes, blankets infected with smallpox, the stripping away of culture, names, languages, and identities followed by decades of mass killings. As I sat with these truths, I felt my heart growing unbearably heavy, and I could not escape the question: how could human beings inflict such suffering on others?

According to a new report by a historian from the University of Newcastle released this year, some of the most unspeakable atrocities were committed by white settlers. They chained Aboriginal people by the neck and forced them to gather firewood. Then, after dousing the wood with kerosene, they pushed the victims into the flames. These acts grew increasingly deliberate and cruel over time. Scientific research now confirms that the trauma suffered by Aboriginal people has embedded itself in their DNA across eight generations. The term 'Stolen Generations,' along with true-story films like *Rabbit-Proof Fence,* makes painfully clear the ways white colonisers treated Aboriginal Australians as less than human. Under the guise of 'civilised education', children were snatched away like stray animals picked up from the streets and forcibly placed into institutions or adopted into white families. They were banned from speaking their own languages and subjected to physical, emotional, and sexual abuse. Many were left so deeply scarred that they struggled to lead normal lives as adults. When I imagine my own young grandchildren being seized from the streets and subjected to such horrors, the very thought makes me feel like I would collapse in anguish. How can one even begin to grasp the unbearable pain endured by those parents? And yet, these atrocities were all carried out at the hands of white settlers.

I came across a song on YouTube titled *January 26*. It was performed by David Beniuk, a journalist, folk singer and songwriter from Wollongong. The song left a profound impact on me. It questions the celebration of January 26, the day Captain Arthur Phillip planted the British flag at The Rocks, marking the beginning of colonisation. The lyrics, which repeatedly ask, "Why do we celebrate a day of tragedy?" are powerfully matched by the video footage. In it, Aboriginal men are shown with thick metal chains around their necks, linked to one another in a harrowing image. A protest poster reads, "Let's celebrate the day that invasion, murder, rape, and theft began", a scathing irony. Do we really need to designate this day of invasion as Australia Day? Surely, we could choose a different day that doesn't reopen the wounds of the First Peoples.

I now see the Aboriginal people through a different lens. In Korean, we simply refer to them as 'Indigenous Australians' or 'Aborigine,' but when speaking in English, I learned from the presenters who visited my daughter's school that the appropriate term is 'Aboriginal'-not 'Aborigine'. They explained that 'Aborigine' is a derogatory term, much like how Koreans were demeaned as *"Chōsenjin"* during Japan's colonial rule. It carries a tone of disrespect and is best avoided.

It was not until 2007 that the federal government officially apologised for the 'Stolen Generations.' Despite backlash from conservative factions and the implementation process was fraught with difficulties, then-Prime Minister Kevin Rudd succeeded in delivering the apology. Peeling back the layers like an onion, the enormous challenges that lie ahead are far beyond my capacity to discuss. However, I can at least hold an interest and offer my heartfelt support. How far does human greed and cruelty really go? It makes my blood run cold. Did the colonial pioneers really have to swallow up this vast land by such means?

(2022)

Natural Disasters and Man-made Disasters

Last night, as the sky seemed to collapse and torrential rain pounded relentlessly on the concrete outside our kitchen, the noise was so deafening that the news on TV-continuously reporting the devastating floods in New South Wales and Queensland and the ongoing war in Ukraine-was barely audible without turning up the volume. Even now, as March has begun, the weather forecast predicts rain or thunderstorms throughout the week. In New South Wales, the northeastern towns of Lismore and Ballina suffered the most damage, and heavy rainfall continues in various areas. There was even talk that Ballina, with some six thousand households submerged, might disappear from the map. We watched with trembling hearts as the heartbreaking news unfolded:

two elderly people had drowned in their flooded homes in Lismore, and countless others were stranded on rooftops, surrounded by water, being rescued by helicopters. The sight of cattle and horses running together to escape the rising waters was almost unbearable to watch without shedding tears. The tragic deaths of livestock are deeply saddening. The ongoing war in Ukraine, now into its second week, also tears at the heart with its horrors.

We can learn about why and how the war in Ukraine started through various media, and thanks to living in the internet age, we receive real-time updates on the progress of the war. Russian forces have bombed over ten cities including the capital, Kyiv, and men aged 18 to 60 are forbidden to leave Ukraine and are required to join the war effort. However, even before the conscription order was issued, numerous volunteers from all walks of life-students, professors, anti-Russian lawmakers, former presidents-stepped forward to defend their homeland. Volunteers also returned from overseas. A newlywed couple married just one day earlier joined the defense forces. Civilians, including housewives, quickly helped produce Molotov cocktails, as shown on news reports. A brave young woman was featured, reporting the situation to Australian media while hiding underground. In the midst of the chaos, a man said goodbye to his wife and children departing by train, wiping away tears as he quickly turned away. Today's TV news showed a man who had lost his wife in a missile strike. Blood ran from a wound on his forehead down his face. In agony over his loss, he raised his fist in despair and struck it against his other palm. Perhaps he drew some small comfort from the fact that his daughter and parents were alive and nearby. Yet I couldn't miss the tears welling in his wide eyes, ready to spill at any moment. Missiles are falling not only on key facilities but also on civilian areas, causing many civilian casualties. Pregnant women giving birth underground. I can't imagine the dangers if surgical procedures like cesarean sections become necessary.

Watching the long lines of refugees walking into neighbouring Poland, I found myself imagining the desperate days my parents endured during the Korean War. During the brutal winter retreat of January 4th 1951, my mother carried me, just a baby then, on her back, with a blanket wrapped over the baby quilt as she walked south with my father, fleeing Seoul. My father would now and then lift the blanket to make sure I was still breathing. The Ukrainian refugees wear padded coats and sheepskin boots, but seventy years ago, in poverty-stricken Korea, women likely wore cotton socks and rubber shoes even in the bitter cold. I can only imagine how freezing, frightening, and uncertain it must have been. I wonder if my mother ever got frostbite on her hands or feet during that escape. At the time, she was only in her mid-twenties, a young and beautiful wife and mother.

As of early March, twelve NATO member countries were offering full support to Ukraine, and countries like South Korea, Japan, and Australia were also sending aid. Volodymyr Zelensky, the 44-year-old President of Ukraine, declared that as a leader, he had no right to fear death, vowing to stay in the capital and fight to the end. International media report that he is rapidly rising as a hero, calling for global support from a bunker deep underground.

During the Korean War, a total of 63 countries supported South Korea through combat troops, medical teams, material aid, or expressions of solidarity. From the United States alone, nearly 1.8 million troops were dispatched to help defend the Korean Peninsula. Thailand sent forces by land, sea, and air, while the Philippines also contributed soldiers. Many lives were lost among these allies. Even Iran, Vietnam, and Cambodia were listed among the countries that sent material aid, and Haiti-now among the world's poorest nations-contributed 3,000 US dollars. El Salvador sent 500 dollars.

Though those amounts may seem small now, they carried great value at the time. Realising how the world came together to support Korea fills me with deep gratitude and humility. The Korean War lasted for three long years, but I sincerely hope the war in Ukraine will come to an end much sooner. President Putin of Russia had expected a swift victory in Kyiv within three days, but the war has been prolonged due to the strong unity and resistance of the Ukrainian people.

Fundraising efforts to support Ukraine are taking place across the globe. In Taiwan, even the President and Vice President have donated a full month's salary, and the national legislature is reportedly contributing a large sum. With China's constant threats looming over Taiwan, it is understandable that their leaders would respond with empathy and solidarity. In Korea, donations are reportedly pouring in as well. In Australia, people can choose to donate specifically to support Ukrainian children, women, or other causes.

Meanwhile, Australia is also facing its own major crisis—catastrophic flooding—and is calling for donations to help the flood victims recover and rebuild. With aid from governments and heartfelt contributions from individuals around the world, we can hope that those who lost everything in the floods may regain a sense of normalcy. Likewise, the global outpouring of support for Ukraine gives hope that peace will return soon. This may not be an unrealistic dream.

Already, the world has been gripped by fear for three years due to the COVID-19 pandemic, and now we are faced with a new calamity: War. On top of this, there are devastating floods here in Australia, leaving many in fear and instability. These days, natural disasters and human-made disasters seem to be taking turns in shaking the world. Since the first humans, Adam and Eve, were cast out of the Garden of Eden, is the paradise we so desperately long for on this earth doomed to remain forever a mirage?

(2022)

We Come From Far, Far Away

One particularly clear autumn day in May, my daughter and I walked lightheartedly toward the Sydney Opera House. The midday breeze brushed gently against our cheeks, and the waters of Sydney Harbour sparkled as if the sun had spilled a handful of jewels upon them. The area bustled with people out to enjoy the glorious weather, and under the white tents lined along one side of the walkway, diners sat at tables draped in linen, their faces aglow with contentment. The play we watched at the Opera House, however, stood in stark contrast to this serene and beautiful Sydney afternoon. It was a powerful dramatisation based on a true and deeply troubling story.

The play told the stories of ordinary people swept up in

the harsh winds of history. Those who had the misfortune of being in the wrong place at the wrong time, and suffered unimaginable consequences because of it. The theatre company, based in Norway, has spent the past twenty years staging such works, often in collaboration with artists from various European countries.

The title of the play we saw that day was *We Come From Far, Far Away*. It was based on real conversations with young Syrian refugees who had fled the civil war in their homeland and journeyed – risking death and countless dangers–all the way to Oslo, Norway. In the play, a 15-year-old boy hides the money his mother gave him beneath a cap pulled low over his head. He and a friend are smuggled in a truck to the coast, where they pay a large sum to board a ship that will illegally take them across the Mediterranean Sea to Greece. The overcrowded ship sets off in the dead of night. With too many people aboard, it soon begins to struggle. Passengers are ordered to throw all their belongings overboard. Eventually, in the pitch-black waters, they are forced to leap into a smaller vessel. In despair, the boy reaches out to steady his friend but his friend slips and vanishes into the cold, dark sea. Stories like this are tragically common. It's said that around 25,000 people have drowned in similar crossings. The life jackets given to them were, in truth, nothing but worthless fakes.

In Greece, the boy bought a small camping tent from a shopkeeper who shouted at him with a frightening expression. One can only imagine how terrified he must have been. Each time he moved to a new place, he battled his fear by pretending to speak with his lost friend, as if his friend were still by his side. These whispered, one-sided conversations became his way of surviving the loneliness and terror. At last, he arrived in Oslo and found his way to a police station, where he applied for refugee status. There, the tears he had held back for so long finally broke free. As the overwhelming fear and tension that had gripped him throughout his journey began to ease, the boy clutched his body and sobbed uncontrollably. Watching him on stage, I felt tears slipping down my own cheeks. I wasn't alone. Sniffling sounds filled the theatre as the audience shared in his pain. The terrifying sea, the friend he had lost, the thought of his mother. This fifteen-year-old boy had endured it all and made it, against all odds, to the distant north of Europe. His sheer will to survive seemed nothing short of a miracle. Eventually, he was sent to a youth refugee centre.

Inside the Opera House's Studio, a vast space in itself, stood a Mongolian nomadic yurt, eight meters in diameter. It had been constructed much larger than the traditional tents actually used by nomads, and while the real ones typically have only one entrance, this version was fitted with four doors to serve the needs of the performance. Though the play itself had nothing to do with Mongolia, the audience was guided by the actors into the yurt to take their seats. Inside, two of the four actors, both men, played musical instruments while the audience settled in. It felt as though we had entered another world. About two-fifths of the tent was set up as a stage, with a small camping tent placed at the centre. Hanging on the surrounding fabric walls were props like life jackets and a police puppet. The audience sat on the floor lined with long padded cushions for comfort; shoes had to be left outside before entering. A few benches were placed along the edges, and we managed to find seats there. The audience consisted of some 80 high school students and their teachers who had booked in advance. For a space that comfortably holds about sixty, it was far more crowded than expected. It is hardly a fair comparison, but as the play unfolded, everyone squeezed into the closed space like an overfilled vessel, wholly absorbed in the performance. I noticed a Middle Eastern girl with her head wrapped in a scarf, wiping away tears as she whispered to her friend next to her.

The Syrian civil war, which broke out in 2011, has continued for over a decade, with no clear end in sight. During that time, it is estimated that more than 400,000 civilians have lost their lives, and over 12 million people (that is more than half the country's population) have been displaced as refugees. The teenagers featured in the play were ordinary youth, no different from teenagers living in Australia today. But simply because they were born in Syria, their homes were bombed into rubble, and precious lives were lost like flies. As waves of people fled in search of safety, Europe struggled under the weight of an overwhelming refugee crisis. Many nations, already burdened, found themselves at a loss, unable to accept such large numbers, yet what other choice was there? And Syria is not alone. Even today, countless regions in Africa and the Middle East continue to suffer under brutal civil wars driven by religious and ethnic strife. Each time the media shows the devastation, the children and the civilians caught in the crossfire, a deep sorrow weighs on my heart.

When the play ended, one side of the Mongolian tent was slightly lifted from the outside, allowing fresh air to flow through. A wave of relief spread among the audience, and many smiled. After the cast took a bow, a Q&A session followed. Listening to the thoughtful questions from the high school students in attendance, I was reminded of the value of experiential learning. "Is this story true?" one asked. "Why did you decide to make a play about it?" another inquired. The lead actor responded, "In reality, the boy's best friend, who had fled with him, was shot and killed at the Turkish border. But because so many others drowned while being transferred to small boats, we chose to represent his friend as one of them." To conclude, a counseling professional stepped forward to introduce herself in case any of the students were feeling distressed or unsettled by the performance. She had a warm, motherly presence that immediately put the audience at ease.

This production has received one of Norway's most prestigious theatre awards. It was clear that the creators had achieved their purpose: to raise awareness through storytelling and to awaken a sense of shared humanity. And yet, as I thought about our fractured world, I couldn't help but wonder, will we ever find a solution? All we can do is hold onto hope and entrust our prayers to a higher power. My daughter and I returned to one of the white-tented restaurants we had passed earlier at noon and chose a set menu that included a glass of wine. We raised our glasses in a quiet toast to Abdullah, the boy whose real-life story had inspired the play, and hoped he was now safe and thriving somewhere as an adult. As we watched people posing for photos with the Harbour Bridge in the background and others strolling past us with carefree smiles, a thought settled in my heart: however unfair the world may seem, each of us must still live the life we've been given. It was a bittersweet reminder.

(2023)

Part Four

The Spirit of Craftsmanship

Every weekday morning, seven fresh sea bream are reliably delivered to a small restaurant in Kyoto. The chef (who I will refer to as Chef M) has been preparing sea bream for the past 35 years. He estimates he has handled over 140,000 of them. His knife, now an extension of his own hand, seems to remember each precise movement. When he slices sashimi, the delicate lift of the blade's tip resembles the fluid motion of an orchestra conductor, so rhythmic and refined that it captivates the viewer. His skill with bamboo shoots is equally artistic. Every morning, he receives ten freshly harvested bamboo shoots, which he alternately boils in two large pots to parboil them. He then finishes the preparation swiftly in front of his guests, serving them while steam still rises from the dish. Each of the various dishes that passes through his hands never fails to move the ten patrons seated at the counter. At first glance, the sight alone stimulates the appetite. The food looks almost too exquisite to eat-something one wishes to simply admire for a long while. Behind the mastery Chef M displays today is a long lineage of dedication, with both his father and grandfather having been renowned chefs. The task of cleaning and slicing sea bream is usually reserved for seasoned chefs with two to three decades of experience, yet Chef M's father, preparing his son to become the third-generation successor, made him do it from the beginning, putting him through a harsh and rigorous training.

There is no easy path to success in any field. When I entered the world of essay writing well past the age of fifty, my writing mentor commented, "You started far too late." I must admit, I often feel the same. To write well, one must read widely, reflect deeply, and write constantly-but my pace is no longer what it once was. Perhaps that's what my teacher meant. But what choice did I have? After immigrating to Australia in my thirties, my priorities were my family and my children's education, not myself. It was for their sake that my husband and I chose this life abroad. So I remained constantly on standby-ready to drop everything and run whenever the children needed me. When they were finally grown and I found myself with time of my own, what did I do? I went back to work. Though I continued reading during those years, time passed before I finally began writing. Still, enrolling in my mentor's creative writing class and taking up literature has remained one of the best decisions of my life. Having lived abroad for decades-knowing I will likely be buried in Australian soil one day-the fact that I can still write in my mother tongue fills me with both pride and emotion.

Most women in their sixties find themselves gradually freed from domestic responsibilities. And given today's longer life expectancy, reaching into the 80s or 90s, there remains a golden stretch of twenty or thirty years, a kind of final bonus time meant to be lived fully for oneself. I began to wonder how I might best spend this time. Joining a writing group turned out to be a fitting choice for me. Of course, I don't dare dream of becoming a master like Chef M. But I do hope to learn from his spirit of craftsmanship. He once said that just as he is deeply moved when he listens to Mozart performed by the great pianist Horowitz, he too believes cooking should evoke emotion-and he has devoted his life to that pursuit. Surely, that is what true craftsmanship is. The process of completing even a single piece of writing is no easy task. In everyday life, I keep my senses sharp, always searching for inspiration. I often find myself sitting in front of the computer, writing a line or two, then spending hours choosing the right words, crafting an opening, and immersing myself so deeply that I lose track of time. Even if the final result is clumsy, the process of slowly weaving words together, shaping them into something tangible, brings a joy that's hard to match. They say the secret to happiness is not in doing what you love, but in loving what you do. If that's true, then perhaps I am already a happy person.

Before our monthly literary gatherings begin, my fellow writers and I sit together to listen to classical music. One of our members, who has a deep appreciation for music, selects a piece each month and hands out printed notes that include thoughtful explanations and background on the work. We calm our minds as we listen, letting the music settle into us. Often, the era and life of the 18th-century composer seem to breathe through the notes, and I find myself reflecting on possible themes for my writing. I was especially struck by the story of Korean pianist Yunchan Lim, who at just 18 years old became the youngest gold medalist at the Van Cliburn International Piano Competition in Boston last year. In preparation for his performance of Liszt's *Transcendental*

Études, he reportedly read Dante's *Divine Comedy* ten times. I feel a sudden thrill in realising once again that literature, music, visual art, and even cooking are all interconnected.

At times, the path I've chosen reminds me of my college days when I hiked toward Nogodan Peak on Mount Jiri, panting with exertion, overwhelmed yet determined. I can't help but wonder: will I truly be able to follow this road to the summit without faltering halfway? And yet, I find encouragement in the community of fellow writers who have become like siblings to me over the years. We support one another, sharing both carrots and sticks along the way. A stream that has begun to flow does not dry up so easily. That is where I place my hope.

(2023)

Welcoming the New Year

The year 2022 has begun. Even amid the noisy buzz of the COVID-19 pandemic, talks of vaccines, lockdowns, and boosters, the indifferent passage of time has marched on relentlessly, and the new year has arrived as expected. The year that begins on January 1st is not ordained by the Creator, but rather the invention of Julius Caesar, who devised the calendar system. And so, thanks to him, I find myself one year older once again. As I drift into another year seemingly without purpose, I find myself half-jokingly blaming Caesar. In my youth, the New Year felt bright with joy and hope, especially as we welcomed it by eating *tteok guk* (rice cake soup) to mark another year of life. I used to make resolutions, dream big, and set plans to achieve grand ambitions. Although more than once my resolutions lasted only three days before veering off course, through trial and error I have arrived at where I am now. With more years behind me than before me, what I once called 'New Year's resolutions' have become little more than hopes.

I hope this year will be one in which we cherish our encounters with others even more. The pandemic, now stretching into its third year, has completely transformed people's lifestyles, and many say we may never return to the daily normality we once knew, which is a sad thought. How frustrating it was when lockdowns forced us to stay home, unable to meet anyone. It truly felt like being trapped with no way out. When the world was shaken by the 9/11 terror attacks in 2001, people embraced one another and did their best to overcome the tragedy through comfort and solidarity. Yet in the face of this virus, the saying 'united we die, divided we survive' seems to ring true, and it unsettles me to think about what kind of world awaits us in the future.

In early December, I went to see the musical *Come From Away*. It tells the story of the 9/11 terror attacks in the United States. I had planned to see it a year ago but had to cancel due to COVID-19. When the production resumed, I quickly bought tickets. The NSW government was set to ease restrictions on

December 15, allowing even the unvaccinated to go outside, so I hurried to watch it before that. Unfortunately, the musical was canceled again before Christmas, so my daughter and I were lucky to have seen it. Based on a true story, with characters using their real names, the musical brought both tears and laughter to the audience.

On the day of the 9/11 terror attacks, nearly 7,000 people of 93 different nationalities were aboard 38 planes headed to the United States. Suddenly, urgent messages came to the pilots in the cockpits that the airports where they were scheduled to land had been closed. They were instructed to divert to a small town called Gander, located on the easternmost Island of Newfoundland in Canada. At that time, the small town had a population of just 9,300, but suddenly 7,000 people arrived. They disembarked without any luggage. The town's hotels combined had only 500 beds. All the schools, gymnasiums, and community centres were converted into temporary shelters, and the ice hockey rink was transformed into a refrigerated storage area. Many volunteers from nearby towns eagerly stepped up to help. A clothing store owner opened the shop and allowed people to freely take any clothes that fit. Those preparing meals worked tirelessly to serve the newcomers. During the five days they stayed, it is said that "on the first day there were 7,000 strangers; by the third day, 7,000 friends; and by the fifth day, 7,000 families who had lost loved ones"-such was the closeness that developed. Thanks to the town's collective love and kindness, everyone was able to leave Gander safely. Today, the musical shares this beautiful and moving story of Gander's people amidst that tragic situation.

Of all times, our family moved during the pandemic lockdown when everyone was confined at home, and only one person per household was allowed to go out once a day for groceries or medical reasons. It was pouring rain that day. As we left the house where we had lived for 26 years, we took cuttings of our beloved plants in pots, as if asking to be taken along. We couldn't stack them all in the moving truck, so we had to rent an additional truck. After struggling to move to our new address, even when the three of us were surrounded by piles of boxes, not even my younger brother, who lives nearby, could come in to see us.

Even though it is midsummer, perhaps due to the torrential rain last night, today feels as cool as early autumn. After finishing a late breakfast, I make myself a cup of coffee and come to my study, picking out a book to read for the day. My lifestyle has changed a lot due to staying at home during the pandemic. The musical about the 9/11 attacks and the miraculous humanity shown by the people of Gander, Newfoundland, taught me many lessons. Both personal histories and global human history reveal a surprising truth: whenever harsh storms of hardship sweep through, hopeful reversals can occur even amidst despair. If things were to continue without any change, perhaps not only desperate hope or progress would wither away, but life might drag on meaninglessly in stagnation until it fades out. Now in the 21st century, faced with a world-threatening pandemic, we can only watch quietly and wonder what astonishing miracles of insight might emerge. But just as the contents of a jar settle back into order after being shaken and tossed about, I want to believe that even if some disaster threatens us this year, once it has passed, a new kind of miracle will emerge. I hold on to that hope.

(2022)

This Too Shall Pass

The year 2021 has dawned, and the COVID-19 pandemic has crossed into the new year with us. We carry hopes that the war against the pandemic will end sometime this year, yet no one knows exactly when that might be. Science seems on the verge of catching up with the realm of the divine, and yet it has failed to conquer the virus, reminding us just how powerful this invisible enemy is. In the midst of it all, life as we knew it has come to a standstill across the globe, and in my own daily existence.

New Year's Day. The sun rose like any other day, no different from yesterday, and yet today marks the beginning of another full revolution of the Earth around the sun. Same but somehow different. Starting with Sydney and following the time zones around the globe, people welcomed the new year with fireworks on TV screens, even if the crowds of the past were missing. In many parts of the world still under lockdown, not only were public celebrations cancelled, but people couldn't even move about freely under tightened restrictions. I find myself suddenly nostalgic for the time I once drove out early to watch the sunrise. This should be a time to make new resolutions and plans. And yet, my thoughts linger on one question: how do I simply live through this year well?

Last year, the pandemic brought the world to a halt as if time itself had stopped and the rhythm of life had broken down. I remember a cartoon that went around on KakaoTalk, joking, "I didn't add a year to my age because I didn't use it." Instead of the usual New Year's greetings hoping for good things, people began wishing that nothing at all would happen.

What is the strength that allows us to endure dark and difficult times? Is hope some kind of magic that comes true if we hold on to it? If the end of the world were to come tomorrow, could I still plant an apple tree today? Recently, my daughter gave me a book as a Christmas present: *Phosphorescence – On Awe, Wonder & Things That Sustain You When the World Goes Dark* by Julia Baird. "Phosphorescence" is a scientific term for the phenomenon of an object emitting light, but in this book, it is used as a metaphor. Julia Baird is an Australian journalist, broadcaster, writer, historian, a Christian, and also a mother of two.

Published during the COVID-19 pandemic, this book brought me courage and hope. Like a firefly glowing in the dark, it reminded me of the light that shines from deep within us: a light made of hope and willpower that we must not lose, no matter the circumstances. The author herself endured a recurrence of cancer, went through multiple surgeries, and experienced pain so intense it felt almost unbearable. At one point she carried a tumour the size of a basketball in her abdomen. Yet she kept writing-sometimes even from her hospital bed. For her, writing became a form of catharsis. Today, she has recovered and now hosts *The Drum*, a current affairs program on ABC TV.

What impressed me deeply was the way she learned to centre her life around faith, cut off negativity, and hold close the people who truly supported her. Having walked so close to death, she came to see each day of life as a profound gift. In her reflections, she reminds us that being alive, and being able to move without pain, is already a blessing.

The book also recounts the story of a Navy admiral who, after being captured in the Vietnam War, survived seven years of unimaginable pain and suffering in the infamous 'Hanoi Hilton'. Despite broken bones and torment, he never lost his will to live. During those years, he drew strength from *Discourses* by the Stoic philosopher Epictetus-a former slave who himself lived with the scars of torture, yet taught the power of inner freedom and resilience. For the admiral, Epictetus became a guiding light in the darkest of times.

Reading this book, I felt a subtle but meaningful shift in myself. Things that once went unnoticed now bring me quiet joy and gratitude. A tiny succulent sprouting in the corner of a pot feels precious. I no longer grumble at the eucalyptus trees shedding bark and scattering leaves all over the driveway, because I see now that this shedding is how the tree stays healthy-and perhaps it even helps the birds. My way of looking at nature has changed. It reminds me of the saying: *If you can't avoid it, learn to enjoy it.*

In the past, I used to greet the new year with long lists of resolutions, only to end up disappointed for not keeping them. But the pandemic has grounded me. My wings of wandering have been clipped, and I now wish to set goals that are small but real. First and foremost, I want to live each day with sincerity and intention.

When the endless days of the pandemic seemed

monotonous, I later realised that no two days were ever truly the same. Each day had its own worth.

On New Year's Day, our family celebrated with *tteokguk* (rice cake soup). The day before, my daughter and I made *mandu* (dumplings), braised short ribs, and a few other dishes. As we finished breakfast, my son's family in the U.S. called on FaceTime to wish us a Happy New Year.

All four of my grandchildren, from age nine down to three, lined up and bowed, saying "*Saehae bok mani badeuseyo* (Happy New Year)." Children are hope itself. Their presence fills me with proud, uplifting energy. And yet my heart aches to know that children everywhere are enduring this pandemic without fully understanding it. Even my grandchildren have been confined at home, with homeschooling managed by my daughter-in-law. Their next-door neighbour had tested positive, and I can only imagine their anxiety. Though far away, my heart could not rest easy.

When will the day come when the whole world can finally celebrate the end of COVID-19? I do not know. But what I do know is this: by holding onto the truth that "this too shall pass," I can face the year 2021 with renewed hope and expectation.

(2021)

Where Do Traces of the Soul Remain?

The house next door has been sold. For the past three months, it stood empty, yet every time I looked at it from our backyard, I felt as if our neighbour Hazel, who had lived alone there for so many years, might step out into her garden at any moment. I could almost hear her voice as she scattered birdseed across the lawn with a flick of her hand, calling out to the gathering birds, "Hungry, are you? Come on, eat up." Even today, the birds may have come for their meal and are now perched on the branches, not knowing why she hasn't come out, simply waiting, and waiting. Beside the fence that separates our yards, the camellia tree still extends its green curtain toward our side, just as it always has. And come April, it generously covers itself with soft pink blossoms, bringing joy to our family. As if prearranged with Hazel, the flowers have bloomed again this year, faithfully. But where has Hazel gone?

Last Christmas, I baked some cookies, wrapped them nicely, and brought them over to Hazel's house next door. Hearing no response at the door, I assumed she was out and would be back soon, so I left the gift by her front door. But when I checked the next day, it was still there, untouched. I thought, *'She must have gone to her daughter's house'*. But it turned out that very day, she had passed away in the hospital-ten days after being admitted, never returning home again.

Hazel was a stylish lady who looked much younger than her 92 years. Every year on Australia Day, at our street breakfast gathering, she would bring two bottles of wine carefully wrapped, each adorned with a small Australian flag. They would be raffled off to neighbours, drawn by house number. This year, another neighbour continued the tradition but who would have imagined that last year's breakfast would be her final one?

The fact that we had once worked at the same bank, though half a century apart, created a rare common thread between a typical Australian grandmother and a Korean immigrant like myself. Perhaps that shared experience made me feel closer to her, and in turn, she may have felt a special fondness for me next door. Every time we met, she would ask after my children, always showing genuine interest. When we first became neighbours and I introduced myself, Hazel asked me to call her by her first name.

In our culture, people of her age are commonly referred to simply as *halmoni* (grandmother), but this Australian grandmother wished to be addressed not as "Mrs" anyone, but by her own name. Though we were living in Australia, it still took time for me to grow used to calling someone older than my own mother by her first name.

Hazel had a son and a daughter, but she never left the home where the whole family had once lived together; staying there until the very end of her life. Even in her nineties, she looked remarkably healthy. Her posture was upright, and conditions I fear as I age like dementia or strokes seemed not to touch her. What was her secret? I often wondered if her weekly gatherings with friends played a role. Every Wednesday, without fail, several cars would be parked in front of her house. Her home had become a cosy hideaway for her circle of senior friends, who gathered regularly. They had likely been playing tennis together since their younger days on the court at her house and continued to spend their

Wednesday afternoons enjoying each other's company. When the coloured lights strung across the backyard flickered on as the sun set, it was undoubtedly time for a barbecue. I often wondered, *What do these elderly folks talk about week after week?* One Christmas, my husband and I were invited over, and I finally had my answer. They talked about movies – many of them. After a lively discussion about films, the conversation flowed easily into current affairs, politics, travel, and many other topics. There seemed to be no end to the energy in their conversations, and they didn't seem to be conscious of their age at all. That evening, Hazel wore a stylish necklace and a beautiful bracelet, dressing up more than usual. Seeing her live so joyfully stirred a sense of admiration in me. After returning home, I thought of my own mother. She had spent her final years bedridden and passed away with much of her life unfulfilled. I made a quiet vow to myself–to live well, not just for me, but also for my mother, and to make her happy through the life I live.

Though living well is important, I deeply feel, as I think of my mother, how much more important it is to die well. But dying is not something we can control with our minds. Hazel's passing, after living a healthy life filled with enjoyment and only spending a few days in the hospital, was a blessing.

She lived alone in a large house with a tennis court and a swimming pool, never settling its affairs or passing it on to her descendants during her lifetime. Even if this is normal for Australians, it stands in stark contrast to the tragic situations I occasionally hear about from news in my home country or acquaintances, cases where retired parents transfer property to their children prematurely, or even hand over house deeds for the sake of their children's businesses, only to face heartbreaking outcomes.

Hazel's daughter looked just like her mother. After her mother passed away and she had sorted out the house, she put it on the real estate market, leaving only the furniture needed for interior decoration. Once the house was sold, she contacted the council to arrange for their cleanup service. In Australia, when you discard appliances like refrigerators or washing machines, you are supposed to remove the doors and leave them out in front of the house. However, the two refrigerators and the washing machine that Hazel's daughter put out were left with their doors intact. This meant they were still usable, not broken. Sure enough, almost all the items left by the roadside were quickly taken by someone. For some reason, I was drawn to the round outdoor table in the backyard of that house, and I decided to bring it home. I felt as if Hazel's spirit had been transplanted into it. Looking at this sturdy table that showed clear signs of long use, I sometimes call out, "Hi, Hazel!" It must have been a table around which family and friends gathered over many years to eat, drink tea, and share time together. I think Hazel would be happy to know that now I, the neighbour next door, am using it.

According to the order of the universe, all living things must face the moment of death, but where do the traces of the soul remain?

(2014)

In the Golden Years of Life

It has been three decades since I put down roots in Australia as a migrant from an ethnic minority. I made the move in my late thirties, and now, according to Professor Hyeong-seok Kim, the philosopher who lived past a hundred, I stand at the midpoint of what he calls "the most beautiful and precious season of life", between the ages of 65 and 75. I wonder if I had heard his words earlier, might I have spent the first half of these golden years differently?

Not long ago, I had the chance to attend a graduation ceremony at a theological college in Sydney. Among the words of advice delivered to the graduates by the NSW Minister for Education, the phrase *"Never stop learning"* lingered with me the most. As graduates stepped onto the stage to receive their degrees, I noticed several who were well into middle age, some leaning on canes or crutches, one woman so bent with osteoporosis that her back was much curved. Yet their proud demeanour seemed to declare that a stooped back or a head of white hair could never be an obstacle to learning. When the student representative, a mother of three, proudly shared that it had taken her eight years to complete her degree, the hall erupted in applause. At that moment, the meaning of lifelong education came alive. I too have long been pursuing learning with the goal of "until the day I die." Many years ago, I began studying a foreign language, at first simply to prepare for a future trip. But as time went on, I found real joy in it, and knowing it might help ward off dementia, I continued with steady persistence. When I finally visited that country for the first time at the age of sixty-five, I was as delighted as a child. Looking back, I now realise that was the very age when I had entered the golden years of life.

There was also a time when I went through a great challenge, yet gained immense fulfillment in return. Through that experience I encountered precious bonds, and those connections have continued to ripple forward like a domino effect of relationships, reminding me that this too was surely a golden season of life. In Sydney, where no alumnae association of my Korean high school yet existed, an opportunity arose when the New York alumnae group organised a concert in celebration of our alma mater's 130th anniversary. On that occasion, seven of us came together to launch the Sydney chapter. We sought out fellow alumnae scattered across the city, and with united effort we managed to fill every seat of the thousand-capacity concert hall with invitation-only guests. It felt nothing short of a miracle. The concert, graced by alumnae who had traveled from Seoul, the United States and Japan, was a resounding success. It carried a level of excellence that silenced the doubts of those who questioned why it had to be held in distant Australia. It remains one of the most rewarding and unforgettable achievements of my life.

A common saying goes that all overseas Koreans are patriots, and it's not far from the truth. The year 2019 marked the centennial anniversaries of several key moments in Korea's independence movement: the February 8 Declaration of Independence, the March 1st Movement, and the establishment of the Provisional Government in Shanghai. A grand commemoration was held in Sydney as well. Had I been living in Korea, I would likely have marked these meaningful occasions by simply watching the ceremonies on

TV or reading about them in the papers. But in Australia, it was different. I attended the commemorative ceremony held at the Korean Society of Sydney and joined the triple cheer of *"Manse!"*. It felt like a truly fitting stride for this golden period of my life.

As one of my seniors once recalled, our high school principal used to say, "Health comes first, health comes second, health comes third, and fourth is study." Now, at this stage of life, I believe that the fourth is health as well. I hope to extend the latter part of this 'golden period' for as long as possible. In the canvas of my mind, I picture our family tree, firmly rooted in Australia, spreading its branches wide and strong. I see myself in many roles-wife, mother, grandmother, daughter, friend and simply as myself. Reflecting on all these roles I'm juggling, I wonder if perhaps I am, like many women, becoming a 'superwoman'!

(2019)

Life Sonata

It's been a while since conversations with friends began to revolve around health issues. Once someone brings it up, it quickly becomes the topic of the hour, with everyone chiming in. The explanation moves from symptoms to treatments; the names of illnesses and medications lining up like notes playing on repeat. It begins to feel as though we've just returned from a tour of a general hospital. As we part, we always say, "Let's stay healthy until we meet again." Well, after all these years of wear and tear, how could our teeth or organs possibly remain intact? In our youth, cracking open a hard walnut with our teeth and splitting it clean in two was effortless. We delighted in rich, delicious foods, oblivious to the cries of protest our bodies may have been sending. For someone like me, born in the analog age, it hasn't been long since I began accessing endless health information online, through YouTube and countless websites. So I can no longer excuse myself by blaming ignorance for having missed my body's warning signs. Even when walking, I no longer look straight ahead like I used to. Now, I glance down at the pavement to avoid a dangerous fall. One wrong twist of the waist or knee, and the pain can be excruciating. This is the time of life when we must truly listen to our bodies and treat them with the care and respect they deserve.

One day, while working in the backyard, my husband injured his back. A slipped disc pressed against a spinal nerve, sending a tsunami of pain all the way down to his foot. He was beside himself, screaming in agony so loud it seemed to shake the house. Looking back, I should have called an ambulance, but I foolishly followed his plea not to. Instead, I phoned our neighbor to ask her not to be alarmed if she heard loud cries from our house. A physiotherapist came to our home several times, but there was little improvement. Then, through a friend who had been a rehabilitation specialist in Korea, we were referred to a physiotherapy clinic equipped with a device designed to restore the slipped disc to its original position. I helped my husband into the car, along with an old wheelchair that had once belonged to my daughter's friend's grandmother. Then I drove us to this clinic. Up to that point, things went relatively smoothly. But as soon as I parked on the street and began pushing my husband in the wheelchair, it suddenly lurched forward. If I had let go even for a moment, it would have rolled straight into the busy road. My heart nearly stopped in that instant. Only then did I notice that the pavement was slightly sloped, but in my panic I had completely forgotten about the brakes. All I could do was brace the wheelchair against my knee and pull it back with every ounce of strength I had. My knee pain began with that incident.

A series of domino effects began from that point. Since my husband had injured his back, he underwent a number of medical tests as well, only to receive troubling results. After scheduling an appointment with a specialist, my mind became a whirlwind of thoughts. Just a few days later, my daughter and I were supposed to travel to Jeju Island to perform a puppet show about female divers, a trip we had planned months in advance. We had already prepared everything: folding tables, screens, props, and were ready to head to the airport. But how could I possibly leave my husband alone, when he couldn't even stand up by himself? The thought of having to cancel the performance at this late stage was deeply disappointing. It was such a rare opportunity, and I felt like I was becoming an unreliable person. In the end, my daughter decided not to go to Korea and to stay behind with her father instead. She would accompany him to his specialist appointments and other tests, pushing his wheelchair. My daughter also prepared a presentation file so that I could still give a brief talk at the event in Jeju. On the night before my early morning flight, neither of us slept a wink.

What I had initially dismissed as a minor issue with my knee eventually became something more serious. While I was traveling as planned to Korea, then Japan, and back to Korea again, I found myself limping more and more. My knee became severely swollen, and I couldn't bend it at all; the pain grew steadily worse. I ended up visiting an orthopaedic clinic and received a mild steroid injection. Back in Sydney, after finally getting an MRI scan, I learned that I had a torn meniscus along with slight ligament damage. It took me eight weeks from the time I was injured to finally begin physiotherapy. By then, the damage had worsened, and I had to rely on a walking stick.

To make matters worse, my husband had another mishap. This time, he slipped on the concrete just outside our kitchen and injured both knees. Thankfully, there were no fractures, but the wounds were so large that each had to be covered with a palm-sized bandage. He dug out an old hiking stick we had at home, and so it happened that the two of us, husband and wife, suddenly found ourselves hobbling side by side with canes; a living testament to the inevitable realities of aging.

There is a Western saying that bad things come in threes, and I can't help but marvel at the mysterious ways of the world. My husband's back injury, for instance, led to a series of tests that uncovered hidden warning signs in his body, allowing him to receive treatment early. It's a true blessing in disguise. His recovery has been relatively swift, but my knee seems to require much longer to heal. Around that time, a card was shared in our high school friends' group chat. It read: *"Even when life is hard, let's smile and carry on."* After coming this far in life, you'd think I would have learned to stay calm in the face of hardship. Yet I still find myself flustered. How many more years must I live before I can finally outgrow this immaturity? Perhaps embracing the process of aging with gratitude is nothing more than a way to console myself. But then again, all of this is simply part of living. My life's sonata, woven through joys and sorrows, is still being played. In the passing years, the music has slowed, carrying the weight of both joy and sorrow.

(2023)

Short Story
Father's Spring

While sorting through my father's belongings, my eyes fell upon a small wooden comb-delicate, crescent-shaped, meticulously carved with fine teeth. It still held a few strands of his silvery hair, as if preserving a fragment of time. I recalled how, on several occasions, I had caught him gently running his fingers over that very comb, as though caressing the hand of a beloved.

"You're playing with that comb again, Dad," I teased softly.

A faint blush would colour his cheeks as he replied, "Oh, hush. It's nothing. I used to have quite a head of hair once… though it's all white now. I'm just trying to smooth out the thinning patch on top with this comb, that's all."

His voice lingers in my ears like a tender refrain, and

memories rise slowly, swelling in my chest. I open the window wide, and the crisp, early spring air brushes gently against my face. A solitary bird perches on the balcony's edge, gazing steadily in my direction as if sent to watch over me. For a fleeting moment, I wonder: could this bird be a messenger from my father?

* * *

I remember the day of my mother's funeral. He stood silently by her grave, watching as the digger placed an empty rice bowl upside down beside her casket-the mark of the place where his own would one day rest. In a voice barely above a whisper, he said, "Wait for me, until I come."

From that day on, whenever he drank, tears would glisten in his eyes as he spoke of his longing to be with her again. I would say, "Dad, there you go again. Do you really want to leave your only daughter an orphan? You have to live for Mum's sake, and for mine." How many winters have passed since then?

I was living close to my father at the time, working as a teacher. During the school holidays, I would bustle about, trying to fill the empty space my mother had left by staying at his side. One afternoon, after several days of heavy snow had blanketed the world in white, my father remained silent, gazing out the window even as I finished washing the lunch dishes and tidying up the kitchen. Then, as if he had come to a decision, he called to me in a voice both calm and resolute.

"Yeonju, stop what you're doing and come sit down. I have something to tell you. There's a favour I'd like to ask."

I wiped my wet hands on my apron and, wondering what this was about, walked over to the sofa and sat down. Then my father, to my utter surprise, shared something I never expected to hear from him at my age of over fifty. What? You want to find your first love? Don't be ridiculous. How could that be possible? You're over eighty now. Please, be sensible. Mother would leap right out of her grave! I wanted to shout those words aloud, but I bit my tongue. I couldn't risk wounding the father who depended on me, for fear he might shut his heart.

That night, tossing and turning in bed, I realised dawn light was already filtering faintly through the gap in the curtains. At his age, without knowing how much longer he might have, how could I deny his wish to visit Tokyo at least once more? Of course, there was no guarantee he could find the first love he had met in the springtime of his life, just by going to Japan. It seemed as impossible as climbing a mountain to look for fish. But my thoughts began to shift. Instead of overthinking it, why not simply take him on a trip? It was the middle of winter, yes, but school was on a break, and if I could help him fulfill a lifelong wish, what did the weather matter? Before I could change my mind, I hurried to book the plane tickets.

* * *

In his early twenties, during the Japanese colonial period, my father, Sangpil Lee, was studying abroad in Tokyo. There was a small general store near his boarding house that he would occasionally stop by, and every time, a young woman greeted him with kindness and warmth. One day, he overheard her calling the woman in the apron behind the counter "*Okāsan* (mum)," and realised she was the daughter of the shop owner. He remembered sensing that the young woman seemed fond of him.

One day, while waiting for the relentless sleet to subside in the university library, Sang-pil quickly closed his book and pulled his coat tightly around him as darkness began to settle outside the window, then headed back to his lodgings. The icy road made him walk carefully and just then, the familiar young woman appeared before him, holding an umbrella. In a shy voice, she said, "If your coat gets soaked and freezes, you might not be able to wear it to school tomorrow. I heard it's going to be even colder." And she handed him the umbrella.

Startled, Father accepted it without thinking. As she turned and walked away, he called out,

"Thank you! What's your name?"

"Mieko. Mori Mieko. And you?"

"Lee··· Sangpil."

"Lee Sangpiru-san. Thank you."

That winter was unusually snowy. Until then, Sang-pil, living far from home and devoted entirely to his studies, had paid little attention to the beauty of snowy landscapes. He only found them bothersome—slushy roads and slippery paths.

But walking down snow-covered trails with Mieko, he felt as if he were seeing a snowy landscape for the first time. He found himself drawn more and more to this gentle and graceful girl. Sometimes, when he stayed late at the library, she would bring him a neatly packed homemade lunch wrapped in a pretty cloth. Sang-pil's life revolved around the small triangle of school, the library, and his room, and her kindness brought an unexpected warmth to his routine. One day, as they walked through a snowy park, Sang-pil remarked on how heavy the branches looked under the snow and shook one with all his strength. A shower of snow tumbled down like an avalanche over them both, and reflexively, he pulled her into his arms. They stood there for a while, holding each other beneath the falling snow.

Yet each time Sang-pil parted from Mieko, he was tormented by the stirrings of his own heart. His parents, who had sent him abroad with high hopes, had sternly warned him against distraction—especially of the romantic kind. The more he tried to suppress these feelings, the more they rebelled within him, leaving him in turmoil.

* * *

By 1944, as Japan neared the end of the Pacific War, Sang-pil was drafted. Faced with the dreadful reality of conscription, he decided he would rather die trying to escape. Every time the names of students who had stowed away on the smuggler's ship were blared loudly through the megaphone aboard the vessel, his lips burned dry, and his whole body shriveled as if it were a deflated balloon. After many twists and turns, he finally managed to slip aboard a smuggler's ship and reach Busan. But just days later, when he arrived in Seoul and saw his family, he was caught by the police and forced into grueling labour at a factory. It wasn't until Japan's defeat that he was finally able to return home.

He eventually married in his late twenties through a match arranged by his family. In such a conservative household, even uttering the name "Mieko" was unthinkable. He vowed to carry the memory of Tokyo with him to the grave. Whenever she came to mind, he chastised himself, trying every way he could to switch off the lingering emotions. After he and his wife had a daughter, he devoted himself entirely to his family. When his once-vibrant wife's hair began to streak with silver, he found it quietly poignant. Then, unexpectedly, she passed away, and with her, his will to live seemed to vanish. Every corner of the house resonated with her absence. Even the potted plants on the veranda seemed to breathe traces of her, and whenever they bloomed, he missed her all the more. She had been steady and devoted, tending their home with care and grace. But when she was gone, it was as if the very pillars of the house had crumbled. Her absence left a vast, echoing hollow. He regretted never having expressed his gratitude while she was alive. "Thank you... and I'm sorry," he murmured to the empty space around him, like a man possessed. Adrift in the house with nothing to do but drink, all he could feel was the aching desire to be with her.

Then, something extraordinary stirred in Father's heart that winter. One quiet night, he stood before the glass door in the darkened living room, curtains drawn aside. As he gazed at the silent, heavy snowfall, a shiver of loneliness ran through him when suddenly, Mieko appeared before his eyes. It wasn't a dream. Startled, he rubbed his eyes and looked at her, the girl from his memories. How could this be? After all these years, buried so deep in his past, why should she appear now? It was as if a spell had been lifted, and from the farthest recesses of his subconscious, Mieko had fluttered into the present. Hadn't he forgotten her? Yet here she was. No photograph remained, but he could clearly see her fair, delicate face, her sparkling eyes, and the soft, rounded lips that had always spoken with such kindness. The snow white world they had once walked through together came flooding back like a vision. He remembered how he had left her in tears, with no time to say a proper goodbye. This was the same Mieko he had tried to push away all his life, unable to face the weight of the past. Where could she be now? When the Americans carpet-bombed Tokyo near the end of the war, there had been no guarantee she would survive. And even if she had, she would now be over eighty. Was she well? Despite the six decades that had passed, Father felt an overwhelming, almost irrational urge to find her. It was as though some invisible force were pulling him forward.

I arrived at Narita Airport with him. He was smartly dressed in dark brown wool trousers with a checked shirt, a cashmere cardigan, a wool coat and a plaid scarf, and wearing a hat. I cheerfully told him he looked twenty years younger. "Enjoy this trip with your daughter," I said, hoping to lift his spirits. In truth, I had no real expectation of finding this woman named Mieko. I only wanted to soften any disappointment that might come. After all, trying to find someone after sixty years in a sprawling city like Tokyo-it felt like searching for a needle in a sandy beach. I thought Father merely wanted a vacation. But I was mistaken. As soon as we unpacked at the hotel, he pulled out a phone book and a map. He wanted to visit the neighbourhood where her family's store had once stood, along with the house behind it where they had lived. Reluctantly, I followed him, but I was hardly prepared for the adventure of navigating foreign trains and unfamiliar streets. The old traces were gone, replaced by modern buildings. That first day felt like wandering through a maze, and by the end, we returned to our starting point and made our way back to the hotel. I was utterly exhausted, ready to collapse into bed. But Father didn't rest. He sat by the hotel phone, dialing each "Mori Mieko" listed in the directory, one after another. He spent the entire day doing just that. Surely this was the power of love.

Eventually, I went out on my own, wandering the streets. As

I walked, resentment welled up inside me. I thought of Father sitting pointlessly by that phone-at his age, why not simply enjoy a trip with his daughter? Why cling so stubbornly to the past?

When I returned and quietly opened the door to our room, he was still by the phone, his face buried in both hands.

"Father..."

He lifted his head, and I saw his face twisted with emotion. Perhaps he had finally realised how hopeless this all was. Surely, it was time to let go.

Just as I was about to offer words of comfort, I heard something from him that I could hardly believe.

"Yeonju... I found Mieko. She has stayed in the same district all these years⋯ waiting, in case I might come looking for her. She never married. She kept her name in the phone book..."

His voice broke, and he could not go on.

I stared at him in disbelief, as though I were dreaming. Could this be real? Such things did not happen in real life.

The next morning, a woman about my age, her hair touched with grey, came to the hotel to pick us up. As she bowed politely in greeting, I glimpsed her face and felt an odd sense of familiarity. In the backseat of the taxi, I sat beside Father and wondered what was passing through his heart. Was it a tangle of emotions? A flutter of anticipation? Was his heart pounding? Would he recognise her? What an extraordinary thing this was. And yet, outside the taxi window, streams of people passed by with indifferent faces, oblivious to the miracle unfolding inside this car. It seemed absurd—and yet there I was, wondering if I had gone mad.

We stepped out of the taxi and followed the woman into a narrow alley, scarcely wide enough for a single car to squeeze through. On either side stood rows of grey houses, neat and plain, giving off an air of modest simplicity. At the very end of the lane, our guide stopped in front of a house. Passing through the gate, we entered a small yard where a bare tree, an empty flowerbed, and a few brick-coloured pots seemed to endure the winter in silence. At that moment, a sudden resistance stirred within me. I didn't want to witness my father's reunion with his old love. He had lived faithfully, happily, with my late mother. So why were we here now? I had never truly believed we would find her, and now I resented myself for coming. Yet it was too late to turn back alone.

She met us at the entrance, seated in a wheelchair.

"Sangpil-san," she said softly.

"Mieko," my father replied.

He walked toward her, bent down, and embraced her. It was as if they had just parted yesterday, as natural and gentle as could be. How could that be possible? They stayed that way for a long moment, not saying a word. Perhaps they were recalling that snowy day, when they had hugged beneath the falling snow shaken from a tree.

Had it not been my father, I might have shed tears from the sheer emotion of the scene. Mieko, brushing away tears, turned to us–no, to my father–and introduced the woman who had brought us there.

"This is your daughter, Mie.

I had never seen such a look on my father's face before. It was a mixture of disbelief and sorrow, a look that struck me to the core. Looking more closely, I noticed the resemblance–her forehead, her eyes, even the shape of her nose reminded me of myself. Her delicate mouth was just like Mieko's. I felt dizzy, as if I had been struck on the head. Mie–who was introduced as his daughter–stood frozen, with her mouth agape, staring at my father. Mieko had kept the truth of her birth hidden from her all these years. Born in 1945, Mie had grown up believing her father had died in the war. That her real father was Korean–how was she supposed to process that now? Mieko had named her daughter after herself, secretly hoping that one day she might be reunited with her father. Over more than half a century, she had raised her daughter alone, seeing Sangpil reflected in her daughter's face.

I, who had always believed I was my father's only child, now had an older half-sister. I was overwhelmed. I didn't follow my father the next day, nor the day after that. I wandered the city alone, needing time to come to terms with this staggering reality. What a bolt from the blue, striking our ordinary, uneventful family life! Was my father a traitor-or a man of honour? My heart was in utter turmoil.

When we returned to Korea, the first thing we did was visit my mother's grave. As my father quietly spoke to her about the trip to Tokyo, I stepped aside to give him privacy. After bidding her farewell with "Until I join you, be well," we returned home. My father threw open all the windows, as if to replace the heavy silence in the house with fresh air and new energy. While unpacking his luggage, I came across some unfamiliar items. Among them was a small crescent-shaped wooden comb, worn smooth and darkened over years of use. Mieko had used it for decades to gently comb up and secure her hair. My father cherished it as if it were a part of her.

Every Monday at 10 a.m., my father calls Mieko in Tokyo. After showering, he carefully combs his thinning hair with Mieko's comb, then dresses as if preparing for a date before taking his seat by the phone. Though I couldn't understand their words, I could sense they were recounting the stories of their lives. Sometimes his voice caught with emotion; other times he smiled. Watching him, I felt a subtle sympathy for Mieko and Mie, my half-sister. Even though I hadn't spoken to them, I felt a subtle pang of guilt. My father said he and Mieko had agreed to wait patiently until Mie and I were ready to open our hearts. Occasionally, he would share bits of their conversations with me.

"Back then," he said, "Mieko's father did everything he could to avoid conscription—he even starved himself to become too thin to pass the physical. One night, overwhelmed by how much he missed his wife and daughter, he snuck back to the family store. But Mieko's grandmother was furious: 'Do you want to bring disaster upon us all?' she cried, and drove him out. Later, when Mieko's pregnancy became obvious, the grandmother took her to a relative's house in the countryside to avoid the scrutiny of neighbours. That's how they managed to escape the carpet-bombing of Tokyo. Unfortunately, not long after, Mieko lost both her parents and became an orphan."

Then he added, "Yeonju, whatever else she may be, Mie is your sister. She has stayed by her mother's side all these years, never marrying. At one point, she worked as a kindergarten teacher. Later, she ran a small general store on her own, and now lives off the rental income from that shop. They even visited Korea once, before Mieko had an accident that put her in a wheelchair. Walking through Seoul, the streets felt strangely familiar to Mie—and it was no wonder. Korean blood runs in her veins. She's now enjoying Korean dramas and learning the language. I believe she'll be a good sister to you, if you allow her. All I can do is hope that someday you'll open your heart to her as well."

The phone dates between Father and Mieko continued for five years. Without fail, they spoke once a week. Mieko recounted with some excitement a trip with her daughter in autumn, where the blazing reds and bright yellows of the leaves were at their peak. She wished Sangpil could have been there with them. After the call, she clutched her left chest and collapsed.

I had strongly urged Father not to go to Tokyo, worried about his health and fearing that another tragedy might strike. In the end, Mieko had spent her final days sharing the beauty of the autumn leaves with her old love. If not a perfect life, then at least she could depart in peace, surrounded by love and beauty.

After Mieko's passing, Father mourned deeply and drank more often. He lost his appetite and almost stopped eating altogether.

Then one day, a thick parcel arrived from Tokyo-sent by Mie:

"… Mother's funeral was quietly concluded. Following her instructions, I opened the drawer of the cabinet that had remained locked. Inside lay a bundle of old letters addressed to "Sangpil-sang." They were her most private thoughts, written over the years, yearning for the lover whose fate and whereabouts she never knew. Each letter was filled with such urgency and longing, as if she believed that, if they could not meet in this life, they would surely be reunited in the next.

Mother gave birth to me in the chaos of war and raised me amid the ruins that followed. From time to time, she would stroke my face and say, "You look like your father." With no photograph of the man she loved, she sought his features in mine and smiled wistfully. For decades she endured, longing for him so deeply that perhaps heaven itself granted them the grace of reunion. I am grateful that you found my mother five years ago.

Honestly, the shock I felt at the time was overwhelming. I even resented my mother for keeping such a truth from her only daughter all those years. Until then, I had taken it as unquestionable that my father was Japanese and had died in the Tokyo air raids. Now, however, I accept that my real father was Korean. I feel sorry for your late wife, yet I pray that in the next world she will welcome my mother with kindness. Even now, with silver in my hair, the knowledge that I have a father and a younger sister named Yeonju in Korea brings solace to my lonely heart.

I noticed that this library holds many books on Korea. From now on, I intend to study in earnest about my father's country. I am planning to visit Korea next spring. Though I am diligently learning Korean so that I may converse with Yeonju, it has not been easy, perhaps because of my age. Yet I long to share a true bond of father and daughter with you.

Enclosed is a bundle of my mother's letters. I sincerely pray for your good health.

Respectfully yours,
Mie Mori

My father told me about Mie's letter up to this point, and

then shut himself away for several days, deeply absorbed in Mieko's letters.

"Yeonju, I beg you. When I'm gone, keep in touch with your sister and live well. She's a poor soul. She suffered a lot with her mother."

These words, like a final wish, were the last he left me. He passed away before he could meet Mie, who had promised to visit Korea in the spring. How desperate and heartfelt must Mieko's letters have been for him to hasten to the other world, eager to meet her? Wasn't he the same father who often said he longed to be reunited with my mother, his wife with whom he had shared a lifetime? I cannot help but wonder what it will be like when the three of them meet again in the next world.

I did not invite Mie to my father's funeral. After all, he was already gone, and I did not want to burden her with such a long journey. Besides, I was not yet ready to explain the complicated truth to my children or to others, and I wished to avoid turning it into a subject of gossip.

On the day I was sorting through my father's belongings, a bird flew in and perched on the balcony, gazing straight at me. That moment has remained etched in my heart, vivid as a photograph. Perhaps the bird was a messenger from Father, urging me to keep in touch with my half-sister and live well together. Just as Father had spoken with Mieko every week on the phone, I now call Mie at a set time each weekend. She speaks in halting Korean, and I answer in broken Japanese, our conversations made up of only a few words.

This coming holiday, I plan to travel to Tokyo to meet Mie who is now left alone in this world. I will not forget to tuck into my suitcase Mieko's wooden comb Father cherished so dearly, carrying with me a fragment of the love and history that binds us.

"Father's Spring" was inspired by a real story that happened in France and Germany.

부록/
APPENDIX

저의 영원한 글 스승 이효정 선생님을 제 수필집에 모십니다.

I am honoured to include my literary mentor, novelist Hyojeong Lee, in this collection of essays. Her guidance and inspiration have profoundly shaped my path as an essayist. For readers who may not be familiar with her, I have included a photograph and a video link from a forum where she was invited as a speaker last year.

원로 소설가 이효정의 생애와 문학세계
The Life and Literary World of Hyojeong Lee, Senior Novelist
제4차 시드니 목요포럼
The 4th Sydney Thursday Forum 8th August 2024, at Epping Club

프롤로그 영상/Prologue Video
(3분26초)

풀영상/Full Video
(1시간 38분)

이효정문학회 단체연혁	Lee Hyo-jeong Literary Society – Group History
1995년 3월: 소설가 이효정 선생 외 뜻을 같이하는 사람들이 모여 시드니문학회 발족 **2001년**: 시드니수필문학회로 개명 **2006년**: 사단법인 호주수필문학회로 개명 **2010년**: (사)호주문학협회로 개명 (수필, 소설, 시, 번역문학분과) **2017년**: (사)시드니한인작가회 Sydney Korean Writers Club으로 명칭 변경 **2023년**: 이효정문학회로 명칭변경 동인지 제12집 발행 교민대상 문예창작교실 제9회 개최 (강사: 본회 상임고문 이효정) 한국중앙문단에 본 회원 30여명 추천 등단	**March 1995:** Founded as the Sydney Literary Society by novelist Lee Hyojeong and others who shared the same vision. **2001:** Renamed Sydney Essay Literary Society. **2006:** Renamed Australian Essay Literary Society (incorporated association). **2010:** Renamed Australian Literary Association, Inc. (with divisions for essays, fiction, poetry, and literary translation). **2017:** Renamed Sydney Korean Writers Club, Inc. **2023:** Renamed Lee Hyojeong Literary Society. **Activities** Published the 12th issue of the literary anthology. Held the 9th Creative Writing Workshop for the Korean community (Instructor: Lee Hyojeong, Senior Advisor of the Society). Recommended and introduced about 30 members to the Korean central literary scene for official debut.

이효정문학회 문우들과 2024년 11월.

With the fellow writers of the Lee Hyojeong Literary Society, November 2024.